Sex, Slander, and Salvation

Investigating The Family/Children of God

James R. Lewis and J. Gordon Melton, Editors

Center for Academic Publication
Stanford, California

Requests for permission to make copies
of any part of the work should be mailed to:
Permissions Department, Center for Academic Publication,
Box 5097, Stanford, California 94309.

ISBN: 0-9639501-2-6

Printed in the United States of America
First edition

Cover illustration courtesy World Services

Contents

iv

Introduction

Meeting The Family: Face-to-Face with an Exotic Species

James R. Lewis
Center for Academic Publication

"I'm your worst nightmare," is an expression that has been popularized by the entertainment media. Despite the popularity of this expression, I doubt that many of us have reflected seriously on what our most frightening "bad dreams" might be. As someone whose scholarship has contributed to the debunking of the "cult" stereotype, and who has tended to defend non-traditional religions against persecution, I have discovered at least one of my worst nightmares. This nightmare is that I examine a controversial religious group, give it a clean bill of health on the basis of my research, and, later, after my study has been published, discover that I have defended the People's Temple, or worse.

In relating my bad dream, I feel that I am articulating a fear that many of us in this field of study share. This unstated anxiety affects our perspective on every new religious movement (NRM) we observe, influencing us to approach non-traditional religions cautiously and even skeptically. For example, despite my decade-long involvement with alternative religions—a ten-year period in which I found most accusations leveled against Moonies, Hare Krishnas, and so forth to be foundationless—I was still ready to believe many of the worst charges made about Elizabeth Clare Prophet's Church Universal and Triumphant. It was not until I spent a week at their Montana headquarters in the fall of 1992 that I realized most of the charges I had read or heard about were little more than media hype. I experienced much the same reaction when I first met The Family, a.k.a. the Children of God.

To those of use who study the "cult" controversy, the Children of God are almost mythological. Aggressive proselytizers in their formative years who were given to dramatic denunciations of established society, the Children of God (COG) were so controversial that reactions to their activities generated the very first "anti-cult" organization, FREECOG (Free the Children of God) as well as the practice of "deprogramming." However, in spite of their historical importance, the Children received little scholarly attention, largely because they left the United States in the mid-seventies at about the same time that "New Religious Movements" was being established as a field of study.

I was thus not a little surprised when, in January of 1993, a colleague and myself were contacted by The Family (the successor organization to the Children of God), who wished to meet with us. It is not often that one gets to meet one of the legends of their field of study, and I approached the meeting with all the anticipation a zoologist might approach a rare species she or he had never before observed. Perhaps needless to say, Family members did not strike me as being particularly exotic or unusual when I actually met them face-to-face.

At that meeting I learned that The Family had returned to the United States a year or two earlier, and had gone about establishing communal homes in major cities without attracting much attention. Their religious/theological reasons for returning were that they felt they would be able to gather one last harvest of souls from the U.S. before the End. However, rather than the original Family members being at the forefront of the new harvest, it would be the next generation—the children of the Children, so to speak—who would be the core of this new wave of activity.

The reason for their wishing to contact scholars of alternative religion was that they were on the verge of "going public," and were seeking advice on how to combat the negative publicity and other attacks they felt certain would result from this bold new public stature. They had read many of the publications of academics who had studied the "cult" controversy, and found that most scholarly specialists were critical of the cult stereotype—especially of the notion that intensive religious groups "brainwash" their members. Because these publications struck them as generally fair and even-handed, The Family felt that scholars of

Introduction vii

new religions, of all the various segments of society they might approach, would be the most open-minded group from which to seek advice.

While I was generally positively impressed by The Family during this initial meeting, I still had many reservations. I was also still bothered by what I might call the "nightmare factor," namely, What if the worst accusations leveled against them were true? The Family had been very frank about their controversial practice of "Flirty Fishing," openly admitting that sexual sharing had been an aspect of their witnessing outreach during the 1980s. Because much of my own scholarship had been critical of the notion of "cultic mind control," I categorically rejected the idea that The Family "brainwashed" their adherents. There was, however, one particular accusation about which I had doubts, namely, Did Family members interact sexually with, or otherwise abuse, their children? This particular accusation had been a central theme in anti-Family literature, and I had little or no way of evaluating it. I called other scholars I knew, but no one had any hard data on the issue.

Because I still had a question on this point, I interacted with The Family cautiously. When we could spare time from our busy schedules, my wife and I visited the Family home in the Los Angeles area. I gathered impressions, being especially attentive in my interactions with the second generation. I found the young adults to be balanced, well-integrated individuals, and the children to be exceptionally open and loving. Over the course of a year of ongoing contact with The Family, including interactions with communities in different areas of the country and abroad, these impressions have been continually reinforced. Thus, while I do not claim formal competence as a psychologist, I can assert with some confidence that The Family does *not* abuse its children.

During 1993, the same year in which I was evaluating The Family, they made international headlines as a result of mass arrests in France and Argentina. The pretext for these raids was a charge of child abuse—precisely the issue I was investigating. Gratifyingly, authorities in these countries came to the same conclusion I was reaching, namely that the child abuse accusation was little more than an emotionally-charged excuse for persecuting a minority religious group. In both countries everyone was eventually released, and The Family given a clean bill of health. Even as I write these words, Argentina is considering impeachment proceedings against the judge who ordered the raids.

The release of Family members has not, however, made headlines. In a pattern typical of the media, dismissal of the same charges that months before had made front page news failed to merit even a back page story. Thus despite their innocence, the public still has the impression that The Family is an "awful sex cult" that abuses its children.

The Family's most vociferous critics have, however, begun to change tactics. Having failed to make the child abuse charge stick, the latest approach has been to accuse The Family of being a racist movement. This charge flows out of The Family's adherence to certain conspiracy theories that postulate a small clique of wealthy Jews (portrayed as a kind of Jewish Mafia) playing a key role in the "one world" conspiracy that will bring in the Anti-Christ. At the time of this writing, adherence to such theories is beginning to be used by The Family's critics to support the contention that Family members are unworthy parents who teach their offspring a doctrine of paranoid hatred. This accusation is, however, as empty of empirical content as the child abuse accusation. To point to a hypothetical group of Jewish financiers as plotters in a worldwide conspiracy does not, at least in the case of the Family, automatically translate into anti-Semitism.

Because this writer's wife is of Italian-Jewish heritage and because of our activity in Jewish religious life (e.g., my youngest daughter is currently preparing for her Bat Mitzvah), I have taken more than a little interest in this aspect of The Family's teachings, and have spent many hours discussing the matter with members and reading relevant position statements and tracts. David Berg, the group's leader, is clearly not anti-Semitic: Berg has no trouble admitting his own Jewish heritage, and Family members from Jewish backgrounds are not regarded differently from non-Jews. Berg is, rather, inclined toward radical rhetoric, and certain of his statements can, when taken out of context, be construed as anti-Semitic.

With respect to all forms of racial and ethnic prejudice, my observation is that The Family is, if anything, on the opposite extreme, going out of their way to be open and accepting of others. My impressions have been strongly reinforced by the observation of other academics. For instance, in a statement prepared for one of The Family's court cases, Stuart Wright, Professor of Sociology at Lamar University, observed that the community he visited was,

> quite diverse, a sort of microcosm of the global community. I was not prepared for the diversity that I saw there. The fact that you have been able to forge a community across so many different ethnic, racial and class boundaries speaks well of The Family and your efforts. You have been able to accomplish this at a very time when societies in Europe and North America are becoming increasingly fragmented along ethnic, racial & religious lines. I do not consider this a small feat, and it should evoke some degree of interest among scholars.

Because of their importance, and because of their often controversial history, a number of different academicians have accepted The Family's invitation to study them. Being aware of both this state of affairs and of the widespread general interest in The Family, I contacted many of the relevant researchers in the early fall of 1993, and invited them to participate in the present volume. Because some of these scholars did not feel that they were far enough along in their investigations to contribute formal papers, the project was reconceptualized to consist of relatively *informal* papers—papers that would present *preliminary* findings rather than the finished products of formal research projects. To this modified agenda, I added the request that participants attempt to write in a less academic style, a style that would make their observations accessible to a broad readership.

The impact of these alterations has been uneven. Some of my colleagues have been able to break out of old habits and write truly engaging prose, while others have not. Also, in cases where their research was more focused on the analysis of documents and past history than on gathering new data from current membership, their chapters present finished products rather than preliminary findings. Finally, the reader will also find that the authors take differing positions toward The Family, depending on, among other factors, their differing sources of information. While these variables may make the volume come across as something of a "patchwork quilt," the net effect of this diversity should provide readers with both a richly textured picture of this fascinating group, and a variety of perspectives from which to view The Family.

As introductory essays, it was difficult to choose between two excellent overviews of The Family's history, namely David Bromley and Sidney Newton's concise, "The Family: History, Organization and Ideology," and James Richardson's more in-depth, "Update on 'The Family': Organizational Change and Development in a Controversial New Religious Group." In the end, a third option, Susan Palmer's "Heaven's Children: The Children of God's Second Generation," was utilized as the first chapter, and the Richardson and Bromley/Newton papers were inserted as second and third chapters, respectively. The Palmer paper was chosen to introduce the book because its descriptive, first-person account made The Family come alive as a group of flesh-and-blood human beings—arguably the best point from which to begin an examination of a movement that has been thoroughly dehumanized in the mass media.

Lawrence Lilliston (a child psychologist) and Gary Shepherd (a sociologist of religion) have, as a team, studied The Family's children.

Their jointly-authored chapters, "Psychological Assessment of Children in The Family" and "Field Observations of Young People's Experience and Role in the Family," provide two differing but complementary perspectives on how the community regards and treats its children—the aspect of The Family's lifestyle most reported in recent media coverage. The other facet of this group's ministry on which the media has focused is the discontinued practice of "flirty fishing," in which Family members would engage in sexual activity with the individuals to whom they were witnessing. Gordon Melton's chapter, "Sexuality and the Maturation of The Family," traces the development of flirty fishing as an outgrowth of the Law of Love through a careful, historical examination of the movement's literature.

Chapters seven, eight, and nine give the reader some sense of The Family's international dimension. Charlotte Hardman studied The Family in England, and her chapter, "Keeping the Faith and Leaving the Army: TRF Supporters of the Lord's Endtime Family," focuses on the sociologically-interesting group of individuals who have dropped out of full-time involvement with The Family, but who continue to receive the movement's literature, and remain affiliated in less formal ways. In his "The Children of God and The Family in Italy," Massimo Introvigne provides an intriguing case study of this movement's history in Italy. And in "From 'Children of God' to 'The Family,'" Stuart Wright discusses how The Family's international presence prompted their transformation from a California-based counter-cultural group to a global religious movement.

The next four essays focus directly on the controversy surrounding The Family. Michael Homer's chapter, "New Religions and Child Custody Cases: Comparisons Between the American and European Experience," compares The Family's current problems with a variety of different conflicts, and especially with child custody cases involving Mormon polygamous groups. Moorman Oliver's "Today's Jackboots: The Inquisition Revisited," is a detailed survey of the outrageous manner in which officials in different nations around the globe have persecuted The Family on trumped up charges of child abuse. In his passionately-worded essay, Oliver concludes that child abuse has indeed been committed—by The Family's persecutors. George Robertson's and James Lewis's chapters examine assaults on two other non-traditional religions in which accusations of child abuse played a key role—respectively, the Island Pond raid and the attack on the Branch Davidian community. Both of these incidents offer constructive parallels with the international crusade that has been carried out against The Family.

John Saliba's "Scholarly Studies on the Children of God/The Family" surveys the limited scholarship that has been published on The Family to date. Though much of what earlier researchers wrote is out-of-date with respect to the current movement, and while some of it is even tendentious, placed in the right perspective this body of scholarship nevertheless provides a useful point of reference for anyone contemplating an in-depth study of The Family, particularly of its earlier years. While parts of David Millikan's chapter repeat historical material covered in preceding chapters, Millikan's in-depth essay, "The Children of God, The Family of Love, The Family," provides details of Family life not found elsewhere. His essay is especially useful for his description of aspects of The Family's theology and eschatology. The volume concludes with an afterward by Gordon Melton that puts many of The Family's beliefs and practices in historical and comparative perspective.

Editor's Note:

As this volume was going it press, it was learned that Father David had passed away. I would like to offer my heartfelt condolences to the worldwide membership of The Family. It is my sincere hope that the following pages will serve to clear up many of the misunderstandings which continue to surround the movement founded by Father David.

Chapter 1

"Heaven's Children": The Children of God's Second Generation

Susan J. Palmer
Dawson College

On September 8, 1993 I was flying over the Grand Canyon to visit The Family in Los Angeles. The leaders in L.A. had found out about my SSHRC grant to study children in new religious movements (NRMs) and had demanded, "*We* need to be studied, so why don't you come out and study *us*?" They had offered unlimited access and cooperation (in contrast to Quebec NRMs I'd approached who definitely didn't want me snuffling around their kids, and even accused me of spying for the Catholic School Board). So, I booked a flight—and then the Argentina "raid" made the headlines.

Looking down at the purple-orange crusts of the Grand Canyon, I thought of my family's warning: "What if you get hauled off to jail in the middle of the night as a child molester?" and my friend's unsolicited advice on how to ward off "flirty fishermen"—and I was a *little* worried. There was nothing written on this group since the articles by Roy Wallis and James Richardson, based on research undertaken in the late seventies—except for Deborah Davis' horrid book (1984) which denounces her prophet-father as a child molester and heretic, and awards him a negative apocalyptic role within mainstream fundamentalist

Christianity. Existing studies categorize this NRM as a millenarian and communal movement—exactly the kind of social organization that is prone to conducting radical experiments in family life and sexuality (Kanter, 1973). So, the point is, I didn't know what to expect—utopia or distopia?

One week later I was back in Montreal, and everyone seemed to inquire, "Well, do they? Do they abuse their children?" "No, they don't, I'm convinced of it." My friends looked doubtful. "Are you sure? That's not what *Time* magazine said. How can you be so sure?" Now that I know the disciples, have studied their literature and tried to figure out their history and communal patterns, my own common sense is telling me these allegations of "kidnapping, rape, sodomy, child abuse" are ludicrous—but it is difficult to convince others. "You've been love-bombed," they joke, "brainwashed!" My mother, horrified that I would contradict *Time* magazine warned, "Don't lose your objectivity!"

My purpose in writing down my thoughts and experiences of the past week is to convey my impressions of life in The Family today, as related by an outsider who at least strives towards the elusive ideal of "objectivity." Next, what I find most extraordinary about The Family at this phase in their history is their success in socializing their children who, it seems, have absorbed their parents' fiery evangelical spirit and intense religious commitment. Since Foster (1981) and other historians have observed that one of the main causes for the decline of two great utopias in American history, the Shakers and Oneida Perfectionists, was their failure in inculcating religious values in their children, I am going to address the issue of how The Family has accomplished this feat. Finally, I feel compelled (more by a feeling of exasperation than by a larger sense of justice) to refute the lies and gross inaccuracies inundating the mass media concerning The Family—and to present my own theories as to why this particular NRM invites this currently fashionable brand of religious persecution—allegations of child abuse.

The media portrait of "the sex-for-salvation cult" suggests aging baby boomers enslaving and molesting little children. What I actually encountered was a society run by dynamic teenagers and young adults born into the movement. Attractive and clean cut, they brought to mind the *Pat Boone Show* rather than the ragged hippies who "forsook all" to become Children of God. Trained in music and choreography from an early age, they perform on the streets and make the outreach videos; they teach the children, preside over devotional services in the Homes, and deal with the public—while many of their parents have left the communes to become associate tithing members (TRF supporters) or have retired to the back bench of the organization. As a participant-observer I felt like I was living with a (drug-free, domestically tidy and sexually disciplined) rock group, for I was surrounded by a flourishing "cult of youth" that in many ways replicates—and even—parodies—the glamorous youth cult conjured up by the mass media.

I will begin with a travelogue, and then attempt to analyze the development of the commune, its family patterns and the satisfactions "Heaven's Children" find within their charismatic community. Some thoughts on the child abuse allegations will conclude this essay.

Travelogue

At the Arrivals gate, I was greeted by a teenage girl with long black hair, and a man in his forties. They were dressed in shorts and T-shirts and led me to their van. After praying for a safe trip ("Thankyou, thankyou Jesus, Praise the Lord") we drove along the beautiful coast towards San Diego where The Family's largest School Home in North America is situated. They were pretty interesting. He had joined as a young Jewish boy in 1968 on Miami Beach when there were only 100 disciples. (His impressions: "It was as if those people had just stepped out of the pages of the Bible!") The girl, "Jimena" was the 19 year-old daughter of a Mexican drug-dealer and Amerindian-Spanish biker's babe who had both "forsaken all" to follow Jesus, but had since split up and left the movement, leaving their children in the care of The Family. (Later I began to see it the other way around—they had left care and future of The Family in the hands of their children.)

The home in San Diego was a large, ranch-style L-shaped house with a swimming pool. After I had been introduced to the 15-odd adult brothers and sisters and finally mastered the ritual hug, I was taken on a tour. It was during the two-hour "Rest & Word" period (2:OO-4:OO p.m.) and all the children were asleep. Jimena had explained The Family's system of age sets, which I was now trying to apply to these rooms of sleeping children. Four little "MC" boys (Middle Children of 6-8) lay in their bunks beside a fan's cooling buzz. I was interested to note that they segregate their children's sleeping quarters by sex at an early age. (Later I was to learn this was a response to persecution: "They'll say we encourage our three year olds to have sex orgies among themselves!") Five pre-teen girls, whom I was later to know as the "JETTS" (Junior End Time Teens, 11-13) slumbered in their bunkbeds, their long silky hair trailing over their pillows, their features ranging from North European to Oriental to Hispanic. The children's rooms were clean and pleasantly arranged, from the YC's (Younger Children of 3-5) to the OC's (Older Children) to the OT's (Older Teens). On viewing the five empty basinets in the Infants & Toddlers' room, I asked,

"Where are the babies?" "With their mothers," was the logical reply.

That evening, the whole commune gathered to watch the NBC NOW Show's special on The Family and its recent controversies. The host set the tone immediately by blurting out, "Family members we interviewed begged us *not* to call them a *CULT*, and not to refer to their homes as a *COMPOUND* [the famous clip of David Koresh tossing his head appears, his chin bristles protruding like ominous portents of social disorder] . . . and *not* to compare them to the Branch Davidians" [the flames of Waco reared up ominously]. He went on to mention that members in Argentina had been arrested on charges of rape, kidnapping, child abuse, sodomy . . . . "Sodomy!" screamed the teenagers in the audience, "Eooh! Gross! That just *proves* they don't know anything about us. Grandpa's *always* been against sodomy!"

"If we're a so-called 'sex cult,'" remarked a gorgeous 18 year-old sitting beside me, "What *I* don't understand is why *I'm* not getting any!" "Yeah!" her peers agreed, "How come there's never any sex coming *our* way?"

"Shhh" cautioned the Shepherdess, "Let's listen."

"Angry ex-members were trying to track down the leader David Berg, who went into hiding in the 1970's," we were told. A photograph of the prophet himself, flanked by his consort Maria and a bevy of low-necked beauties during the Flirty Fishing heyday at Tenerife flashed on the screen. The disciples gasped. Later, reading through their literature, I was to learn that they *never* show Father David's face for fear his enemies will recognize him. "Dad" (or "Grandpa" for the second generation) went underground with Maria in the mid-70's, and has not made a public appearance since (except for a short time in Tenerife in 1977). In The Family's "pubs" (publications), his face is sometimes concealed beneath the caricature of a lion. From his hiding place, as a "prophet on the mountain," he has kept up a prolific stream of "Mo Letters." These "pubs" convey a wealth of detail concerning the private domestic life of the charismatic duo. In the early days their intimate life and the trials of "flirty fishing" were frankly discussed, and advice to disciples on handling jealousy and acheiving sexual satisfaction was offered. Since 1987, however, there has been a distinct change in their tone and content. Wholesome, family-oriented comic strips have appeared relating tales from "Grandpa's" childhood. Didactic comics written for children introduce new role models in Techi and Davidito, the charismatic duo's children, and document their daily life as they learn to cook, wash, sew and avoid domestic hazards.

Two young teachers introduced me to The Family's rich and extensive literature on childrearing and education. Parents consult the three volume *Childcare Handbook* (1982), and the book *Raise 'Em Right*, which is a compilation of writings and theories from secular sources. The educational materials used in their home schooling program contain a broad range of information in the same subject areas found in public schools. The main difference lies in the rejection of Darwin and the emphasis on Bible studies, prophecy and prayer. Various teaching methods are employed—books, workbooks, Family produced "GAP" videos, a (secular) *Skillbank* computor course on reading, comprehension, dictionary, language tutorial, composition, grammar, spelling ("We consider it pretty godly") and field trips. The Family's schooling has been registered under an umbrella school, and they periodically hand in samples of work, put out report cards and have been examined by schoolboard officials in five or six countries ("They have told us our program is *superior* to most regular programs").

Children are carefully guarded. I noticed that during "family time," when one parent had to go indoors for a moment, he or she would always make sure that the other parent kept a close eye on the kids—who looked perfectly safe sitting on the grass or playing ball. Since the garden was surrounded by a fence, and other adults were playing nearby, I felt this was oversolicitous, but then it occurred to me that the tiniest scrape or bruise (which my own children are constantly receiving when they play outdoors) might be analyzed as evidence of "physical abuse" in the event of a "raid."

Witnessing Expeditions

On the third day I was invited to accompany the children on a Get Out. The KIDS (Kind Inspired Dedicated Soldiers) and the JETTS (Junior End Time Teens) were well-groomed and dressed like any middle-class kids but in matching T-shirts, jeans and sneakers that were factory-donated, not personally chosen. Throughout the trip the teachers kept brushing their hair and spraying their small hands with an alcohol bottle. This latter custom, they explained, was picked up in Asia, where it was used as a safeguard against tropical diseases when children rode on subways or played in parks. After the KIDS had sung and danced in a Philipino restaurant, they needed a hat for the collection, so I offered mine. Afterwords, to my surprise, the teacher apologized profusely for soiling the hat with "money which is so dirty" and sprayed the inside with alchohol before returning it.

The next evening I drove the van for the Senior Teens and the YA's witnessing/provisioning expedition. The girls resembled all-American upper middle class teens in shorts and blouses, their long hair brushed neatly. Eight young people and two guitars piled into the van and, before setting off, we prayed for safety. Sometimes the team would stop at a restaurant that knew them and had invited them back. Sometimes they couldn't remember its location and we'd have to "pioneer it." We had already sung in a few restaurants, when they decided it was time for "provisioning." I pointed out an expensive-looking restaurant as a joke, and they said, "OK, stop!"

I panicked, "Come on, there's no *way* we can barge in—nine strangers—and ask for free food!" But we pulled into the parking lot, prayed for the Lord to "soften the manager's heart," and then the girls went in, asked to speak to the assistant manager, explained they were from a "Christian missionary movement," got permission to sing a few songs and started right away. The guests, surprised by the high quality of the performance, put down their forks and clapped. The girls performed exhuberant choreography, and waiters and cooks gathered at the kitchen and stared. The eyes of some were tearful, evidently moved by the singers' intense religious expression. After a few songs, everyone in the room was charmed by these talented, attractive, clean-cut kids—who then mentioned they were hungry and asked the manager to provide some food . . . "just something simple."

To my surprise, heaping plates of burritos and salad arrived at our table, with sugarless drinks. While the boys wiped their mouths, the leader girl got them organized: "You go take those cooks in the kitchen. You take the manager and the waiter—take them into the hall, and I'll talk to this table." It was now serious soul-saving time when receptive "sheep" would be warned of the impending End Time and invited to repeat a prayer so that Jesus could come into their heart. I watched puzzled Mexican busboys in stained white aprons gazing up at tanned blonde Valkyries who patted their shoulders and directed their prayer in fluent Spanish.

"Great! We saved twelve souls tonight! We sang in five restaurants, *and* we got provisioned!" the beautiful Hispanic-Amerindian leader girl exclaimed as we crawled back into our van, said the "Thankyou, thankyou Jesus" prayer.

"How do you know whether those guys were really saved or not?" I asked the sixteen year-old guitarist. He looked suprised, "Well they prayed didn't they?" He thought for a minute . . . "They were saved," he nodded confidently.

Like the Mormons, The Family sends out its restless youth to sow their wild oats by preaching; to assuage their longing for adventure and travel through missionary activity, which reinforces their commitment to the religion of their parents.

During the mid '80s, when Family children reached thirteen, they celebrated the completion of a stage of their formal schooling with a ceremony attended by their parents. The graduates wore white, were presented with a diploma and enjoyed music and ice cream. The first Teen Training Camp (TTC) was organized in 1986 in Mexico in response to the growing number of teenage members. Much of the movement's success in socializing their children seems to hinge on teens' experiences at the TTC's. During these months the youth forge strong ties with their peers, make friends with the opposite sex and participate in an intense, supervised regime involving Bible study, hard manual labour in the areas of renovations and gardening, and witnessing expeditions with singing and dance, under the guidance of Shepherds and Shepherdesses. Eschewing higher education in "the System" they move back into the communal homes (not necessarily the one inhabited by their parents) where they perform different tasks until they find their favourite or "ministry." On reaching eighteen and becoming a young adult ("YA"), they are considered sufficiently mature to embark on their first sexual relationship, which is viewed in the context of seeking a mate (although on occasion they have married before 18 with parental consent). To this end, they may enter into a "trial period" where they live and work with another YA of the opposite sex for six months, while they make up their minds whether or not God wants them to be together. If they feel that He does, they become "betrothed." Obviously, this highly supervised and cautious courtship is not what one would expect to find in a movement currently branded as a "sex-cult."

Family teenagers appear to be far more cautious and conservative than their parents' generation in their attitudes towards sexuality. The Shepherdess of the San Diego home who counselled YA's and Teens, having grown up in the permissive society of Denmark, commented: "They are very different from the way we were. In the sixties if you just made friends with a guy, you'd usually end up in bed together, and with our children today, it is always *baby steps*, never a leap. They never take a risk." I interviewed two pretty girls in their late teens who were concerned about the shortage of young men on the West Coast. "We decided to organize a big dance, and we were sitting there adding up all the boys in the States we could invite, and we realized there weren't very many and we knew them all. We'd heard all about them from the girls they'd liked at Teen Camp, so it was hard to get excited about them." While listening to these teenagers' various romantic histories, I was able to piece together an elaborate web of emotional intrigue dating back to the Teen Training Camp in Mexico. The girls related how shy and inexpressive boys, after months of patient coaxing, had finally admitted in rare climactic moments that "He liked me." The girls were so worried about selfishly hogging an eligible boy that, in true communal spirit, they had offered him to their girlfriends first before experiencing their first kiss. In *Children of the Dream*, Bruno Bettelheim comments on the sexual inhibitions of the Kibbutzim children who grow up with no privacy as brothers and sisters, and interprets their repression as an incest taboo. It struck me that I might be seeing the same phenomenon here. When the first disciples joined, there were many single adults of the same age to choose from, new faces appeared every day, and the surrounding cultural environment encouraged sexual freedom and experimentation. For The Family's second generation the situation is quite different, they must contract endogamous "betrothals," courtship is supervised and regulated, and their choice is narrow.

There appears to be a generation gap between the 25 year-olds and their parents' generation. Disciples in their thirties were hard to find. The first generation, flower children of the sixties, and were now in their forties—many of them grandparents as their oldest children reached their twenties and became "betrothed." This came about because the Family of Love moved east to Europe and spread in small family teams throughout South East Asia and Japan in the mid seventies. There does not appear to be many interracial, intercultural marriages, and some of the original American disciples returned home with their families in 1989, leaving their mission posts in the hands of nationals, many of whom, presumably, would be in their thirties.

The second generation appear to regard their parents' time of sexual excess with a kind of amused indulgence. A group of YA's showed me their albums and pointed to photographs of their parents in their hippie heyday with pride. "There's my Dad. He used to be a drug dealer before he got saved. "Did you see my Mom? She was in a biker gang when she met the disciples on Miami beach." "*My* Dad was from a very old Argentinian family, they were very wealthy and he was a famous guitarist, but he forsook all because he really loved the Lord." "My Mom was feeling really depressed and guilty when she met the disciples because she's just had an abortion. She was so grateful to the Lord when she met my dad and they had me." Whether their parents had been down and out or aristocrats, the point was they had *forsaken* all for Jesus, and their children looked back on them as legendary heroes and pioneers.

The rather wild impression I had received of the Children of God in the '70's was of an erratic band of rebellious hippies-turned-Jesus Freaks who indulged in what Roy Wallis (1979) dubbed "antinomian" behaviour in pursuing "short-term, pluralistic sexual relationships" inside the group and evangelical strategies as "Happy Hookers for Jesus" in the outside world. So, naturally, I wondered how they had arrived from *there* to *here*—to developing this rich, highly organized and elaborate culture of childhood. In attempting to chart the changing communal patterns and the development of parental roles and models of childrearing I relied upon three sources: 1. Interviews (two female YA teachers, two teens, four mothers and Shepherdesses who shared their FF-ing remniscences, and one father, a longterm disciple); 2. 50 questionnaires were filled out, 35 in the San Diego Home and 15 in the L.A. Media Home; 3. A study of a cupboardful of COG to Family literature was undertaken with the assistance of a YA who pointed out important passages in the Mo Letters, the *Book of Remembrance* and the children's comic, *Life with Grandpa*. Through perusing the pubs, and listening to members' biographical accounts it became clear that this movement has always been engaged in self-conscious experimentation; as the community matures its changes appear to depend *less* on the prophet's revelations and *more* on collective decision-making as information flows smoothly from the bottom up as well as percolating down. The "pubs" are remarkable for their candid discussions of individuals' shortcomings and abuses of power in the community and in their trial and error approach to problem solving.

Patterns of Communal Living and Family

Like most communes, this one sees itself as a large, extended family. Adults call each other "Brother" and "Sister" and are addressed by the second generation as "Auntie" and "Uncle." While older members refer to their 74 year-old founder-prophet as "Dad," for their children he is "Grandpa." It is interesting that Maria, who at 47 is of the first generation of disciples, is titled "Mama," but that her own son and daughter address her prophet-consort (and their acting father) as "Grandpa."

Marriage ceremonies in the movement are called "betrothals," a term which reflects the ideal of group marriage and the members' primary commitment to Jesus as Spouse. In the early years (1968-1978) men and women slept apart and Moses David insisted on celibacy for the new Bible students ("Babes"), but also pressured his followers to find mates in preparation for traveling in the mission field. Group betrothals were celebrated, and couples often based (or confirmed) their choice on prophetic dreams, on the recommendations of the Shepherds and Shepherdesses (leaders), on the advice of angelic apparitions or spirit guides, and a form of divination called "Gideon's Fleece." By the late seventies betrothed couples living in communes (called "colonies" then) began sexual sharing based on the "Law of Love." Between 1978 and

1987 women were encouraged to extend sexual freedom beyond the boundaries of the commune by offering sexual favours to lonely businessmen in order to prove Jesus' love for them in a new soul-saving strategy called "flirty fishing" or "FFing." Many of these girls developed warm and long-lasting relationships with their "fish" who moved into the commune or—more frequently—became "friends" or patrons, sometimes contributing financial aid to the Family of Love. (I received conflicting accounts of this phase; some members insisted that sexual sharing was a consequence of flirty fishing, a consolation for lonely jealous husbands; others suggested the leaders were already experimenting with "free love" before FFing was instituted.) FFing was discontinued in 1987 due to the AIDS threat, and sex with outsiders became punishable by excommunication. "Sharing" between consenting adults still continues today, but only within the individual Home, not between Homes, and it seems to be a practice confined to the first generation.

In January to February, 1978 Father David sent out the *RNR* letters, instituting a number of dramatic changes in the movement. Claiming there were reports of local abuses of power, he fired over 300 leaders who made up the international "Chain" (Kings, Queens, Visiting Servants) and sent them out to pioneer new fields. Nationals were encouraged to take the lead in their native countries, and "Grassroots" leaders were appointed or elected by the local congregation. With the disbanding of the large communes, the number of Homes worldwide increased from 879 to 1634 in 1979 (*The Book of Remembrance*, Vols.I & II, 1983:387). Many of the top leaders defected, including the prophet's daughter Deborah, her current husband Bill Davis and former spouse Jethro, Watchman who became one of the main career apostates currently lionized by the Cult Awareness Network, and Rachel, the prophet's top consort after Maria. The official membership figures demonstrate a high rate of defection, from 8068 members in 1977 to 5742 by the end of 1978. There was a wave of persecution and media attacks on the Family of Love in 1978 in the wake of Jonstown, and members were jailed in Mexico. Members packed their "flee bags" and "went underground." Dad, Maria and their entourage fled from Spain to Portugal, and on to Switzerland, Malta, and France.

During the *RNR* phase (1978-1981) the Homes shrunk to the size of 4-8 members, mainly nuclear families living with one or two friends. Many of these families drifted away from the movement, neglected to pay their tithing or send in reports and subscribe to the Mo Letters. As one informant noted, "many of the couples were having a hard time finding jobs and raising their kids without the support of living in a colony." There was a minimal supervision over members by the Visiting

Servants who toured the Homes, but were in no position to enforce rules. *The Book of Remembrance* reports "Sexual freedom! FFing witness booms w/worldwide results!" right after the *RNR*. The letter *DO YA WANT THE LETTERS OR DON'TCHA?!* (DO No. 667, Feb. 1978) complains that donations to World Services have dropped from 20-50% to 10% and the movement has swung from "total tyranny to total anarchy." This letter features a cartoon of Father David sadly standing in the snow outside a home where a wild orgy appears to be in progress, with women in baby doll pajamas and men swilling beer beneath a banner which reads "RNR Liberation Party." On the basis of interview data, I received the impression that sexual sharing was an important means for the disciples to preserve their close emotional bonds despite the collapse of the communal structure; to reaffirm their unique identity and elite status as distinct from mainstream Christians at a time when they were "invading the Churches" (infiltrating mainline denominations) and many of the distinguishing features of their culture seemed to be threatened with extinction. Also, women continued to witness through "flirty fishing" and the subsequent donations would often go towards maintaining their husbands and children rather than towards "the work"—a situation which contributed towards a general impression of sexual license.

In 1981 the Homes began to group together and consolidate into large communes (40-45 members) in the "Fellowship Revolution." Homes were directed by Shepherding Teams of three unrelated members, in order to avoid the abuses of power that were believed to have resulted from having married couples Shepherd the Homes in the pre-RNR days. New channels were established whereby information could flow upward like the letter drop for Dad and Maria, and counselling and discussion played a major role in decision-making.

Integrating the Biological and the Spiritual Family

In The Family it appears that emotional bonds between parents and progeny are reinforced by certain institutions and yet weakened by others. Children above toddler age sleep in rooms with their peers and attend classes and eat with their age set during the week. Every day has a "Family Time," however, just before dinner (or at other times, depending on the needs of each Home) when the biological parents will play in the garden with their offspring. The private family is enlarged by adding single adults or solitary teenagers who participate in childcare responsibilities to make up a "Family Team." Every Saturday evening, all the children will "sleep over" in their biological parents' room, and will spend all day Sunday with their parents and adjunct members of the

Family Team. It is understood that the kids belong to the commune first, and to their parents second. One father described how his youngest toddler would see him going out and would cry to be picked up, and how he longed to pick him up and take him with him, but "that would be depriving him of the opportunity to get the Victory. His teachers are doing what's best for *him*, and I must respect their input." He added, "We are all Uncles and Aunties to all the children. I would never go out and buy toys or sweets and come back and give them to my *own* kids. Every kid is equal and they all have to learn to share."

The "Childcare Revolution"

Previous studies of American communal/millenarian movements that espouse the ideals of sexual sharing and freedom seem to suggest that a "typical" pattern is to censure pregnancy and to discourage parental roles. The 19th century Oneida Perfectionists practised *coitus interruptus* and abhorred "philopropogativeness"; the Rajneesh banned childbearing, encouraged sterilization and separated existing children from parents by setting up a "Kids Commune." The Raelian Movement made the use of condoms obligatory in 1977, and advises members to refrain from procreation in anticipation of being cloned when the extraterrestrials descend. The Family, therefore, stands out as an example of a "free love" commune that has always welcomed babies, rejected birth control and condemned abortion.

In 1971 the Children of God numbered around 175, lived on the TSC (Texas Soul Clinic) ranch and had produced only 6 children. By 1972 there was a population explosion of 108 babies. Deborah, Berg's oldest daughter, who had several children by then, produced the early writings on childbirth and baby care (which are still used despite her "enemy" status), and a Montessori-based program was set up for toddlers. A Mo Letter from that period condemns the free-wheeling ex-hippies as men who "scatter seed" and mothers who were "spending their time making love and don't mind bearing children, but they don't give a damn about taking care of them. Let someone else do that!"—and admonishes them to adjust to their new responsibilities as parents. The concern is expressed that COG will become "an orphanage for brats instead of an officers training school." Mo suggests the solution is to decentralize into smaller colonies where parents can look after their own progeny (*Decentralization*, 9/1O/71. GP.No.122).

The first self-conscious efforts to found a commune are expressed in a class Dad gave at TSC (Texas Soul Clinic Ranch), called "A Sample, Not a Sermon":

We are learning to be a living example ... of how God wants His Children to live ... We are pioneers ... This is like a great experiment and we've got to make it work. We are organizing a society. We're in the experimental stage of organizing a nation with every minor detail involved, from how to take care of babies to ID cards .... This is the kingdom of God ... right here on this desolate piece of land in the middle of Texas wilderness—'as it is in Heaven' (*The Book of Remembrance*, Vol.II. 1983,55-56).

An ideological emphasis on the subordination of the biological family to the spiritual family—what Kanter terms "defamilialization"—is found in Dad's revelation concerning "what it meant to be one family and really one in the Lord—replacing one of the main causes of this selfishness, the private family, with God's Family unit, the Church, of whom Jesus is the Head and we are all membets." Dad declared, "God is in the business of breaking up marriages in order that He might join each of the parties together with Himself" (*The Book of Remembrance* Vol. II. 1983:67).

The issue of the ownership of progeny had to be addressed, and Dad's policy on illegitimate children, called "Jesus babies," became clarified as the group gradually moved into sexual "sharing" *within* the commune, and also into providing sexual favours *outside* the commune to potential converts and supporters through "flirty fishing."

By 1974 Dad and Maria had left America, gone to Enland, Israel and Cyprus, and then began living in Tenerife of the Canary Islands where they were "pioneering" the flirty fishing ministry. Maria became pregnant from one of her fish and gave birth to a boy, Davidito, in 1975. Although Dad reveals that her first reaction to pregnancy was to "moan and groan" and worry about how she could continue her ministry, he concludes that God will only permit pregnancies according to His Will, and rejoices in Davidito as compensation for their sacrificial ministry of FFing:

HE WAS ALMOST LIKE OUR REWARD. Hallelujah! Thank You Jesus! He was like our reward for all the suffering and agony and everything else, the sacrifice she had to go through to do what she did to show those men love. We were rewarded with about as sweet and cute and smart and funny little baby as you could have!

The leader's acceptance of his own "illegitimate" son set a precedent for the communal responsibility of children: "I couldn't possibly love Davidito any more. Some people talk about him as if he's some kind of physical freak ... but ... He's God's little love-gift to us—Amen? Shouldn't *you* feel that way about a child of *your* own family, a child of your brother or sister?"

The charismatic duo's interest in setting up guidelines for rearing children was evidently stimulated by the birth of their own children:

It wasn't until *she* got pregnant that we found out there was virtually *no childcare* ministry! . . . Davidito was to become an example to the world and inspire *loads* of Childcare material! Thank God! *(The Advantages of Having Children* DO 688, 4/78).

Careful attention was paid to the needs of children in the ensuing pubs. The statistics or "stats" from 1971 to 1981 claim that 4800 children have been born into the movement, 1000 have joined with their parents, and "346 Jesus Babies have been reported." By 1982 the Family of Love claimed to number 5,8OO kids and 21,000 adults. In contrast to this ratio (1:3), the ratio now (1993) is even higher in favour of youth; it is 2:I in favour of children out of around 9,000 or 1O,OOO disciples.

Dad's ideas on child education at that stage were obviously very different from Maria's. He vacillates between advocating large and small communes, and between awarding the care of kids more to parents or more to the collective. Having recently disbanded the "monster blobs like 250 at TSC [where] we had nurseries and . . . schools " he recommends that parents "pioneer their own Home amd take care of their *own* children the normal way in the normal home" (*The Advantages of Having Children,* May 1978 MO-DO 688). He also discourages investing in many educational materials and promotes religious training:

People think that Schools are where to pool all your Money to buy all this expensive equipment that isn't even suitable for our children. Much of that expensive Monttessori junk is not even worth putting in your house!

A HOME SHOULD BE A PLACE WHERE THE CHILD CAN LEARN ABOUT JESUS . . . So if the kids [here Dad is referring to the adults, who he often called "kids" in the early days] get the MO Letters and the Davidito series and some of the new Family Care material they'll know how to teach the children. . . . *STICK TO THE NEW TESTAMENT AND THE MO LETTERS* and teach the Children at *hoe*. Take the children *litnessing,* take the children *provisioning* . . . then the kids will be getting the best school possible every day!

Maria, however, seems to have pursued a different course, and became increasingly interested in pedagogy. At this point she emergences as the more dominant figure in the charismatic duo—at least in the area of childrearing. An increasing emphasis is placed on the importance of children, so that more time, money, energy and air space is allotted to children's care and concerns.

It is generally agreed that "Mama Maria" was responsible for the "Childcare Revolution," and she was also instrumental in implementing the "School Vision." When the children of the original disciples began to reach school age, she set up a team of researchers to examine different philosophies of education, from Montessori, Doman to Spock, the range of child development theories and training available in "the System," and the first materials for the current Home School program appeared in 1982. Communes which specialized in childcare and schooling were established, called "School Homes" as opposed to "Media Home"s or "Outreach Homes." Young adults attended teachers' training courses and took up the new "ministry" of home school teaching.

The communal sharing of parenting responsibilities was increasingly emphasized:

OUR CHILDREN BELONG TO THE FAMILY and *all* of us, and we are *all* their parents and they are *all* our children, so no "unwed" mother need fear for herslf or her children . . . .

MARRIAGE IN THE FAMILY IS TO JESUS and they are *all* "Jesus babies"! And we are *all* married to each other in His Love.

In 1978 611 babies were born into the Family of Love, and the pubs began to lay down new standards for caring for children and their mothers. Dad continually stresses the importance of taking children out litnessing (*Happy Housekeeping!* DO 671, 31/1/78), but makes it clear that they should *not* be used as sexual bait in FFing: ". . . they must be of legal age for sexual involvement, usually at least 21 to 23 depending on the state or the country. Watch out!" In an important pub called *HAPPY REBIRTHDAY!—RNR RULES* (DO 663, 18/2/78), the *THE FAMILY OF LOVE CHECKLIST* was sent to all the international colonies, requiring that each colony check the following procedures and report on a monthly basis to headquarters:

THE FAMILY OF LOVE CHECKLIST
VIII.Children; Have or do the children:
A. Have the necessary amount of neat, clean clothing—coat, hat, sweater, pajamas, good right-size shoes, bedding, underclothing, dia[pers, etc.? Yes__ No__ B. Sleep with helper in *separate bedroom* if parents schedule differs. C. Have sufficient *school* accomodations and supplies? Yes--No-- D. Have a good *bedroom* with the right kind of bed, bedding, ventilation, heating, and lighting? Yes__ No__ E. Have their *educational needs* been met? Yes__ No-- F. Read good *educational materials?* Yes__No__. G. Encouraged to *witness* to others? Yes__No__. H. Taught Bible and Mo Letters daily? Yes__No__. I. Get out for freash air and exercise daily? Yes__No__. J. On a regular eating, sleeping, school schedule? Yes__No__. K. If *sick,* isolated from others and well-supervised, fed and medically checked? Yes__No__. L. Get daily at least two glasses of whole milk, meat, hard cheese, yogurt, fresh fruit or juice, greemn or yellow vegetables and vitamins? Yes__No__. M. Get nutritious *snacks,* good wholesome *drinks* and safe water? Yes__No__.

Explain any No's:

The first indication that children were not merely an asset to the movement, but would actually play a millenarian role in the group's apocalyptic expectations, appears in Dad's *Prophecy for Davidito!* (DFO 619, 2/3/1977). At this time, Dad and Maria were fleeing from Tenerife to escape arrest resulting from their FFing activities in the local nightclubs, and were leaving their son behind. As they were kissing him goodby, Dad prophecied: *"FOR THIS CHILD SHALL SHINE AMONGST MEN* [he will be] a prince among men . . . a standard bearer before God."* A cartoon of Davidito as a young preacher appears in this pub. The millenarian theme became even stronger after the birth of Maria's daughter, Techi.

In the fall of 1977, Dad was sick and had a dream in which he beheld a five year-old girl who introduced herself as "Techi." When he became very ill the subsequent year and was thought to be dying, Techi reappeared and prayed for him, whereupon he was healed. In 1979 Maria gave birth to a little girl whom they named Techi. In 1985, Techi's sixth year, a number of pubs appeared proclaiming woman's dominant role in the End Times:

> Our women are going to be the leaders of tomorrow. They're going to be the salvation of this outfit, they already are . . . . Our women are the ones who are going to do the job, the real Heaven's Girls! *(TEENS! THE FUTURE OF YOUR FATHER!* (DO 2056 9/85).

The same pub announces that the pre-school Techi is "just like a teen" and features a cartoon of Techi, her blond pigtails flying, leading a millenarian gang of Amazonian teenage girls:

> Techi shall lead them . . . she is the greatest . . . she's going to lead them like she's leading them now. She's the best proofreader we have. I mean nobody is as anointed as she is reading those Heavens Girls texts . . . She's the heart & soul of her father and has the anointing & the mantle of me.

In October, 1990 Maria began writing the "Techi's Battles and Victories" Series. These pubs became important didactic literature for children, and were introduced to the disciples in a dramatic way:

> Recently he [the Devil] has attempted to . . . cause trouble in the King's house, by viciously attacking dear Techi . . . As a result of these battles, the Lord has been transforming Techi from a previously rather passive & spiritually easygoing little girl into an aggressive *fighter* for the Lord. . . And though the personal victories in Techi's life have been a great blessing, perhaps the greatest blessing to come out of these battles is the volume of

priceless lessons that Grandpa & Mama have shared . . . and that Techi herself has shared in her reports, reactions and times of pouring out her heart to Mama (*Good News,* October 1990).

The series is illustrated with cartoons of Techi kicking bad habits out the door, or sliding down a chute perilously close to an awaiting devil. These cautionary tales of a 9 year-old's "trials, battles and victories" contain moral lessons summed up by Maria in the section "Blessings from Battles!" Young readers are given assignments in writing their own confessions, questions and reactions. Maria writes, "Mama wants you JETTS & Teens to know that this GN . . . is especially for *you*.! Seeing how Techi has won different battles should encourage & help you with any similar battles that *you* may be going through."

A contrasting "sample" for child disciples is provided in the "Tony series. ("Tony's Last Chance," *Good News,* October 1991). These recount the battles of a rebellious young man who is unable to "get the victory" and is consequently threatened with expulsion from the community.

"Heaven's Children," The Future of the Family

The empowerment of youth is a theme that runs through the movement's history. Teens and young adults are praised in the pubs as Biblical scholars with prodigious memories, precocious prophets, intrepid ascetics and fiery evangelists. A retrospective account of the witnessing adventures of David Berg's three teenagers, Hosca, Aaron and Faith is presented in the videocassette, *The Acts of the Revolution for Jesus,* and the teens' early decision to "forsake all" (drop out of college, sell their livestock and witness across America)—as their own decision, with their father a mere shadowy, background figure giving Bible classes by night and driving the bus or "Ark" by day.

Today this pattern has returned. Now that the second generation have reached the same age as the original Children of God, they are being groomed to take over the administration and executive posts of the movement, and to assume the main "burden" of witnessing. Their parents' generation (now in their forties) are retreating and working behind the scenes. I observed tense moments between bossy YA's and adults in their forties who had been running things since the early seventies and appeared reluctant to relinquish their territory. It was explained to me that the YA's (no longer called "EA's" or "Experimental Adults") were undergoing "leadership training" because the reins of leadership were being placed in their hands, a deliberate policy announced by Dad:

I know they'll be our flame when I'm gone. All I know is that they've got it, they've got the anointing & they're the new wave, the Future, our tomorrow. They're going to do it no matter what because they love the Lord and they love me (*TEENS! THE FUTURE OF YOUR FATHER!*) (DO 2056 9/85).

A pub known as the "PER" ("Personal Encouragement Revolution," *Good News* July 1993, GN 553 DO) is a declaration of the coming of age of Family children and tells them they will henceforth be judged on their individual merits regardless of age. It begins with a note of encouragement: *"Grandpa and I Love You and Are Proud of You! We think you are the greatest teens on earth!.* Then it outlines their role in the coming Endtime:

> How applicable to you, the Lord's Endtime children, are His Words, "Ye are a *chosen* generation, a *royal priesthood, an holy nation, a peculiar people. . . Never before in history has the world been so utterly engulfed in spiritual darkness & so desperately in need of you—God's anointed children* . . . He needs you & you're going to be some of his key witnesses, & He's constantly watching over you with great care & love . . .

One of The Family's responses to external persecution has been to place even greater emphasis on the millenarian role awarded to children. When I asked the teachers how the possibility of another raid was affecting the children, they replied, "Well, we had to prepare them. Some of the kids in Australia were told that they would never see their parents again, that they're parents were bad and didn't love them. They all have their little flee bag packed with their Bibles, toothbrushes, the lawyer's number and our number. and they've been instructed how to behave—to be a good example." "That's in case we are woken up with guns pointed at our heads, like they did in France," the other teacher said.

When I noted, "They must be scared!" the first teacher answered, "We were worried about that, but they seem—sort of excited! It's as if they're *hoping* to get raided. One boy packed some rope, and when I asked him what it was for he said it was to tie up the legs of the guard, trip him up, then tie another guard to a chair, so they could all escape out the window. The other children saw it as a fun game and I had to tell them to calm down, not to get violent! They were getting over-stimulated."

I sat in on a class for the MC's and OC's in which they read aloud from a recent pub, *Victory in Babylon!*. This didactic comic mythologized the "raid" that had taken place in Australia the previous year, and prepared Family kids for a similar emergency:

> In 605 B.C., young Daniel, Shadrach . . . were taken from their homes in

Jerulasem by the invading army of Nebuchadnessar, & carries away to be captives to Babylon . . . Now in Heaven over 2000 years later, they have been looking back at the mighty miracles the Lord did at their time of captivity.

Youthful readers are reassured that, "A huge team of Angels and spirit helpers are sent to Earth to look after the children during their captivity. They warn the homes through dreams to prepare the children spiritually and physically for the coming persecution." Real events which had occurred to the Family children in the "raids" in Australia and France are woven into the narrative. A certain Judas-like character named Simon wins the children's sympathy by pretending to injure his foot during a basketball game. After they helped him bandage his foot, he convinces them to entrust him with secret messages to be smuggled out to their lawyer and parents, and hobbles off on his errand. One boy, happening to glance out of a bathroom window, sees Simon in the parking lot walking normally, presumably about to hand over their messages to a "Mrs Rotweiler" of Social Services, and the children express their shock and indignation at his betrayal. This parable illustrates the untrustworthiness of some Systemites (or, at least, the untrustworthiness of some social workers). This real-life social worker has unwittingly become a legendary figure for perhaps centuries of future generations of The Family.

The vital millenarian role of their children in uniting Heaven and Earth is further elaborated in *HEAVEN'S CHILDREN* (DO 2133, 9/85) and *HEAVEN'S CHILDREN IN THE MILLENNIUM* (DO 2126, 9/85). These pubs predict that the second generation will be the leaders in the millennium, and describe the world reverting to stone age, primitive societies after the Great Tribulation, and promise that Heaven's Children will take charge, clean up the mess, and rebuild a new civilization. Videosassetes like *Twenty Minutes to Go* and *New Worlds to Discover* dramatize The Family's postmillennial apocalyptic expectations. We see the Mark of the Beast, the One World Leader, the rise of the Antichrist, and the Children of God fleeing into the wilderness and receiving the crown of eternal life from Jesus, while America is destroyed.

These rock videos are an important tool in their outreach, but their significance in defining and reinforcing their own culture of youth cannot be overemphasized. Teens I interviewed were astonished that I had never seen nor heard of their key videos like *20 Minutes to Go*, and hastened to fill this gap in my education, pointing with pride to their older brothers and sisters who were starring in some of the numbers. In this way the group avoids the problem besetting many sectarian fundamentalist communities: the seductive influence of the mass media on their youth. Instead of outlawing movies and popular music, this

NRM inundates its children's daily life with its own tapes, videos, and select only those movies and news broadcasts from the secular world which lend themselves to an apocalyptic interpretation. Thus, the signing of the peace agreement between Israel and Palestine was taped and shown to the whole community. I heard comments like, "Wow! So the prophecy really *is* becoming fulfilled," and "It'll be broken in 3 1/2 years for sure; then we'll have the Great Tribulation!."

The technology of the mass media is used by The Family to reflect and replicate the glamorous youth culture supposedly happening outside the boundaries of the sect. Musical and dance idioms are borrowed from the mainstream, while some songs convey deeply counter-cultural messages -"Forsake all for Jesus" and "We're Living in the Endtime!" Every teen and YA gets their turn to be a narcissistic rock star and a selfless missionary at the same time. In the larger society, teens watching television can only yearn for fame and glamour; in The Family they participate in the creation of their own glamorous cult of youth through coopting the technology, but rejecting the values of the mass culture. Forestalling that sense of social deprivation through exposure to the media, the movement makes its own videos to convey a joyful sense of belonging to an exciting, elite youth club; of being on the inside looking out.

It occured to me that a new religion's success in socializing their children might depend on the thickness of the boundaries separating their community from the outside world. If these boundaries are too thick and formidable, children become curious, feel deprived and rebel against captivity. It they are too flimsy, children absorb the secular attitudes of their friends. The Family children mix with outsiders, but always within the framework of their witnessing role as the Lord's Endtime Children.

Reflections on the Child Abuse Allegations

On returning home I felt somewhat disoriented by the discrepancies between the reports appearing in newspapers and the reality I had just experienced. *The Gazette* (Montreal, Saturday, September 4, 1993) conjured up monsters born out of a primal stew of incest:

> "It's horrible. Nationalities are all mixed up." said Emilio Senise, of the investigating team. "There might even be children born of (incest between) fathers and daughters and other things like that."

The careless disregard of accuracy and history was disturbing:

> The U.S.-based Cult Awareness Network, which monitors such groups, says the sect's adult members and its children sleep with each other indiscriminately, believing that salvation comes through sex (*The Ottawa Citizen* Saturday, September 4, 1993: A7).

The New York Times International (Sunday, September 26, 1993) describes this NRM as "combining a belief in the Bible as the truth of God with a free exchange of sex, including encouraging young children to engage in sex . . . Former members say they were forced to have sex as minors with adults."

There was the uncritical citing of embittered ex-members' who dished out salacious glimpses illicit sex:

> There was abuse of children, actual penetration of girls under 10 years of age," says Ed Priebe, a member for 19 years, "there was incest." His wife, Amy . . . said children were pressured into sex. They were told Jesus "who died for us, he was willing to go all the way. So would you be willing to go all the way?" (*The Ottawa Citizen,* Sunday, September 5, 1993:D11).

Their stories were often inconsistent. In her book, Deborah Berg Davis makes it clear that she *never* succumbed to her prophet father's incestuous advances, and yet. . .."Appearing on the *The Geraldo Show* last week, Davis, 47, denounced her father as a child molester who continually raped her from age eight" (*The Ottawa Citizen,* Sunday, September 12, 1993:D11).

How could I reconcile these nightmares with the clean, peaceful, fun-loving households I had just stayed in? There seem to be three different notions as to the origins of the child abuse rumours:

Members invited to explain the origins of the child abuse allegations were of the opinion that they referred to private abuses possibly occurring in the small, unsupervised homes during the RNR period, whose members had probably left the movement by now. If any child abuse had occured, they argued, it was a result of secularization and contamination by a morally chaotic and selfish society upon members in the process of defecting.

The Family's accusers point to David Berg's *Letters to Davidito* as evidence that the charismatic founder not only expressed pederastic tendencies, but justified them in religious terms, encouraging his flock to experiment in this direction.

Religious minorities with unconventional marriage patterns (such as the Mormons, the Sullivanians, the Oneida Perfectionists) appear to stimulate fears in the surrounding culture and invite the accusation that they are exposing their children to inappropriate sexual behavior, or are corrupting their morals (Homer, 1993). During the Family of Love phase children were seen litnessing on the street, and their possible involvement in FFing was a concern.

After living with The Family for an action-packed week and poring over the Mo Letters I decided that perhaps these people were, after all, merely Christian Fundamentalists with a heavy millenarian and communal emphasis. Roy Wallis emphasises David Berg's originality, and claims that after his mother died and he left his wife (the Old Church) for 22-year-old Maria (the Young Church), his new consort recorded and validated his prophetic visions, and encouraged charismatic displays, thereby facilitating in "the full flowering of his heretical imagination." Richardson and Davis, on the other hand, insists that this NRM—while definitely unusual in its *praxis* (the experiential focus on sex)—still belongs to traditional fundamentalism in terms of its *beliefs*.

The Mo Letters at first browsing certainly *look* like heresy. UFOs, angels and spirits of gypsy kings float through the landscape of primitive Christianity. God's End Time prophet entertains us with frank disclosures of his own sex life and antinomian impulses, his poster-like prose voluptuously festooned with cartoons of naked ladies. But, despite recent accusations, these are not so much "pornographic" as aesthetically disquieting simply because of their *context;* surrounded as they are with PTL's (Praise the Lord's) and Bible quotes. They "mess up" our categories, our preconceptions concerning the sexual repressions and hypocrisy of Christian Fundamentalists, particularly those who (like Father David) are inclined to denounce sin, doomsday, abortion and "sodomites." Judges, journalists and juries take a quick glance at these letters and are inclined to believe something perverse is going on.

A survey of small societies, past and present which have been known to use harsh discipline on their children or sanctioned sexual relations between adults and pre-pubescent girls suggests they share two conditions in common: the subjugation of women to men and a denial of age as a meaningful category, as in the Love Israel commune and Aries' description (1962) of the court of Versailles. The Family, as it is currently structured, lacks both of these conditions, and exhibits a highly developed awareness of age sets, which separate its members into age-based categories which precise codes of etiquette and ethics governing their daily interactions. The "patriarchal control" theory used by feminist scholars (Jacob, 1984) to explain sexual abuse of young females in religious minorities does not apply to this NRM where women and men share leadership positions and domestic work, and the theology promotes the feminine aspect of the sacred.

The arguments for the child abuse allegations rest heavily on an oversimplified model of charisma. The assumption is that Mo is a perv and a pederast (look at his letters!) and hence he is cloning a whole society of pervs and pederasts. The main problem with this notion is that more sophisticated studies of the charisma-building process have demonstrated that many different models of charisma are possible; that decision-making process vary from group to group, and that followers participate in a dynamic relationship with their leader and wield considerable power in dictating the future course of their budding culture. The Family's pattern of charismatic authority departs from the anticult stereoptype in many important respects. First, it is not composed of *one* person, but two. "Grandpa" and Mama Maria *both* hold the gift of prophecy, they both write letters. Her letters, in recent years, have been given equal weight to his, and certainly in the area of childcare and education, it is *her* voice, not his, that is listened to. It was her idea to invest heavily in school equipment like the KIDDIE VIDDIES, the computer tutorials and the "Montessori junk." She directed a large-scale research project on compiling and combining the various theories on pedagogy and child development available from the "System," choosing that which was compatible with a fundamentalist Christian education. She set up training courses for teachers. It is out of her conversations with her daughter that the Techi series originated, and her voice heard in the pubs outlining standards of sexual conduct for teens (*Child Abuse: A Final Warning!* 6/89; *Flirty Little Teens Beware!* 10/89). The charismatic career of Moses David is not typical of the "cult leader," but highly idiosyncratic. Wallis (1982) traces the deviations in Mo's career, his abrupt about faces, his series of prophesied "End Times," his doctrinal improvisations, as explicable in terms of strategical responses to the perennial problem every charismatic leader confronts: that of "creeping institutionalization." Wallis has argued that, by pruning his followers so that only the most loyal remain, by overturning the institutions that core group leaders have laboriously constructed, and by depriving local Shepherds of "tenure of office," that "Mo" is able to keep his creativity unbridled, and to remain the sole direct access to truth. His followers are not so much loyal to *what he says,* Wallis notes, but rather to whatever comes out of his mouth at that particular moment. Wallis' theory appears to be a promising framework for atudying Father David's *modus operandi.* It would explain why he fired the Chain in 1978 (see the *RNR Letters*), why he destroyed the "blobs" (large colonies). These actions suggest a determination to avoid the rigidity, compartmentalization and complacency that tend to "settle in" once a movement becomes large, successful, and institutionalized.

Another useful model for understanding these divagations in found in Feuerstein's new study (1991) of the "holy madness" or "crazy wisdom" type of charismatic leadership. Feuerstein presents this enigma as a radical style of initiation that demonstrates spiritual values, and as (hitherto) unremarked ancient tradition that can be found in Hinduism, Buddhism, Islam and occasionally in Christianity. "Crazy wise" masters deliberately jolt their apprentices out of their cognitive boundaries by using trickery, clowning, obscenity or threats, and frequently employ the ritual breaking of taboos associated with sex, intoxication and nudity as a teaching device. Dad tells us in his own inimitable prose that he is deliberately and self-consciously adopting this pedagogical method, in the hope that those remarks which are in exceedingly poor taste will ". . .

wake'm up and shake'em up amd jar'm loose and shock'm":

> "I'm an extremist and I exaggerate a little bit sometimes, I shock you!" (ML
> #1031:36, Jan.1976).
>
> "I figure if I shock you with the opposite extreme, it may wake you up. . ."
> (MOP 109:8).

Examined within the context of our postfeminist, politically-correct age, the Flirty Fishing and Davidito letters are inflammatory and in exceedingly poor taste. But it is important to understand them as representing transient phases within the experimental process of this developing movement. One must consider that religious founders often display unconventional approaches to the moral dilemmas and obsessions of their age, and an uncanny ability to predict future trends through setting up laboratories of social, sexual and familial experimentation. Thus, the changing sexual mores and patterns of marriage and parenting from the COG days to the present might be analysed as reflecting, magnifying and occasionally even parodying social tensions and moral trends in the surrounding culture.

David Berg's letters explore the boundaries between adult sexuality and childish need for affection. This boundary shifts as one moves through different cultures and decades. For example, Ina May's book on natural childbirth at The Farm quotes Stephen Gaskin, who frankly states that a breastfeeding mother and infant are "getting it on." This statement was made in the sixties, but in 1992, a woman in Montreal phoned a CSLC (family clinic) to ask whether or not it was normal for a woman who was breastfeeding her baby to feel sexually aroused. The Social Services arrived the same day and her baby was taken away from her, and she was charged with sexual abuse (she eventually got her infant back). A similar concern was expressed by a pregnant friend of mine who worried about what effect her orgasms were having on her embryo, and whether she was corrupting her baby's innocence. As absurd as these stories sound, they reveal the extraordinary preoccupation of our age with the sexual education and exploitation of children. The Mo Letters mirror and magnify these larger shifting social dilemmas and it would be fairer to treat them as an exploratory narrative, rather than as evidence of pathology when quoted out of context.

It is clear that David Berg intends to shock, to test the boundaries of morality and taste—from his literary wallowing in morning orgasms with she-monsters in the 70's, to his more recent graphic complaints of geriatric incontinence. The sex, sci-fi and scatology might be expected to appeal to your average, rebellious teenage non-reader, while "grossing out" more mature Christians in the mainstream. For this reason, it "makes sense" to consider the Mo Letters as performance art or "show biz," rather than as biography. While David Berg remains an enigmatic character whose private domestic life and personal conduct is an enigma, it cannot be assumed that he is necessarily acting upon the antinomian impulses he highlights in his letters. To arrest his disciples for sexually abusing their children on the basis of the Davidito letters would be equivalent to arresting the youthful audience of an Alice Cooper concert on the charge of infanticide, because they had listened to and applauded the (admittedly revolting) song in which Alice throws stones at a doll in a pram.

It is understandable that alarm bells begin to ring when outsiders listen to the exagerrated horror stories of career apostates groomed by the Cult Awareness Network. It is not surprising that the mass media and its audience would tend to regard The Family's troupes of little children who are out singing and provisioning in the streets as equivalent to trained beggars; they would examine the queasy blending of heavy-handed Fundamentalism with psychedelic cartoons of sexy spirits and monsters in the Mo Letters, and consider them pathological; they would listen to ex-members' tales of Flirty Fishing, and easily interpret this "ministry" from a secular perspective—as evidence of a prostitution racket or the sexual subjugation of women. Once this religion has been effectively stigmatized and demonized through the media's dissemination and amplification of misinformation supplied by its detractors, the public is ready to believe—in spite of the lack of evidence—that here is yet another ring of "ritual" child abusers. In another hundred years, however, with the Endtime reinterpreted by Heaven's Children, it appears likely that The Family will enjoy the social status of a small Christian church or denomination—quite as respectable, upwardly mobile and certainly less "heretical" than Christian Science or the Latter Day Saints.

Susan J. Palmer received her Ph.D. from Concordia University in Montreal, Quebec, where she worked on a research project involving new religions, directed by Frederick Bird. She is co-author (with Arvind Sharma) of *The Rajneesh Papers*, 1993) and has published articles on various movements—including the Raelian Movement, ISKCON, the Unification Church, I AM, La Mission de l'Esprit Saint, the IDHHB, Friends of Osho—which have appeared (or will appear) in anthologies and journals.

display unconventional approaches to the moral dilemmas and obsessions of their age, and an uncanny ability to predict future trends through setting up laboratories of social, sexual and familial experimentation. Thus, the changing sexual mores and patterns of marriage and parenting from the COG days to the present might be analysed as reflecting, magnifying and occasionally even parodying social tensions and moral trends in the surrounding culture.

David Berg's letters explore the boundaries between adult sexuality and childish need for affection. This boundary shifts as one moves through different cultures and decades. For example, Ina May's book on natural childbirth at The Farm quotes Stephen Gaskin, who frankly states that a breastfeeding mother and infant are "getting it on." This statement was made in the sixties, but in 1992, a woman in Montreal phoned a CSLC (family clinic) to ask whether or not it was normal for a woman who was breastfeeding her baby to feel sexually aroused. The Social Services arrived the same day and her baby was taken away from her, and she was charged with sexual abuse (she eventually got her infant back). A similar concern was expressed by a pregnant friend of mine who worried about what effect her orgasms were having on her embryo, and whether she was corrupting her baby's innocence. As absurd as these stories sound, they reveal the extraordinary preoccupation of our age with the sexual education and exploitation of children. The Mo Letters mirror and magnify these larger shifting social dilemmas and it would be fairer to treat them as an exploratory narrative, rather than as evidence of pathology when quoted out of context.

It is clear that David Berg intends to shock, to test the boundaries of morality and taste—from his literary wallowing in morning orgasms with she-monsters in the 70's, to his more recent graphic complaints of geriatric incontinence. The sex, sci-fi and scatology might be expected to appeal to your average, rebellious teenage non-reader, while "grossing out" more mature Christians in the mainstream. For this reason, it "makes sense" to consider the Mo Letters as performance art or "show biz," rather than as biography. While David Berg remains an enigmatic character whose private domestic life and personal conduct is an enigma, it cannot be assumed that he is necessarily acting upon the antinomian impulses he highlights in his letters. To arrest his disciples for sexually abusing their children on the basis of the Davidito letters would be equivalent to arresting the youthful audience of an Alice Cooper concert on the charge of infanticide, because they had listened to and applauded the (admittedly revolting) song in which Alice throws stones at a doll in a pram.

Chapter 2

Update on "The Family": Organizational Change and Development in a Controversial New Religious Group

James T. Richardson
University of Nevada, Reno

Introduction

"Cult controversies" such as the one surrounding "The Family" are nothing new in contemporary history (Beckford, 1985). This paper offers a sociologically and social psychologically oriented assessment of The Family organization, also known previously as the Children of God (COG) and the Family of Love (FOL), in order to furnish more information for those in policy positions or the media, which plays such a major role in telling the public what it should think about exotic religious groups.

The report is based on earlier research on the precursor groups to The Family, as well as on reading of recent scholarly, legal, and popular media materials about The Family, along with conversations with members and leaders of The Family in several different countries. Included in my recent reading about The Family have been news reports from America, the U.K., Australia, and other countries, materials published by The Family, and some court documents relating to a number of legal actions involving The Family in several different countries. I have had recent contact with members of The Family in America, Hungary, and Australia.

Earlier particularly relevant work included two papers in which I and Rex Davis dealt quite specifically with the Children of God, as well as several papers in which the COG were discussed along with several other new religious groups. The two more focused papers were: "The Organization and Functioning of the Children of God" (Davis and Richardson, 1976), and "Experiential Fundamentalism: Revisions of Orthodoxy in the Jesus Movement" (Richardson and Davis, 1983). Other papers in which the COG and its newer forms were specifically discussed focused on recruitment, fund-raising, personality assessment of members, and other organizational and individual considerations (see Richardson, 1982b, 1985a, 1985b, 1985c, especially.)

This assessment will offer comments on several aspects of The Family, including an examination of changes undergone by the organization of The Family and its earlier renditions, from the point of view of social movements research and theory. This section will make use of a common theoretical perspective in the study of social movements, known as the "natural history" approach to social movement organizations. That approach focuses on the kinds of usual changes that occur in virtually any social movement organization, be it religious, political or otherwise. The history of The Family exemplifies such changes, and I will assess what has happened with the group, as well as comment on further changes that might be expected.

I will also discuss briefly the scholarly and legal status of claims that members of new religious groups such as The Family are "brainwashed" into participating in such groups. These claims have been made often, especially in the U.S, but they have come under heavy attack by most scholars who study such phenomena. Related to this is material summarizing the effects on individuals of participation in such groups. A brief scholarly interpretation of what happens when people leave such groups will be included, as well. Particularly I will assess problems with treating accounts developed by defectors as completely factual.

Evolution of the Children of God/Family of Love/ The Family

The Family has followed a rather predictable course in its evolution as an organization, even though it has, of course, had its own unique history (see Drakeford, 1972; Enroth, et al, 1972 for two popularized brief histories). That unique history results from the interaction of leadership decisions with other influences from both inside and outside the group, and over which groups such as the COG/FOL/Family often have little control.

The scholarly study of social movement organizations is replete with examples of significant organizational evolution occurring in a relatively short period of time. Nearly all textbooks and scholarly monographs dealing with social movements and social movement organizations discuss patterns of organization change. This perspective is sometimes referred to in the scholarly literature as the "natural history" approach to the study of social movements (see Lang and Lang's 1961 classic text, *Collective Dynamics,* for instance).

Two other social science scholars who have studied the COG in some depth, Roy Wallis and David van Zandt, make use of the natural history approach in some of their writings about the group (see Wallis, 1976, and van Zandt, 1985). Van Zandt, for instance, talks about twelve stages in the history of the COG/FOL. Rex Davis and I used the natural history perspective, as well, in our 1976 article on the COG, as does Enroth, et al. (1972) in their treatment of Jesus groups, including the early COG.

Davis and I described the organization and functioning of the Children of God, and concluded the following (1976: 327):

> We do not mean to imply that the present structure . . . is permanent. In fact, we are sure that modifications of this structure will be made, and that some changes are already taking place. The structure described is thus somewhat provisional in nature, but we do think it important to "freeze the moment" and at least describe the COG organization and functioning as of mid-1976.

That caveat was offered because of our knowledge of social movements derived from studying other movements, as well as the scholarly literature on this phenomenon. Indeed, the COG/FOL/Family and other new religious movements serve as good examples of how such organizations change, sometimes quite rapidly.

The changes that occur in social movement groups do so for two broad reasons, both of which are described in "The 'Deformation' of New Religions: Impacts of Societal and Organizational Factors" (Richardson, 1985b), which makes the point that changes occur because of both *internal* and *external* factors, not usually just because of the actions of an authoritarian leader. The COG were used as examples of many of the points made in this article, which makes use of the "natural history" perspective.

External factors were characterized as "a generally negative response from some major institutions within society" (1985b: 168). The institutions referred to included particularly: the "expansionist state," which was exerting control over larger areas of life than ever before, and thus impinging on activities of religious groups more than before; and the rise of the religious right, which made others in society more sensitive to the actions of religious groups. General social and economic unrest also played a role in the negative reaction to new religions, leading to less tolerance from many people for unusual groups and activities such as those exemplified by newer "high-demand" religious groups, of which The Family is one.

The generally negative response led to a "deforming" of some newer contemporary religious groups—including The Family—as they had to change in response to the pressure from these external factors. Considerable resources were expended in defensive efforts demanded by attacks from the state or from other quarters such as traditional religion or the newly developed "anticult movement" (see Shupe and Bromley, 1980, 1994).

Internal factors also played a crucial role. When most of the new religions started they were relatively homogenous in membership: mostly young middle class single white males from America. Then, many of the groups, including the COG, began to attract many different types of members, as they evangelized around the world. Also, more women were affiliating and families were being formed. Children were born, requiring attention and resources to care for them properly.

The COG/FOL/Family, as well as many other of the new religions, were getting "domesticated." This also "deformed" the groups from what they set out to be and do. No longer could they expect all members to spend their time and energy evangelizing in far away lands. Some members had to take care of their families, and ways to support the diverse membership had to be found.

Davis and I closed our first paper on the COG with some comments about changes in the group, a discussion that pre-dated yet informed the 1985 "deformation" paper. We noted (1976: 336-37) that changes were occurring in the COG not just because leadership dictated them, but for other reasons, including the following:

1. encountering different cultural realities around the world, and being forced to adjust to them;
2. working with the many different religious traditions was bringing about greater tolerance of other perspectives and ways of life;
3. the strong emphasis on radical evangelical techniques was being tempered by the realities of working in other cultures which are more positive toward other approaches to recruitment;
4. the development of families within the COG had a growing "domestication" effect, as COG leaders and members learn the reality of having to maintain husband-wife relationships and take care of the growing number of children, all of which detract from a singular emphasis on mission activities that dominated the COG in its earlier history;

5. the rapid growth and spread of the COG led to including many members from different societies and cultures, which in turn led to the development of new organizational patterns to handle the larger size and the increased diversity within the organization.

Thus, we knew in 1976 that the COG would change, and could see the general direction that change would probably take. We were correct, but there was a significant delay in implementation of the type of change we expected, brought about by directives from leadership, particularly David Berg. I refer here to a number of changes Berg proposed, but particularly to the development of the "flirty fishing" period in COG history, when they were also referred to as "The Family of Love." This development occurred just as our paper was being published, so the 1976 work does not discuss this aspect of group life. Flirty fishing lasted until about 1988, when it was terminated.

Some court documents not readily available to the public at this time trace this development, as do other papers in this collection. However, this phase of COG/FOL organizational life was analyzed by myself and Rex Davis in our 1983 paper, focusing particularly on the theological justifications offered for "flirty fishing" (Richardson and Davis, 1983).

We attempted to explain the apparently anomalous fact of the combining of fundamentalist Christian beliefs with a strong experiential orientation which has been found in some Jesus Movement groups. Most fundamentalist groups emphasize a specific set of beliefs to which a person must adhere to be a member. The beliefs or "fundamentals" take precedence over other possible sources of authority, including personal experiences with deity. Other groups, for instance charismatics (groups which "speak in tongues"), usually emphasize the experiential, and draw ultimate authority from personal experiences with their God or spirit.

In my research of the two largest Jesus Movement organizations, this creative melding of two sources of religious authority is well evidenced (also see Adams and Fox, 1972). One group was the COG/FOL/Family; the other one was known as Shiloh (we used a pseudonym of "Christ Communal Organization") about which I and two others wrote a book and a number of articles (see Richardson, et al., 1979 especially). Both these large groups combined a strong belief in what are usually called fundamentalist beliefs with a heavy emphasis on the experiential side of life. This was a somewhat unusual confluence of approaches to religious life that had typically been thought at odds with each other.

These studies led me to conclude that this unique confluence was a result of the backgrounds of most participants, who had come from the heavily experientially oriented youth culture in America. Heavy drug, tobacco, and alcohol use, as well as sexual promiscuity were common among the youth subculture from whence came most Jesus Movement members, including those in the COG and Shiloh (see Adams and Fox, 1972). Sex and drugs were part of a libertine experientially oriented lifestyle prior to many of the members "getting saved," and *they did not completely drop this experiential focus as they became Jesus Movement participants*. Participants partially substituted the experience of Jesus for other personal experiences, but remained open to other ways to relate their experiential focus to their new set of beliefs.

In the Shiloh organization the experiential co-emphasis took the form of "speaking in tongues," whereas in the COG, which was the only Jesus Movement group not to stress speaking in tongues, the experiential emphasis developed in the form of much more openness toward sexuality. That openness toward sex was manifested through "flirty fishing" and through the "sharing" concept. "Flirty fishing" involved witnessing to outsiders in such a way that it might even involve sex between female members of the FOL and those outsiders. The women involved had to be willing (as did their husbands) for them to "go all the way" if it was deemed necessary in order to "reach someone for Christ." Such decisions were made very seriously, but they were made nonetheless. "Sharing" refers to an openness towards sexual activity between adult members of a commune. If a partner was gone for a time, such as overseas on a mission, then another member might offer temporary comfort through sexual sharing, with the understanding and blessing of the missing partner.

It should be understood that COG members and leaders thought that acting out their sexuality as they did was sanctioned by God, and that sex was a way of expressing God's love to others, including, during the "flirty fishing" period, selected others from outside the group (see theological justification discussed in Richardson and Davis, 1983). The "sharing" practice probably still continues to some extent, but there is no data of which I am aware indicating its frequency or pervasiveness. My saying this is not to approve or condemn the practices of "flirty fishing," or "sharing," but to offer a perspective that may not be easy to appreciate for many observers.

The apparent openness toward sexuality in the COG/FOL could not last, of course. External pressures by governments and other institutional structures against such free sexuality combined with the worldwide spread of AIDS and other sexually transmitted diseases to bring about significant changes. Internal pressures brought about by demands of family life also interfered, especially the birth of large numbers of children who had to be cared for by their mothers. David Berg, under these pressures, directed that "flirty fishing" stop in 1988.

Not everyone in the FOL had been involved in "flirty fishing," and some, including a few current detractors, had left the organization over it. I think it is safe to say, based on my conversations with group members, that a significant portion of those who sanctioned the practice, either by involvement or not arguing against it, were pleased when the practice ended and a more normal life was allowed to develop. This led to less outside pressure, and allowed more concentration of resources, time and energy on taking care of family obligations of the group's communal houses, including especially the many children being born into the group.

The Family presently seems especially solicitous of its children's welfare. The organization has developed sound educational programs for their children in communes around the world, several of which I have observed first hand. They obviously expend significant amounts of their resources on such matters. Such concern cannot coexist for long with a radical evangelical thrust which demands that all be involved in missionizing activities. "Something has to give," and it seems that much radicalness is being shed in favor of doing well by the families of members.

My recent observations, coupled with reading other materials, lead to me think that The Family has evolved into a relatively stable pattern of managing sexuality in a manner much more in keeping with the values of ordinary society. "Flirty fishing" has been abandoned, and some earlier, controversial writings dealing with children's sexuality have been repudiated and withdrawn. The process of "sharing" seems to continue, at least with some adult members. However, I am not prepared to say that even the Family's practice of sexual sharing within the group is particularly radical within the context of relatively sexually liberated contemporary society. I do not think that the actual practices of ordinary society comport very well with the typically expressed sexual values of the greater society that sanction only sex in marriage and monogamy. There is a great deal of sexual activity outside the bonds of monogamous marriage in ordinary society, and the Family's practices do not seem as strange when viewed in that comparative light. What is strange is that The Family admits to the practice, makes no apology for it, and even offers a theological justification to those who care to listen.

In concluding this section, I will reiterate that all groups, including the COG/FOL/Family, go through a "natural history" of organizational evolution. They start out more radical, in part because the originators are typically younger, healthier, and unfettered with families and responsibilities, not to mention more idealized (Drakeford, 1972 best chronicles the colorful early history of the COG). Then the groups evolve, sometimes in fits and starts, toward a more normal existence. They are forced to do this because of external pressures and as a result of internal demands put on the group by increasingly diverse types of members, including particularly the presence of large numbers of small children in groups such as The Family, which does not practice systematic birth control.

The Family now seems much more "normal" than they once did. If that word ever gets out through the media, The Family may well fade into obscurity, simply because they are not doing as many strange things anymore, and few people will be very interested. Such relative obscurity will be a mixed blessing, of course, and at present some may think it could never happen. However, the history of many social movement organizations, some of which were quite radical indeed, suggest that The Family may well follow a similar path.

Brainwashing Allegations Against New Religions

A common accusation levelled by opponents of such new religions as the COG/FOL/The Family is that they "brainwash" people into joining the groups, and then use "mind control" to retain them as members (Shapiro, 1977; Shupe and Bromley, 1980; Richardson, 1982a). These pseudo-technical terms are used regularly in the controversy over new religions, typically as "social weapons" in efforts by some to encourage or seek more control over the groups (Robbins, et al., 1983; Richardson and Kilbourne, 1983). Users of these terms (and other synonyms) assume that few people would participate in such groups of their own free will. Such magical explanations, which often incorporate psychotechnology supposedly derived from the communist regimes, serves well for those who do not want their children or others to participate in such groups.

If people believe that the groups have some magical techniques against which there is little recourse, then this seems to justify taking harsh actions that would otherwise not be contemplated. Such actions may interfere with the free choice of individuals who are of age, and freedom of religion in society may be threatened, as well (Richardson, 1980; 1985a; 1991). However, scientific evidence concerning the brainwashing thesis is problematic at best (Anthony, 1990; Richardson, 1991). There is a basic incongruence between participation in most newer religious groups and being in a prisoner of war camp in Korea, that being the presence of physical coercion in one setting and its absence in the other. Most scholars reject such notions about why people join and participate in new religions. They cite the low membership figures and high attrition rates for those groups alleged to use the psychotechniques. (If the techniques are so powerful, why are the groups so small?) Also discussed by scholars are the processes whereby members are recruited and resocialized, which can be rather easily described in terms of ordinary social psychological processes (Solomon, 1983).

A recent summary of this evidence, "A Social Psychological Critique of 'Brainwashing' Claims About Recruitment to New Religions" (Richardson, 1994), summarizes the evidence, and offers an alternative view of what happens when people participates in new religions. This view is more "active" in its orientation, and involves an *active, seeking person,* wanting to try out a different lifestyle, ethic, and set of beliefs, at least temporarily (see Straus, 1976, 1979; Richardson 1985a).

Richardson (1994) includes, as well, an analysis of the types of *negotiation* in which most people are involved as they decide whether to join a group or not. Individual potential recruits usually retain considerable autonomy as they decide if they want to do the things required of members in a particular group. And research evidence reveals that most potential recruits simply refuse the entreaties and leave, and that many others leave rather soon after joining, factors which in combination explain the relatively small size of most groups (Bird and Reimer, 1983; Barker, 1983, 1984; Galanter, 1980).

This more active orientation was arrived at empirically from years of research on new religions, including the COG, which I first researched while spending a year in England in 1974-75. I started my research on new religions in the early 1970s with a view that something was indeed happening that seemed inexplicable and problematic. However, as I did field research with several major new religions, interviewing many members and leaders, I became aware of a simple truth: *Most of the participants were there simply because they wanted to be,* and further, that *they would leave when the experience was no longer rewarding for them.*

The theoretical papers deriving from this research offer an explanation of why people participate in such groups, and why they often leave, as well (Richardson, 1982a, 1985, Richardson, et al., 1986). This theoretical perspective offers a more adequate explanation of participation than other theories that stress trickery and magical techniques such as brainwashing and mind control (Anthony, 1990; Richardson and Kilbourne, 1983). Such approaches that stress volitional choice by participants undercut the anti-cult movement's efforts to get such groups declared as deviant and in need of social control. Nonetheless, the volitional perspective is much closer to reality than the view that participants in new religions such as The Family are there through trickery.

Personality Assessment of Participants

In 1983 at a conference at Wolfson College, Oxford, on "New Perspectives in the Psychology of Religion," I reviewed the personality assessment and clinical evidence from research in America and other countries on participants in new religions, including the COG. The resulting paper (Richardson, 1985c) is of interest since it includes research on the COG in Germany (Kuner's work; p. 214-215). Kuner's conclusion after his comparative and quite sophisticated research was:

As far as an influence on mental state and psycho-social development can be traced, the (new religious movements) prove themselves rather "therapeutic and/or resocialization groups" for socially alienated. The results . . . give little support for the Anti-Cult Movement's point of view.

The overall conclusion I developed after the review by Kuner and other work, some of which also included COG members, was (p. 221):

The personality assessments of these group members reveal that life in the new religions is often therapeutic instead of harmful. Other information suggests that young people are *affirming* their idealism by virtue of involvement in such groups. Certainly there is some "submerging of personality" in groups which are communal or collective, simply because they do not foster the individualistic and competitive lifestyle to which we are accustomed, particularly in American society. However, there is little data to support the almost completely negative picture painted by a few . . . who have been involved in the controversy over new religions.

That research did not, of course, take the view that no one with a mental problem ever joins a newer religion. That would be an indefensible claim. Newer religions have their share of people with mental difficulties, just as do more traditional groups. The research does, however, take issue with the frequently made accusation by anti-cultists that the new religions *cause* a great number of mental problems. This effort to "medicalize" participation in newer religious groups has been relatively successful, even if it is misguided (Robbins and Anthony, 1982).

Indeed, there is evidence that some people with mental problems are attracted to such groups, but that the groups serve an ameliorative effect for most of those (see discussion of this in Kilbourne and Richardson, 1984, as well as Galanter and Diamond, 1981). I would not, of course, claim that all who needed help obtain it in a newer religious group, but the research reviews show that often such is the case.

Some would like to paint all participants as having a mental problem caused by or exacerbated by the group's influence. This claim cannot be substantiated. Indeed, there is strong evidence of bias on the part of some who would make such a claim, and that the basic theoretical perspective used to base such a claim is itself faulty (Kilbourne and Richardson, 1986). In a recent article, "Religiosity as Deviance: Negative Religious Bias in and Misuse of the DSM-III" (Richardson, 1993), the point is made that there is a pervasive anti-religious bias in this major listing of mental disorders, and that the bias is especially noteworthy regarding newer religions. Any effort to apply the DSM-III (or more recent versions) to participants of newer religions should be looked at with considerable caution, and the self-interest of those making the claims should be examined.

Accounts of Why People Leave Groups

Two points will be briefly made in this section. One deals with what people think, in retrospect, about their experience in a group to which they no longer belong. A related point is then made about the credibility of accounts of former members, especially in circumstances in which their self-interest becomes involved.

As discussed in an article done by myself and two scholars in The Netherlands (Richardson, van der Lans and Derks, 1986), the accounts given about a particular episode of living in or leaving a group depends on who is making the account, and *for what purpose*. The veracity of any account is subject to question, and should be verified by a method of "triangulation," which means the researcher needs to ask different people who have different perspectives, comparing the views of all in order to understand what really happened in the group and during the leaving episode (also see Beckford, 1978a, 1978b).

An illustration may be helpful. If parents think their son should not have joined a religious group, then they have a bias and are self-interested. They may think of themselves as failures if, after raising their child for years, that son decides to give up everything, including educational opportunities and join a group such as The Family. It is in the self-interest of those parents to adopt a "brainwashing account" of how and why their son joined the group.

If the parents kidnap their son from the group and put him through "deprogramming" in a way that results in the son staying out of the group, then it is also in the interest of the son to adopt a "brainwashing account" of why he joined. If the son does not "successfully" deprogram, and returns to the group, the parents can claim he was brainwashed too thoroughly, while the son will perhaps adopt a view that his parents are interfering with God's will for him. Which of these accounts is true depends on the perspective of the person making the claim.

Research by Solomon (1981), Wright (1984, 1987), Lewis (1986), and Lewis and Bromley (1987), some of which includes former COG/FOL members, on the process of leaving new religions shows that there is a strong relationship between the way in which people leave groups and the type of account they adopt. Those who are deprogrammed out of the group tend to adopt a "brainwashing account," while those who leave voluntarily do not. Those scholars suggest that *the deprogramming process itself teaches what an acceptable account is,* offering an explanation that lets all the parties (except the allegedly brainwashing group) "off the hook" in terms of personal responsibility.

Those who leave voluntarily, which most members eventually do, tend to take a view of the experience that accepts responsibility for their decision. They also are more prone to define the time in the group as a positive learning experience for themselves (Wright, 1987).

Some former members do develop an account that is negative. One key factor in the development of an account that is negative about experiences in the former group seems to be the contact with others who share a negative view (Wright, 1984, Lewis, 1986). Also, if there was some sort of conflict while in the group (perhaps a clash of personalities or a difference of opinion over some issue) which led to the person leaving, then they may develop a more negative account of what happened to them, and blame others for the decision to have participated.

The conclusion about accounts, then, is that care must be taken in accepting accounts as totally factual. Those leaving the groups and needing to be accepted back into their normal niche in society develop an explanation of what happened that will ease the transition. Some who enter quasi-professions such as deprogramming (or "exit counseling") need to develop especially strong accounts that justify what they are doing. They might even be classified as "cultphobes" because of the strong reaction they develop (Kilbourne and Richardson, 1986).

The need to be suspect of post hoc explanations includes, as well, accounts of those who remain in the groups, as they too have a perspective on what happened that may involve self interest. All parties have their own point of view, and those who review such situations must base their assessments on a combination of accounts, as well as on the independent assessments by professionals and independent scholars.

Conclusions

I will make one major point in conclusion, after a review of key areas of research concerning The Family. This group and its participants can be understood in rather ordinary terms from the social sciences. There is nothing so spectacular about these groups that cannot be grasped using common theories from sociology, social psychology, and psychology.

It serves no useful purpose to "demonize" new religious groups such as The Family, and claim that the participants act like robots, or engage in behavior that threatens the very roots of society. Certainly a group can "go bad," whether it be religious or otherwise. When that happens, the ordinary rules and laws of civilized society should allow recourse. However, it does not appear from this review and recent investigation that The Family has "gone bad." Indeed, by nearly any standard that could be imagined, The Family has become much more ordinary in their approach to life in general, and sexuality in particular. They have been "domesticated" by pressures from outside and inside the group. The Family certainly has had a colorful and even controversial past, but it seems to this scholar that its future looks much more normal. Indeed, years from now scholars may wonder "what all the fuss was about" concerning The Family.

James T. Richardson is Professor of Sociology and Judicial Studies at the University of Nevada, Reno. He has been researching new religions for over twenty years, and has published five books and nearly seventy-five articles in journals and books.

Chapter 3

The Family: History, Organization, and Ideology

David G. Bromley and Sidney H. Newton
Virginia Commonwealth University

During the late 1960s and the 1970s, the Children of God, together with the Unification Church and the Krishna Consciousness movement, was a major focus of the controversy over "cults" or New Religious Movements. For most of the past twenty years, however, the group has been located abroad, out of the public's eye. But the members of the movement, now known as The Family, have recently begun returning to the United States. This return has renewed the controversy surrounding them and they are again the focus of public attention and "anti-cult" criticism.

History and Organization

The New Religious Movement known currently as The Family was founded in the late 1960s. It has undergone several transformations since that time and has been known variously as the "Teens for Christ," "The Children of God," and "The Family of Love." Any discussion of the history and organization of the group must begin by looking at the movement's founder and spiritual leader, David Brandt Berg. Through the years he has been known by members of The Family as "Uncle Dave," "Moses David," "Mo," "Father David," and "Dad." David Berg has led the movement since its beginnings in Huntington Beach, California. Berg was born in 1919 to a family tradition of evangelical ministry. His mother spent much of her life as an evangelist and had ties to the Christian and Missionary Alliance Church. Berg followed this tradition and, for a brief time, served as pastor to a Christian and Missionary Alliance congregation in Valley Farms, Arizona. However, as early as 1952, Berg began to receive prophecies of the "end-time." This, coupled with a growing distrust of the "system" and "churchy" religion, led Berg to develop a more radical approach to missionary work.[1] For several years up until 1967, he worked for T.V. evangelist Fred Jordon, booking his show across the U.S.

In 1967, Berg moved his wife, Jane Miller (known in the Family as Mother Eve), and their children to Huntington Beach California after hearing his mother's description of the "hippies" who had begun moving into the area. The family began witnessing to the "dropouts" and "druggies" and soon had enough help to take over a beach coffeehouse that had been run by Teen Challenge. An iconoclast himself, Berg was ideally suited to his audience. He and his followers demonstrated their opposition to the "systemite" churches by visiting services and in some cases challenging the beliefs and behaviors of the local parishioners. Then, in 1969, the group left California and traveled around the U.S. in several missionary teams before finally regrouping in Canada.

It was in Canada that Berg revealed his Old Church/New Church doctrine. According to this pronouncement, the Old Church, represented by Berg's wife Jane, was hopelessly corrupt and must be replaced by the New Church, represented by Karen Zerby (known in the Family as Maria), a young woman who had, according to group leaders, joined the group in Tuscon, Arizona. After this announcement, the work of building the "new church" began in earnest. From 1970 to 1971, the group lived a very disciplined life at the Texas Soul Clinic Ranch (a property owned by Berg's former employer, Jordon) and developed a strict training program for new members. During this period, the group emphasized the boundary between the movement and the outside world. The goal of witnessing efforts was the total commitment of the "sheep." Joining required that the prospective member "forsake-all" worldly goods to the group and sever worldly ties. It was in reaction to this standard that the first anti-cult organization in the United States, FreeCOG, was formed. Despite the rigors of membership and the high level of dedication demanded, membership grew to about fifteen hundred during the three years after the move from California in 1969 when the group numbered less than one hundred.[2]

In 1971, Berg and Maria left the United States and moved to Europe and, within one year, much of the membership followed. Prior to this time, the financial support for the movement had come from members "forsake-alls" and "provisioning," the solicitation of support from local businesses and organizations. After the move to Europe, Berg began to encourage members to sell samples of the groups' literature, or "litness," in order to fund the growing movement. Berg himself withdrew from an active leadership role and established a hierarchical structure to maintain the day to day operations. Much of the control was delegated to members of his immediate family who were known as the "Royal Family." Local control was in the hands of appointed leaders known as "Shepherds." Berg kept in touch with the membership and maintained authority over the movement through the "Mo Letters" which were by this time received as the 'Word.' "I am with you in spirit through these words that I speak unto you! They are my spirit & my life, by His spirit & His life—& if you will read them & study them, prayerfully & diligently, you will have more of me than you've ever had before."[3]

The movement has undergone many organizational changes during its history. The most dramatic of these, the Reorganization and Nationalization Revolution (RNR), was effected by Berg at the end of the 1970's. The RNR involved the elimination of all intermediate leadership between Berg and the membership. "Which would you prefer? A low job or no job? Pretty soon you'll be surprised to discover that all the upper-crust offices & their bureaucracies have been totally wiped out along with the exalted staffs . . . ."[4] The new regulations required that the leadership in local homes be elected and include citizens of the host nation. It was also at this time that Berg began encouraging the controversial practice of "flirty fishing" (FFing), a new approach to witnessing which allowed the use of sexual contact in order to save souls. Both "flirty fishing" and the increased emphasis on "litnessing" demonstrate a change in the movement's perception of group boundaries. Both techniques 'won souls' and raised money for the group however, especially in the case of "flirty fishing," the contacts made were not usually expected to "forsake all" and move into a Family home. In fact, since the early 1980's, the Family has had only limited recruitment success and children have accounted for almost all growth since that time.[5]

At the end of the 1980's members of the Family began returning to the United States. "All right! Things are tightening up & we've been forced out of country after country . . . . A lot of Westerners are going to be forced to go home."[6] Currently, the use of "litnessing" has been largely supplanted as a money making technique by the distribution of videotapes. "Provisioning" continues to be an important means of support. At this time the Family claims a world-wide live-in membership of about nine thousand, two-thirds of which are teen-age or younger. The current emphasis placed on child rearing and teen missionary work reflects these demographics.[7] However, allegations of child abuse have placed the group at the center of a new controversy. The charges, stemming from selected quotes and art from old literature, as well as stories told by disaffected former members, have triggered a number of police raids on Family homes around the world. Investigations in a number of countries have all exonerated The Family of abuse charges. Nonetheless, the publicity has renewed earlier criticisms of the groups sexual morality, especially the practice of "flirty fishing" which was officially discontinued in 1987. The Family has responded with a major public relations campaign and open door policy.[8]

Ideology

The formal ideology of the Family may be described as antinomian and premillennial.[9] It is produced by David Berg with the help of his close associates. All members are expected to read the Bible and "Mo Letters" daily and new members, or "babes," must memorize verses. The millennial nature of the Family's ideology has remained consistent throughout the group's history. However, the antinomian character of the group's beliefs was not expressed until after the early 1970s.

Berg's prophecies of the "end-time" predate the movement by a number of years and early witnessing efforts were aimed at the distribution of the "Warning Tract," a prophecy received by his mother. The Family predicts an imminent deterioration of world order which will enable the seizure of power by the Antichrist. Following the "Great Tribulation," Christ will return to defeat the forces of the Antichrist and reign on earth for one thousand years. After one thousand years, Satan will again attempt to defeat the forces of Christ. After the Battle of Gog and Magog" the living and the dead shall be judged. Then, the heavenly city, New Jerusalem, will descend to earth to become the home of all those who have been saved.[10]

The Family's interpretation of world events reflects their belief in the imminent rise of the Antichrist. Any disaster or crisis is viewed as a sign of the impending Tribulation and as an indication of the identity of the Antichrist and his forces. This outlook is well suited to conspiracy theory and The Family has incorporated some familiar examples. Notably, The Family has adopted portions of several anti-semitic conspiracy theories. Berg states that "the Jewish world-antichrist banking system has managed to loan out enough money to make the whole world its slaves."[11] Berg also contends that the Holocaust, and indeed all of WWII, was staged by Jews in a bid for world domination. "Constantly talking about the Holocaust! They're still playing on the sympathy of the world to get what they want." In the same letter, Berg directs those who wish to know more about the way 'they' operate to read "the famous 'Protocols of the Elders of Zion' and some of the other things about the World Jewish Conspiracy."[12] The group has denied charges of anti-semitism; Berg argues that "to be truly anti-semitic you'd have to hate all the Orientals, be against them all."[13] Ironically perhaps, Berg himself comes from Jewish heritage.

It is the sexual morality of The Family which demonstrates the antinomian character of their ideology. While there is a great deal of emphasis placed on 'works' in other areas of Family theology, in this area, The Family has interpreted the doctrine of 'salvation through grace' in a more radical way. Berg's letters have recommended "sexual sharing," and "Flirty Fishing" (FFing), and questioned societal standards regarding the sexuality of children and the incest taboo. The main basis for such practices is the "Law of Love," the commandment to love one another which is believed to take precedence over all other laws. Berg also offers Old Testament support for his beliefs. "If you'll take a look at Bible history, you'll make the shocking discovery that most of God's greats had oodles of wives, women, mistresses, harlots & what have you, as well as multitudes of children!"[14]

In other respects The Family's sexual morality is more in line with traditional fundamentalism. Homosexuality is condemned by the group and is an excommunicable offence. Birth control and abortion are seen as offenses to God and, consequently, most women have large numbers of children. And, in recent years, the group has moved away from some of the more controversial expressions of its sexual morality. The practice of FFing was officially discontinued in 1987 and any teenage-adult sex has been banned as well.[15]

Prospects

The Family's membership is quite different today than that of the "Teens for Christ" and the Children of God. The group has focused much of its attention on its younger members with home-schooling, teen missionary activities and the inclusion of teens within group leadership. However, while group efforts have been focused on the retention of the second generation, the current controversy over the Family has centered around allegations of child abuse. Despite Family reports that the more questionable of their practices have been discontinued, they continue to be accused of religious prostitution, child pornography as well other forms of sexual child abuse. The group has responded with a major public relations campaign claiming that the controversy has been fostered and funded by anti-cult activists. Because this controversy is unlikely to die down quickly, it remains to be seen how increasing attention and pressure, as well as continued police raids on The Family's homes, will affect group membership.

David G. Bromley is a Professor in the Department of Sociology and Anthropology at Virginia Commonwealth University. He has studied and written extensively about cults in America. Among his books is *Strange Gods* (1982) written with Anson D. Shupe Jr.

Sidney H. Newton is a graduate student at Virginia Commonwealth University.

Chapter 4

Psychological Assessment of Children in The Family

Lawrence Lilliston and Gary Shepherd
Oakland University

In his recent highly acclaimed book, *The Culture of Disbelief*, Stephen Carter writes about the trivialization of religion in America. Carter suggests that as we have moved through the last half of the twentieth century, it has become less acceptable for people to base important life and value decisions on religious principles. He goes on to suggest that for many Americans, political stands based on religious values are viewed with suspicion. Carter is well aware that there are enclaves of religious people who do make important life decisions and that there are many people who are influenced as voters by candidates who argue political positions from a religious perspective. He is also aware that we have the highest church going country in the world and that an overwhelming majority of Americans profess a belief in a god of some sort. However, his analysis suggests that most Americans prefer a rather bland, unchallenging type of religion that is embodied in comfortable platitudes and that does not call upon people to make sacrifices or to change lifestyles in dramatic ways. From his perspective as a constitutional lawyer, Carter suggests that the real attitudes of Americans toward religious issues, including that most important issue of religious freedom, are seen in the legal struggles that are waged around religious rights. Carter concluded that an examination of legal arguments, court decisions, and the reporting of this process in the media betrays the real consensual American attitude toward religion, that of trivialization as a basis for important life decisions.

Many social critics preceding Carter have written of a change in the basic standards for conduct and values in this country. This change has seen us go from religious-based standards of conduct, values, and world hypotheses to standards based on modern psychology. Thus, instead of evaluating our own and others' conduct and perceptions in terms of religion-based morality, we now measure these attributes against a standard of mental health. What is right for me and my adjustment? How is my self-esteem affected? Will my children grow up able to cope with emotional stresses? Social psychologist Roy Baumeister has written convincingly of the modern preoccupation with "self" and the way this preoccupation, and the corollary dynamic of escape from this preoccupation, is played out in a variety of self-avoidant and self-destructive behaviors such as drug and alcohol abuse, masochism, and suicide.

In an interesting interaction of these two trends—away from religious standards and toward mental health standards—those who are proponents of either set of standards attack proponents of the other set. Thus, those who continue to cling most fervently to strong religious standards of conduct attack those who adopt mental health standards as sinful, ungodly, or satanic, and those who are devotees of mental health standards attack those who adopt religious standards as being fanatical, narrow-minded, and emotionally sick. Polls showing a high level of belief in god and church membership notwithstanding, most social critics feel that there are many more people who adopt psychological criteria for human conduct and values. Indeed, some of the strongest proponents of these psychological criteria may be seen in the pulpits of mainstream religious institutions. And although it is probably possible at some level to work out a compromise between the two sets of standards, such a compromise would be a weak one at best because the two sets of standards reflect a basic conflict between absolutism (strong religious) and relativism (strong psychological). Carter and several others have pointed out that support for the psychological value system is currently dominant and that this dominance can be readily seen in reporting in the mainstream media as well as polls measuring attitudes toward, for example, the Branch Davidians in Waco.

In light of these factors, then, it is no surprise to see attacks on those minority religions that stand at odds with the larger cultural view of conduct and values. Because some minority religions, such as several New Religious Movements, call upon their members to alter their lifestyles in important ways and to place religion clearly and uncompromisingly at the center of their lives, they stand in marked contrast to the type of relatively undemanding religion endorsed by most of the general population. Such a posture by these minority religions casts them as deviant in relation to larger societal values, and this deviance makes them vulnerable to attack. Although individual members of the larger society do not attack these groups in any great numbers, there is a receptive attitude toward charges against these groups of wrongdoing and of practices damaging to the psychological well-being of the members. As in the infamous and tragic case of the Branch Davidians, these charges are frequently featured in an uncritical fashion on television and in newspapers and news magazines, and they are received just as uncritically by the majority of consumers. These charges are particularly likely to arouse negative feelings toward these minority religions if they include allegations of child abuse and neglect. Virtually all researchers on the topic of child abuse, including sexual abuse, agree that abuse occurs at a regrettably high level in the general population. Moreover, most researchers believe that the data reliably shows an increase in abuse, including sexual abuse. Because of the unfortunate level of abuse in our country, the charge of abuse has a high degree of plausibility with the public and, as such, this charge is frequently made when someone wishes to attack another's character, such as in divorce proceedings or among disgruntled students and parents. It is not surprising, therefore, that such charges are commonly made against minority religious groups, and charges of child abuse and neglect have been made against New Religious Movements for the past twenty-five years. Even groups such as the Hare Krishnas, who have a theologically-based, restrictive approach toward overt sexuality, have been charged by critics over the years with sexual abuse despite the evidence that abuse occurs among devotees at no higher rate, and probably at a much lower rate, than in the general population.

The Family has been particularly susceptible to such charges and has historically been targeted by critics because of their liberal attitudes toward sexuality, although these attitudes and practices have not remained static over the years. This liberal attitude toward sexuality, along with the commitment to communal living, has been sufficient to cause The Family a great deal of trouble over the years. Moreover, some critics have suggested that the liberal attitude toward sex has not been restricted to adults but has involved sexual relationships between adults and children. In 1993, the American media highlighted these charges in several news stories involving children being removed from homes around the world and adults being charged with sexual abuse. The basis for these charges lies in the testimony of ex-members who report that they were sexually abused as children in The Family. As supporting evidence, these ex-members frequently cite *The Story of Davidito*, typically referred to as the Davidito Book, which is a work describing the early life of David, the adopted son of founder and leader, David Berg, and the natural son of Berg's wife, Maria. Critics suggest that this book is a manual for sexual abuse of young children. It is worth noting that in all cases in which children have been removed from homes of The Family around the world, no evidence for sexual abuse has been found. The Davidito book does relate David's early witnessing of sexual behavior and encouragement to explore his own sexuality, and while these experiences would be characterized as sexually abusive or neglectful by most child abuse experts, there is no report of his having been actively molested or abused by adults. Moreover, there is no evidence of long-term negative effects on David. The first author, a clinical child psychologist with thirty years of experience, recently administered a psychological evaluation to David, who is now nineteen, and found him to be a bright, well-adjusted, and emotionally strong young man.

With these considerations in mind, the authors studied thirty-two children in two Family homes in California. It is worth noting that although these two homes were located in California, the residents had an international background. Thus, virtually all children and adolescents had lived in other Family homes around the world, including Mexico, South America, Europe and Asia. Since the attributes we discuss below are not primarily influenced by short-term situational factors, the findings regarding these young people are quite probably reflective of child rearing and educational practices found generally in Family homes. Subsequent to the study reported here, the authors also visited three more Family homes, and the observations reported here are supported by our impressions of the children in these three additional homes. During the time of the study, we lived in each of the homes and observed behaviors in every aspect of home life. Both authors observed and interacted with children at play, during academics, during outreach and witnessing, devotional services, and leisure time. We were given completely free and open access to all children and adults and were allowed to talk about anything we chose with every member of the homes. Additionally, the first author administered psychological assessments, including cognitive tests and personality tests, to the children, and the second author conducted in-depth interviews with teenagers and adults to assess their attitudes toward child rearing and socialization, education, and values, including sexuality. The second author also made extensive videotapes of all members of the homes during all activities. These videotapes are available on request and provide probably the richest source of data currently available on the normal daily lives of children in The Family.

On the basis of this study, we found no evidence for child abuse among these children. Assessment by the first author of preschool and elementary-aged children indicated no psychological signs of abuse. Children interacted well with adults, including Family members as well as the authors. They displayed no anxiety or unusual fears or phobias around close interactions. This comfort in interaction was consistent with intensive clinical interviews which revealed no anxiety related to adults. On a measure involving identification and function of body parts, presented pictorially, no children indicated abnormal responses to bodily sexual areas as displayed in the pictures. No unusual themes were elicited and children's attitudes toward and understanding of the functions of the vagina, penis, and anus were age-appropriate and revealed no unusual patterns. It should be noted that this assessment was undertaken only after we had been in the home for several days, and the children and the authors had developed a comfortable relationship. Moreover, there was no indication that the children had been coached to provide appropriate answers. Such an approach in all likelihood would not have worked because the adult Family members had not been informed of the exact nature of the assessment in advance.

In interviews with adolescents in the group, the authors found no evidence for past sexual abuse despite intensive questioning. Again, the children at this age were quite comfortable with adults, showed no particular patterns indicative of unusual sexual experience, and in fact seemed somewhat more conservative regarding sexuality than age cohorts in the general population.

Apart from the issue of sexual abuse, psychological assessment indicated a general pattern of absence of pathology. None of the children displayed symptomatology of clinical significance. Emotional development was generally age-appropriate, and there were no indications of either significant anxiety or depression in any of the children. Ego functions were well developed: impulse control was appropriate indicating neither undercontrol nor suppression of spontaneity. Ego regulation, according to the important work of psychologists Jack and Jeanne Block, is the ability to adapt behavior to different situational demands and changes and to changes in ongoing situations. Both observational data as well as clinical assessment, using problem-solving fantasy measures, suggest that these children are generally high in ego regulation. Importantly, the Blocks' research suggests that levels of ego control and ego regulation in childhood are predictive of those same traits in adulthood. Thus, these children seem to be developing adaptive traits that will serve them well throughout their lives. Consistent with these developing personality traits, aggressive acting out was at a very low level and cooperative, prosocial behaviors were at a level considerably higher than found among age cohorts in the general population. Curiosity and creativity were high, and cognitive flexibility, the ability to approach situations and stimuli from different perspectives, was good. Functional skills for coping with stress were well developed and even superior, and social interactions with both peers and adults were excellent.

In the areas of cognitive and educational functioning, these children were well in advance of the norms. The Wechsler Intelligence Scale for Children and the Wide Range Achievement Test were given, and most children were above average in intelligence and all children were working at or close to potential. Children were typically two to four grades above age norms in reading and arithmetic. Problem-solving skills were very well developed, whether on abstract, concrete or interpersonal tasks. In general, these children and adolescents function at a considerably higher level than age-cohorts in the larger society. Virtually all children display what child psychologist Carol Dweck calls a mastery orientation toward cognitive tasks, and viewed failures and successes on the cognitive tasks in positive terms. The typical response to failure was a determination to work harder and the typical response to success was satisfaction in achieving competence as well as a determination to become even more competent. Goals were realistic, and behavior was generally task-oriented. In brief, the children were good workers who did not feel defeated by failure and who saw success as a sign of growth.

In sum, on the basis of psychological testing, clinical interviews, and behavioral observation, these children appeared to be emotionally well adjusted, cognitively advanced, and quite adaptive in interpersonal functioning. Moreover, because of the authors' opportunities to live in the homes with the children and to establish rapport to an uncommon degree, it is unlikely that deception could have occurred at a sufficiently important level as to not be detected by experienced researchers. Indeed, no such instances of deception were apparent.

The reasons for these levels of functioning are several. First, the homes provide a very supportive and caring environment for these children. Contrary to critics' claims, these children are treated quite well. They clearly have the impression that the adults are committed to them, and a loving and nurturant atmosphere is pervasive. And even though these homes operate with minimal material resources and little room for waste, there is a strong feeling of togetherness in the homes. This sense of mutual helping and support provides a strong and healthy context for growing children. Much criticism of The Family has involved the fact that children are moved around too much. However, there are other factors that suggest that this criticism is unfounded, not the least of which is the fact that Family children are moved no more often than are many children of parents who work in corporate America. For instance, the authors live and teach in a geographical area heavily dominated by the automobile industry and automobile-related businesses, and we commonly have many neighbors who have moved their children around fully as often as Family children. Many people who would be skeptical of The Family's moving children raise no such reservations regarding the children of corporate America. But just as the children of corporate America understand that their moving is related to parental values and goals, so do children in The Family clearly understand how their moving fits into the life of missionary work. In the final analysis the question is whether or not the children feel comfortable and relaxed in their home and whether they feel cared for and valued. It is clear that the children studied display such positive feelings. The children have clearly developed a sense of basic trust, they are strongly attached to their parents, and they have a strong sense of bonding with both natural siblings and peers in the homes.

Socialization practices in the homes are clearly based on the teachings of the religion. Through a combination of scripture and the writings of their leader, Father David, a strong authoritative support for the lifestyle is communicated clearly to the children. Moreover, the children see these teachings played out in the lives of their parents and other adults, and they are thus exposed to models for behavior and guides toward internalization of values. They also see how these religious values and beliefs are embodied in adults' relationships with them, the children. Emotional support and affection are clearly communicated, and discipline and correction are gentle and instructive. Children receive clear guidance from teachers and other adults, and adherence to the basic rules of the home and the religion is expected; however, autonomy is very much encouraged. Two points are noteworthy here. The first is that like all children, these over extend themselves, fail, have conflicts, and generally get into unpleasant situations. However, these situations are extremely well handled by adults, and through discussion and encouragement, problems are resolved. Thus, the children have relatively few arguments or conflicts of long-lasting significance. A second important point is that independence and leadership are strongly reinforced in the children and adolescents. Their opinions are sought and they play an important role in the functioning of the home. As a consequence, these young people are optimistic and feel quite empowered to take control of their lives. It is, in fact, difficult to imagine a healthier, more growth-enhancing milieu than exists in these homes. Although the teaching of positive values for living is stressed, this socialization is in no way authoritarian. Indeed, based on universally-accepted research findings on the effects of patterns of parental socialization on personality development, the personality traits of the children, as described above, *could not* result from authoritarian socialization practices. The children are friendly, relaxed, spontaneous, and appropriately attached to parents, and these attributes are simply not found in hostile, authoritarian homes. Indeed, in many respects the Family homes provide a living laboratory in support of Urie Bronfenbrenner's Ecological Theory of Development. Bronfenbrenner theorizes that development is sociocultural in nature and a function of the interaction between the individual and environmental systems, ranging from the fine-grained influences of direct interactions of the child with specific defined socialization agents (e.g., parents, school, church, etc.), through a layer of influence reflecting the interactions of these socializing agents with each other and their interactive effect upon the child (e.g., the coordination of values between school and parents and the communication of this coordination to the child), on through a layer of larger influences (e.g., social services, neighbors, friend of family, media) as these are filtered through the layers that are most immediate to the child. Bronfenbrenner then theorizes that the greater the coordination and consistency of influences and messages through these layers to the individual child, the greater will be adaptation and healthy development. In The Family, we seem to see these predictions of Bronfenbrenner being played out in a naturalistic environment.

As mentioned above, in addition to being well-socialized and emotionally healthy, children's performance on cognitive and educational tasks is remarkable. Again, observation in all five Family homes makes clear the reason for this good performance. Education has a high priority among this group, and this is reflected in performance on tests. The basic core of the educational system is the Standardized Home Based School Program. Children are tutored in these materials by several people in the homes, ranging from teenagers to adults. The tutoring is supportive and facilitative. Expectations of good effort are communicated, and natural reinforcers, such as praise, run throughout the process. There is a strong emphasis on a close tutor/child relationship, and the process seems to enhance positive feelings in both child and tutor. The classrooms are well maintained, and the children have a broad array of educational materials upon which to draw. Much of the material for preschoolers on up reflects the influence of Montessori, and in addition to the physical materials, the Montessori philosophy is clearly reflected in the style of teaching and tutoring. Children work at their own level and pace, and there is a great emphasis on the intrinsic motivation of insight and discovery. At the same time, social interaction is not ignored, and the presence of what Vygotsky calls the "zone of proximal development" is clearly salient. This process deals with tasks that are too difficult for the child to master alone, but which can be mastered with the guidance and assistance of adults or more skilled children. The flavor of Vygotsky's approach runs throughout the whole educational process.

One final variable plays a significant role in the social, emotional, and cognitive development of these children. That variable is the restricted use of television. The Family produces excellent videotapes featuring values training for children, and these tapes are sold worldwide in addition to being used for their own children. The Family also makes selective use of commercial films for entertainment and, in the homes we studied, they typically watched the evening news. However, virtually all other television is forbidden to children on the grounds that most television productions are harmful to the development of children as well as being unchristian. By now, it is acknowledged by most child development and educational experts that much television material is harmful to children in a variety of ways. At its worst, much of television programming teaches aggression and antisocial behavior, a distorted view of the world, and simplistic solutions to complex problems. In addition, in terms of simple time demands, time spent before the television takes away from learning cognitive skills, such as reading, as well as the learning of interpersonal skills. Although the relative absence of the influence of television is surely not the only variable to the healthy development of children in The Family, we believe strongly that these children provide strong naturalistic support for the validity of more controlled research studies pointing to the possible harmful effects of television on children.

In summary, our study suggests that the critics of The Family and their approach to child rearing and education are misguided. We found no evidence for child abuse or neglect. Rather, the evidence for a healthy environment for children was overwhelming. This evidence may be found in terms of our observational data, our interviews with members, and the direct assessment of the children themselves. Because The Family lies outside the mainstream of American religion, they have been targeted by critics for persecution, and because the general public, including representatives of the legal system, have little familiarity with these relatively small minority religious, they too easily believe the critics, who are disgruntled ex-members. The authors are well aware that individual cases of abuse may have occurred among members in the past and may well occur again in the future. Given the base rate of child abuse in the world, it would indeed be surprising if it never occurred among any given group with a few thousand members. However, the charges of widespread, institutionalized child abuse are clearly unfounded. The children we studied are simply too healthy to be products of a system in which abuse occurs at a high level. Perhaps in the future, critics, including especially those in the media, will draw upon resources such as this volume of writings by people who are not members of The Family but who have a scholarly interest in religion and religious freedom as background material for their analyses.

Lawrence Lilliston is Professor and Chair of the Department of Psychology at Oakland University in Rochester, Michigan, and a clinical-child psychologist in private practice. He has published research on the psychosocial development of children in new religious movements and in the areas of religion, values, and coping.

Gary Shepherd is Professor of Sociology at Oakland University in Rochester, Michigan. He has published extensively on Mormonism and religious socialization.

Chapter 5

Field Observations of Young People's Experience and Role in The Family

Gary Shepherd and Lawrence Lilliston
Oakland University

In this chapter we wish to expand on observations and conclusions presented in the preceding chapter with two objectives in mind. One is to shift focus from younger children to teens. The second is to amplify our account of activities, interaction patterns, and socialization experiences of Family young people based more on informal observations than formal testing. In so doing we occasionally replicate ourselves, but this tends to occur with regard to points that bear repeating.

Youthful Face of The Family: Implications and Consequences

The Family's young people—infants through teens and early twenties—are immediately its most notable element. For outsiders who know only of this religious group through sensationalized media portrayals, the young have become a paramount focus because of persistent allegations of child abuse. In this view, the young are understood only as tragic victims of religious perversion who must be rescued from a life of unspeakable degradation enforced upon them by their own parents. For outsiders who come into direct contact with Family homes, young people dominate one's initial perceptions by their sheer numbers, appealing interpersonal qualities, and the overwhelming degree in which they are involved in virtually all aspects of home functioning. In this view, the young come to be understood as representing remarkably well socialized new generations who constitute The Family's best hope for survival against the weighty opposition of detractors and secular authorities.

Full-time membership in The Family as of this writing numbers about 10,000 people (scattered in approximately 50 countries). Of this number, somewhere between six and seven thousand are young people under the age of eighteen. These young people are not recruits who have been converted into The Family. They are the second, and even third, generation of children born into The Family during the last thirty odd years. These numbers point to several facts of importance about this new religious movement.

The first fact is that The Family is not really preoccupied with recruiting new members (or "disciples") into the organization as a result of their missionary activity. Rather the primary objective is simply to "save" as many souls as possible prior to the "End Time" via the evangelical mode of urging listeners to repent and accept Jesus as their savior. Individuals thus "saved" are not required, nor routinely urged, to forsake their current social obligations and join The Family.

A second numerical fact is that the family has been very successful in retaining the faith and commitment of its young people. Most new religious movements (including the Church Universal and Triumphant, which we lived with and observed intensively in Montana just prior to our initial stay in Family homes in California), experience difficulty in infusing the second generation with the equivalent motivation and conviction of the parent generation (individuals who *were* converted as adults). In contrast to this usual trend, our observations suggest that The Family's older youngsters are an increasingly vitalizing force, in some ways perhaps even more committed to the missionary work than their elders. (As many as 2,000 people may have dropped out of active Family home participation during the last five years, presumably because of the high level of commitment expected relative to the hardships and opposition that often must be endured in many parts of the world.)

Thus the face of The Family is a predominantly young face, and it is likely to remain so for several reasons. Birth control practices are not generally acceptable whereas sexual relationships are valued. The result is a high birth rate. It was not uncommon among adults we talked to of long-time Family membership (over 15 years) to report having ten or more children. Furthermore, young people are encouraged to marry soon after reaching the age of 18 and to begin having their own children soon thereafter. Finally, it is the case that even when some adults choose to leave The Family some of their teen-aged children elect to remain.

The result of these factors is a skewed age pyramid that is not likely to shift away from its youthful base in the foreseeable future. The San Diego home we stayed in provides a somewhat typical illustration: Of a total of 40 home residents (as of July, 1993), only ten people were over the age of twenty-one. Fourteen of the residents were under the age of eleven, and three mothers were expecting new babies (all of whom were successfully delivered in the fall after our departure). In the Michigan home we have more recently been visiting, only eight of 44 residents are over the age of twenty-one, and twenty-five are under the age of thirteen.

The age imbalance portrayed in these numbers in turn has several important consequences for The Family. Internally, it means that (1) a proportionately very large amount of time, energy and other resources is allocated to child care and socialization; (2) that home rules, interpersonal relationships, and Family philosophy have all undergone significant adaptive changes that reflect and accommodate problems associated with a burgeoning child-youth population; (3) and finally that The Family has perforce become unusually dependent on contributions of young people in both the operation of homes and in the performance of missionary and other outreach activities. Age imbalance also contributes to at least one important external consequence: It reinforces rumors, allegations, and public perceptions of Family-sanctioned child abuse.

Charges of child abuse, particularly sexual, do not, of course, originate in the mere existence of an usually large younger population. As pointed out in the preceding chapter, such accusations most obviously gain credence because The Family teaches a radically liberal view of sexuality and sexual relationships (at least from a traditional religious perspective) and actively practices these views. Two fundamental notions are invoked: One, that God created our sexual nature, so that it cannot be inherently bad; in fact it must be inherently good. And two, the law of love is the operating principle of human life and, appropriately applied, extends to heterosexual relationships between consenting adults outside the constraints of marriage. When these beliefs and certain applications are combined with communal living arrangements that feature a disproportionate number of young people, most outsiders don't think twice about accepting whole cloth the worst tales of anti-cultists and disaffected ex-members.

Reprise of Conclusions Regarding Charges of Child Abuse

The fundamental reason for our initial agreement to visit the California homes was to address these charges through direct observation of Family life. Our more clinically focused report summarizes assessment results (particularly for younger children) that produced no evidence of abuse. Here we want to emphasize the extent to which this outcome of more formal testing was corroborated by constant informal observation of interaction patterns and activities in the households in which we lived. We ate meals with Family members; engaged in simple household chores and recreational activities; observed daily devotional meetings and children's home-school classes; traveled with missionary outreach teams of young people to such destinations as restaurants and fire stations where they "witnessed" through song and literature; and we interviewed many members (both young and old) about their lives in the family and their attitudes concerning a multitude of personal and public issues. In all of these activities we were particularly alert for indications of potential abuse occurring. We detected none.

It is conceivable that a troupe of trained actors, while under constant observation for a period of days, might be able to sustain convincing, coordinating performances that would conceal the true nature of their lives and characters. But as we previously argued, it is inconceivable that young children and toddlers would be able to do so: It strains the bounds of credulity to believe that children who are physically and/or emotionally mistreated on a regular basis could suddenly be made to behave toward their putative abusers in such a way as to avoid giving off the slightest clue that anything was wrong and to instead consistently respond to older household members in persuasively secure and affectionate ways.

It is true that sexuality is not a repressed topic of interest in Family homes. Again, extra-marital relationships are condoned between adult members of households (although it has not been our impression that such liaisons are incessantly engaged in). Discussions of sexual issues and problems are open and candid. Family members did not avoid such discussions in our presence, nor did they inhibit normal behavior patterns tinged with sexual overtones, such as occasional wearing of a moderately revealing article of clothing, physical expressions of affection (a kiss, a hug, holding hands; but not "making-out" between couples), moderately sensual dance movements, etc. Teens are well informed about sex and are capable of talking about it without being either silly or mortified. After the age of 18 it is clear that young people engage in complete sexual relationships with one another, because a number of them are already a marital couple with a baby on the way. However, since 1986, Family rules prescribe instant excommunication for engagement in sexual relationships between adults and young people under the age of 21.

Our initial California observations have since been supplemented by visits to three additional Family homes (one in Michigan, two in Washington, D.C.) totaling approximately 100 other members and resulting in similar conclusions. Our overall sample of homes still remains small and non-random, but, as suggested in our earlier chapter, we nevertheless have several reasons to think that what we have observed so far is likely to be typical of Family homes throughout the world. The Family is a small, culturally homogeneous population that operates on the basis of a very standardized set of rules and values. High levels of geographic mobility insure circulation of membership between homes and countries, and this is also an important standardizing force. (In every home so far visited, we have seen the arrival of new members to the household from previous stations in such countries as Canada, Greece, Japan, Mexico, Brazil, and Argentina. These migrants appear to be quickly integrated into their new homes. They easily assume tasks and roles with which they are utterly familiar, and their smooth merger into the new home is further facilitated by the fact that they often already know many of the extant household members from previous associations over the years.)

Two additional considerations bolster our confidence in the reliability of our conclusions about the absence of child abuse. First, similar inferences are starting to be drawn by other colleagues (some of whom are represented in this volume) from their own recent observational experiences with The Family. Second, the succession of police raids, arrests, and formal changes brought against The Family by authorities in four different countries over the last four years have all failed to yield any acceptable proof of abuse. With the latest such case in Argentina rapidly unraveling at the time of this writing, more than 700 minor children have been removed from homes around the world, placed in state "protective" custody, examined for signs of abuse, and subsequently reunited with families after authorities have not uncovered evidence that would justify the original accusations.

We repeat: None of the above considerations mean that individual instances of abuse can't or don't occur. All long-term groups must be presumed to harbor a wide range of personalities and are subject to individual acts of deviance from established norms. But the above considerations do greatly decrease the likelihood that there are systematic abuses occurring throughout The Family as a matter of policy, custom, theology, or isolation.

Summary of Teen Educational and Social Functioning

We have previously described some of the personal characteristics of young people (particularly children) that we observed in California homes, some of the child rearing practices of parents, and the system of home-education for the elementary and nursery grades. Here we will summarize selected qualities, activities, and patterns of social interaction characteristic of the older youth, including the JETTS (Junior End Time Teens, ages 11-13), Older Teens (ages 14-17), and Young Adults (ages 18-20).

As a general rule, The Family's young people seem above average in intellectual and social development. In the preceding chapter we summarized younger children's performance profiles on several educational and psychological tests and noted the effectiveness of home schooling that children receive through the sixth grade level. We did not formally test teenagers, but as a group they did strike us as bright and creative problem solvers. However, while teens are encouraged to continue a series of self-study programs that can lead to high school certification, this objective is not accorded the same priority and institutionalized support as the mandatory elementary education program. Most teens are eager to become more deeply involved in basic Family work and missionary activities. Indeed, this orientation is shared by adults who also assume that the nearness of the End Time precludes the need for preoccupation with higher levels of education. Consequently our discussions with teens and young adults revealed them to be rather bereft of accepted notions of history, politics, economics, social science, and literature, i.e., the traditional liberal arts areas. For the most part, these young people do not seem to be critical thinkers. Virtually every subject they have learned at home is linked to or understood in light of a biblical or Family perspective.

We have seen very little evidence of ordinary teenage sloth and whining in the homes we have visited. To the contrary, one is immediately struck by the degree of disciplined responsibility assumed by teens of all ages within Family homes. The general impression conveyed is not that of fearful subservience, but rather of genuine acceptance (and usually enthusiasm) while carrying out a variety of tasks that tend to be outside the expected realm of performance for same-age counterparts in modern society. Of course enthusiastic task performance over a limited time period for the benefit of strangers is probably among the easiest of behaviors to simulate. And even when performances are collectively authentic there are bound to be surly exceptions.

Such exceptions are in fact discussed candidly in Family home literature. "Rebellious" young people—especially among the JETTS age group—emerged as a topic of considerable concern about six years ago. Typical concerns centered around the flourishing of such undesirable personal qualities as selfishness, pride, cynicism, faultfinding, complaining, defiance of authority, susceptibility to worldly allurements, and so on. This is a list of traits for pre-teenagers and teens that is not at all remarkable in the modern world. But in an intimate "gameinschaft" society that depends upon consensus, solidarity, and the subjugation of personal wants to collective needs, these are precisely the kinds of individualistic expressions that are perceived as most threatening and therefore most in need of being quelled.

An initial approach to this problem was the establishment of special youth centers in certain areas of the world (e.g., Japan, Mexico, and Brazil) where young people who had been identified as "problems" could be sent for an intensive period of social and spiritual "retraining and strengthening" under the direction of adult teacher-supervisors). (Contemporary jargon distinguishes between a teen who is "DT," meaning a "determined teen," which is bad; and one who is "IC," meaning "intensive care," which is very bad.) These centers were called "Victor" programs, signifying the hope that those who entered the program would be able to gain a "victory" over personal problems and return to their homes in a "yielded" state, with heightened motivation to make more positive contributions.

But the real solution to the problem of building high levels of commitment and conformity in a new generation has not developed from focusing resources on reformatory style rehabilitation programs for a minority of "delinquents." What has apparently happened instead is simply recognition of the need for parents and other Family adults to seriously devote much more systematic attention in every home to socialization issues that affect every young person. This recognition first began to be officially articulated about four years ago by Father David's wife, Maria, in a series of articles that promoted the now widely implemented "Discipleship Training Revolution" and resulted in the dissolution of the Victor Program. From a social psychological perspective, the essence of the DTR, as we observed it being applied in California, may be reduced to such basic principles as emphasizing positive rewards, listening, soliciting opinions and suggestions, conferring important responsibilities, and respecting decisions of young people when conscientiously made in the performance of their duties. When consistently experienced, the cumulative effect of these practices is to strengthen feelings of both personal worth and attachment to the purposes of the group.

These effects were in full blossom at the time of our California

observations. According to one only slightly hyperbolic Family adult:
"Eighteen-year-olds are running the whole show now. It's a challenge to
keep our kids. There are some drop-outs, but with so much good
training, the Lord will still find ways to make use of them." Below we
present a brief sampling of some of the activities in which the operation
of these integrative socialization policies are manifest.

Observational Examples of Youth Integration Activities

One of our first Family experiences in California was sitting in on
the daily home devotional—an hour-long session of singing, praying,
scripture applications, testimonials, and occasional skits. Older teens
were completely in charge of these activities in both homes we visited.
They selected the songs to be sung, provided the guitar accompaniment,
dictated the format for collective prayer and scripture recitation, and led
the discussion of goals that had been accomplished versus those that had
not. These activities were carried out with natural ease and authority.
Adult family members complied with directions, did not intervene in the
programming, and in general responded to the young as one would to
peer and status equals. At the conclusion of these sessions, a round-
robin of hugs and verbal expressions of affection and personal
encouragement were exchanged among all members—young and old,
male and female.

The most important devotional of the week is the Sunday
communion service. Given the spiritual significance of this event, and
the traditional assumption of sacramental officiating by the clergy in
established religions, we anticipated that an adult leader might take
charge on this occasion. Instead, a fourteen-year-old girl led the service
with casual aplomb. She began with a few extemporaneous comments
about the significance of communion, uttered an informal sacramental
prayer, and then initiated the passing of a platter of bread and a glass of
wine from which every household member except infants partook.

Older teens (particularly eighteen- and nineteen-year-olds, who are
now accorded the status of "Young Adults") assume virtually the full
range of "ministries," or roles, necessary for the functioning of Family
homes. Some of the more visible of these roles include meal
preparation; home maintenance and repairs; "provisioning" of food,
clothing, and household goods; child care supervision; pre-school and
elementary education; and finance and home budgeting. One eighteen-
year-old girl was apprenticing to a traveling midwife (who in turn
delivers a large percentage of Family births throughout the United
States: Approximately 700 babies over the last eleven years). The young
apprentice in fact successfully supervised the delivery of a baby in the

temporary absence of the midwife after our departure. Younger teens and older children also make household contributions through regular chores such as house clean-up, laundry, table setting and dish washing, assisting in yard care and child care, and singing gentle wake-up songs for morning reveille in the various home sleeping quarters.

One more particularly good example of the implementation of youthful responsibilities may be cited in the area of finances. Individually Family homes do not open banking accounts: they do not have credit cards or write checks. All goods, services, and supplies that cannot be "provisioned" are paid for in cash. In one of the California homes, a young man who had just turned eighteen had been designated as the "money person," the person responsible for keeping the home's available cash, budgeting its expenditure for routine needs, and making decisions about its allocation to individuals who make requests for items that must be purchased. On one occasion we observed an older adult male—the home cook and one of the longest tenured members in The Family—approach this eighteen-year-old with a request for a small amount of money to buy an ingredient that was lacking for a meal entre he was planning to prepare. The young man checked his cash flow record and denied the request: Current cash level was low and other budgeted items and requests, in his judgement, had priority. He suggested the cook substitute a different ingredient that was on hand or prepare something else. The older man began to bridle, then stopped, grimaced, and without further argument accepted the decision.

Outside the home, young people also make substantial contributions to missionary and other outreach efforts. In so doing, they can concretely identify themselves at an early age with the fundamental purpose of The Family's existence. Outreach efforts may take a variety of forms for the young. It may be as simple as having children regularly create batches of drawings, cards, poems, or letters to send to people who have made donations, or to organizations that have permitted Family member visits, or to institutions that may have some other kind of potential relationship to The Family. Older teens assist in clerical computer tasks necessary for conducting the "mail ministry"—sending out of regular literature to "Turf Supporters" (former but non-alienated members), "Friends," and other sympathetic parties, solicitations and acknowledgements of contributions, etc. Older teens may also be sent considerable distances to offer volunteer relief aid in the aftermath of various natural and social disasters such as Hurricane Andrew, the Mississippi floods of summer '93, or the Los Angeles riots of spring '92.

But the most frequent, visible, and uniquely effective form that youthful outreach and missionary contributions take is through group musical presentations. Over the years, talented Family musicians and composers have created an impressive body of religious songs (emphasizing a folk-rock style) that virtually every member appears to know by heart. From an early age children are trained to sing and dance unself-consciously before audiences, and many also learn to play musical instruments, particularly the guitar. "Performance teams" of various youth age groupings are formed. Specific numbers are imaginatively choreographed and rehearsed. A wide variety of organizations and institutions (local businesses, shopping malls, senior citizen complexes, nursing homes, hospitals, prisons, juvenile homes, police and fire stations, etc.) are contacted to inquire about performance opportunities (which are especially forthcoming during Christmas, Easter, and other holiday periods).

The religious pitch linked to these performances is typically kept very general and low key, sometimes involving nothing more than the generic Christian religious content of the songs themselves. These performance opportunities are esteemed, however, because (1) they do convey a positive outreach message of Christian affirmation and hope; (2) they may open the door to further missionary inroads among receptive listeners, whose "hearts may have been touched"; (3) they convey an extremely positive image of The Family to the larger community that challenges stereotypes of debased cultists; and (4) they provide an ideal vehicle for introducing children and teens to a working conception of themselves as actual missionaries.

We accompanied performance teams on two separate occasions. The first was with a combined group of a dozen JETTS and older teens in a jam-packed van to a fire station in downtown San Diego. A musically talented married couple was in charge of the expedition, participated in the performance themselves, and maintained a constant stream of advisory suggestions and comments on lessons learned during both the drive into the city and the return home. The half-hour performance itself was polished, touching, and very well received by an audience of about 30 fire station personnel. Among the most affecting numbers was a rendition of "The Fireman's Prayer," composed and set to music by the adult male team supervisor.

The second outreach performance we observed was significantly different in several respects. The group was smaller, consisting of just female JETTS (who were under the supervision of an 18-year-old girl, the younger girls' designated "Shepherd"), and was not a pre-arranged performance date. This team drove to a community some 15 miles distant from their home and began searching for a promising restaurant where they might inveigh permission to perform. A modest Italian place was located, a parking lot prayer for success was offered, and an impromptu meeting with the manager was skillfully negotiated by the 18-year-old team Shepherd.

The manager's initial suspicion was mollified by demonstration of a photo album crammed with pictures of Family young people performing in other locales (including the White House for the Bushes during the 1992 Christmas season). When the manager said they could sing in a back room where no customers were currently seated, the 18-year-old asked if they might take a quick poll of customers themselves to see whether there would be any objection to the girls performing in a more central spot nearer the customers. The poll was taken, no objections were registered, and suddenly, in the middle of the restaurant, these six young girls between the ages of eleven and thirteen were confidently launching themselves into a mini-version of the same performance given previously at the fire station.

Reactions at tables ranged from indifference to pleased attention. As soon as the last number was completed, the girls quickly fanned out with literature in hand, trolling their audience of diners for potential receptivity to a more pointed religious message. Two of the youngest girls claimed later they had gotten two men to pray with them and were elated at having "saved" them. Meanwhile, the manager had ordered up deluxe pizzas "on the house," and the team sat down to feast. Prior to leaving, the team went into the kitchen area and serenaded the cooks. The expedition ended with a follow-up parking lot prayer of thanksgiving for its success. (Two days later, when the authors volunteered to treat the entire home to carry-out pizza, in order to reciprocate the hospitality provided us, a youthful provisioner was careful to choose this same restaurant from which to order over a dozen large pizzas.)

While the above observations clearly emphasize the degree to which young people are socialized to serve Family organizational needs, one should not imagine that life for the young is a relentless round of unrelieved work, religious indoctrination, and weighty responsibilities. The daily schedule allocates an hour of private "quiet time" and an hour of "get-out," or recreational exercise, for every home member. Sundays are designated as "Family Day," during which smaller nuclear families are expected to interact together in some enjoyable and relaxing activity. (In cases where adults or older teens are living in a home separate from their "flesh" families, they are "adopted" into one of the existing nuclear units.) Swimming, picnics, and intra-family soccer matches were the activities of choice we observed in California.

Parties are also popular forms of diversion. One regular occasion for parties is a collective birth celebration, held sometime during the appropriate zodiac period, for all home residents who share the same astrological sign. Such a celebration was planned in one of the California homes midway during our visit. Various activities involved in bringing this party to its conclusion are worth mentioning here, because they illustrate additional small but telling ways in which Family values are manifest in young people's routine home experience.

Basic ingredients (including some imaginative substitutes) for making a half dozen "carrot-chocolate" cakes from scratch were identified and prepared by a group of JETTS. A creative older teen adapted a Black and Decker power drill for mixing the batter in a large tub. What was missing was ice cream. The lack of ice cream for the party was presented to a group of younger children (who had elsewhere been engaged in a competitive team game revolving around knowledge of Bible passages) as an opportunity to pray for a "miracle"; i.e., the obtaining of the needed ice cream. The children enthusiastically bunched together and united their voices in a prayer for ice cream. An older teen provisioner then retired from the children's classroom to call local ice cream parlors listed in the phone directory, explaining that she represented a missionary organization that depended on contributions for its sustenance. Would the store consider donating ice cream for the party? Within a short time the teen returned with the news that "we have our miracle": Two different stores had each agreed to donate two gallons of ice cream. This announcement brought cheers from the children, followed immediately by a session of writing and illustrating thank-you notes to the store managers.

The party itself clearly represented a significant entertainment and social outlet. This was a "new" home, only established and operating for about a month prior to our arrival. This meant that at least some residents were still probably in the process of establishing personal relationships with one another, and a party—this was apparently the home's first—presents a number of different relationship opportunities that are not available in routine work settings. Additionally, a traveling Family film crew of four males (two YAs and two older adults) had just arrived, and the temporary presence of more males in a home where women outnumbered men contributed a small portion of extra excitement. Several females—particularly the YAs—exchanged jeans, shorts, and sundresses for dress-up apparel and make-up. Social dancing—including slow and cheek-to-cheek modes, "jitterbugging," and more contemporary, uninhibited movements to a hard rock beat and pulsating strobe light—quickly became the predominant activity. Dancing partners usually rotated between musical selections, and both males and females actively solicited new partners.

Concluding Comments

Space limitations preclude a fuller account here of additional relevant details from our initial, exploratory study of Family relationships. We are engaged in on-going research that we trust will soon permit a more comprehensive, comparative, and analytical assessment of this group's unique capacity for incorporating the creative energy and enthusiasm of its youth in its so-far successful struggle to survive in a world hostile to its existence. From the perspective of many outsiders who share such a hostile view, the preliminary report offered here will be a disappointment: No confirmation of sex crimes, nor of pathetic dupes being hypnotically controlled to serve the malevolent purposes of psychotic leaders. However, our report does point to at least two social truths that are always crucial to remember.

One truth is that things are rarely as they seem on their surface. A very old dictum in interpreting social behavior says that if people perceive something to be true it will, for them, become true in its consequences. If, in this case, we construct a general stereotype of destructive, religious "cults," we are very likely to begin applying this label to every new religious group we encounter that appears to depart from "normal" religion. We assume the worst, fail to make critical distinctions, are receptive only to evidence (oftentimes shaky at best) that supports our assumptions, and respond to members of groups thus defined in exactly the objectionable ways that characterize racial, ethnic, and gender prejudice.

The second, related truth is to acknowledge the difficulty in arriving at critical, rational judgments about complicated issues in a diverse social world. When issues arise outside the boundaries of our own direct knowledge, we typically seek advice or suggestions from sources that are presumably knowledgeable about these issues. For many, the mass media are such a source. In the area of new religious movements, however, the media's usual approach has been to elaborate upon and strengthen the very stereotype of religious "cults."

We can cite one personal example. After completing our observational visit in California, the authors were contacted by CBS television news to provide an interview for a special program they were doing on The Family. We agreed and the interview was video taped—a sober 20-minute summary of our research observations and conclusions. When the program aired, none of our interview was included. Nor was the information included from any other scholarly or objective sources to which CBS had easy access. The story presented to viewers was completely negative, lacking even a passing nod to the existence of evidence or views that might contradict the lurid opening program previews that trumpeted "Story coming up on a bizarre California sex cult!" When one of the authors called the producer to complain about such unbalanced, unprofessional reporting, the producer sheepishly agreed and lamented the need to employ a National Inquirer approach to the news in order to attract viewers.

A fierce struggle is being waged in many nations, our own included, to define what constitutes "valid" religion. This is, in some ways, simply the continuation of a very old struggle in modern guise. In past times, and in pre-modern societies, this conflict is couched in terms of religious heresy. In our own time and society, the conflict has been redefined in the language of secular criminology and psychology. The modern version of this struggle is not just being waged on television screens and in the pages of newspapers or magazines. It is also occurring in courtrooms and within all levels of government concerned with issues of social control. Perhaps it is too naive to hope, as expressed in the concluding statement of the preceding chapter, that some officials and opinion shapers prominently involved in this conflict will heed the cautionary notes sounded by scholars in volumes such as this. But in the aftermath of the Waco debacle, it seems worth a try.

Gary Shepherd is Professor of Sociology at Oakland University in Rochester, Michigan. He has published extensively on Mormonism and religious socialization.

Lawrence Lilliston is Professor and Chair of the Department of Psychology at Oakland University in Rochester, Michigan, and a clinical-child psychologist in private practice. He has published research on the psychosocial development of children in new religious movements and in the areas of religion, values, and coping.

Chapter 6

Sexuality and the Maturation of The Family

J. Gordon Melton
Institute for the Study of American Religion

Observers of first generation religious groups have repeatedly noted the rapid rate of internal change to which such groups are subject. Such change usually centers upon the development of a full doctrinal perspective, the expansion of administration and bureaucracy, and the change of behavior surrounding the care of the children born and raised within group. The Family, an international Christian communal group founded some 25 years ago as the Children of God, has gone through such a period of rapid change. The group is of particular significance for scholars of new and unconventional religions, however, for the completeness of its public record. For most of its life, the Family has been scattered around the world and tied together by a set of communications generated in its international headquarters and sent to all the members on a monthly and, at times, even weekly basis.[1] These publications, primarily epistles by Father David[2] called "MO Letters," chronicle in some detail the organizational, doctrinal, and behavioral life of the group and offer an unusually fruitful resource for bettering our understanding of new religions.[3]

While it has experienced alterations in every aspect of its life, one important set of changes have concerned the group's sexual teachings and behavior. The sexual mores of The Family have, during the 1980s, largely taken center stage away from the standard anti-cultists' attacks centered on brainwashing charges. This study derives from a scrutiny of The Family's literature with special reference to its teachings on sexuality which it places in a doctrinal framework under what it terms the Law of Love, how those teachings have altered through the years, and how the more recent changes have come about as part of a process of maturation into its second generation.[4]

The process of maturation can best be seen as occurring in three stages. During the early and mid 1970s, Father David developed his perspective on the Law of Love and its primary expression, an evangelistic technique called flirty fishing or FFing. Then in 1978 the totality of the Children of God leadership was fired and soon afterward a doctrine of complete sexual freedom declared. The period of sexual freedom was brought to an end in April 1983 with the issuance of a Mo Letter, *Ban the Bomb!*, the first of what has become a decade-long stream of letters which has placed a number of limits on The Family's sexual conduct and brought it into what is today a much more conventional pattern of conduct.

I. The Early Teachings on Sexuality of the Children of God

To understand the origin of the Law of Love, of course, some background is necessary.[5] The Family originated as the Children of God, a teen ministry in Huntington Beach, California, during the heyday of the hippie era, and as the Children of God grew, it consisted almost entirely of older teens and young adults who had placed themselves under the guidance of Father David. The converts came out of a subculture which prized sexual freedom and were all at the age in which some degree of sexual encounter was the norm and the regulation of sexual behavior was among the first important issues to confront the group's leadership. Among its earliest surviving pieces of literature is the transcript of a talk given by Father David in the summer of 1970 to a group of couples who were together announcing their engagements to the larger membership. Adopting the widely used metaphor of "revolution" to describe the life in the Children of God, he delivered a lengthy lecture reviewing much of the ground normally covered in standard marriage counseling.

By 1973, the rapid expansion of membership, most in their late teens or early adulthood, and all of whom had to be integrated into the Children's communal lifestyle, necessitated a return to a consideration of sexual matters. Thus that year Father David issued three Mo Letters on the proper sexual behavior of a "Revolutionary."[6] Of these,

Revolutionary Sex was the most important, as it indicated a next step in Father David's rethinking of broad issues of sexual behavior. Father David declared that the key to the system's erroneous teaching on sex was the "false doctrine that sex is sin." In sharp contrast, he emphasized a doctrine of positive sexuality. The Children's basic problem would be their establishment of a proper attitude toward sex. From the acceptance of that new perspective, one could then make judgments on proper action and gauge the acceptability of various forms of sexual behavior. Sex, asserted Father David, was "Normal, healthful, natural, God-created, God-given, and God-permitted. . . " It should be seen as a normal activity, just like eating, exercising, or sleeping. Problems resulted from having either too much or too little food, exercise, or sleep. In like measure, we needed some sex, and both denial and over indulgence was harmful. Sex was also a healthful physical activity and should be enjoyed just as swimming or hiking. It was as natural as breathing. The world's system corrupted sexuality by making it a matter of law. In addition, the laws concerning acceptable behavior varied widely from place to place since they were dictated by local custom and tradition.

Biblically speaking (and the Children of God was and The Family remains a biblically-based group), there were only four forms of sexual behavior forbidden and/or limited by God—fornication, adultery, incest, and sodomy. Fornication included a variety of sexual behavior indulged in outside of marriage. Adultery was illicit sex with a married person. Incest was intercourse with a close relative. Sodomy was male homosexuality. Of these four, there were exceptions to the first three, and bigamy and polygamy was allowed. Jesus seemed to frown upon bigamy and held the monogamous couple as the ideal. Only male homosexuality was totally condemned. Even lesbianism was not specifically prohibited by the Bible. Father David was most insistent about the acceptability and naturalness of masturbation (not discussed in the Bible) and nudity (discussed most favorably in the Bible). To the contrary, birth control (including the practice of "coitus interruptus") and abortion were an abomination to God, and were to be avoided.

Revolutionary sex provided guidance for the young married couples among the Children. Father David intended to free couples sexually and he invited them to enjoy their life together uninhibited by guilt, false modesty, and unbiblical pronouncements of the system. By this time, the discouragement of the use of birth control methods, had had an unthoughtout side effect among the married members. An increasing number of infants were becoming a part of the family units. By 1973, the question of sex education now demanded some attention. In offering a solution to the problem Father David reached back into his own childhood experiences, some contemporary reading about sexual development, and his most favorable impression of the Kibbutz.[7] He suggested that children should be allowed complete sexual freedom, by which he meant that, first, they should be taught that their body was the beautiful creation of God and that the sexual parts were just as good as the rest of their body. They should learn that the pleasurable feeling that emanated from their sexual parts, even during the prepubescent years, were normal and should be enjoyed without threats of punishment or the imposition of guilt. Also, parents should allow the natural curiosity about the different body parts of members of the opposite sex to be satisfied, as long as it does not lead to anything harmful. However, as they mature, they should be warned of the unlawful or excessive use of their sexual organs.

In advising the COG parents concerning their children, Father David reacted to his own childhood experience of sexual suppression, and he sought to free the COG children from suffering in a similar manner. He had come to believe that ignoring and denying the sexual life of children amounted to a form of suppression that led to their growing up to be sex-obsessed adults.

Flirty Fishing

Father David's original writing on sexual ethics were prompted by the realities of colony life. However, at the same time he was writing the early Mo Letters on sex and marriage, he was developing a new form of evangelistic outreach which would become an additional factor contributing to his mature statement of the Law of Love. What would be known as flirty fishing (or FFing) originated in London in 1973. At some point during the year, seeking a little recreation, he and his wife Maria began attending ballroom dance classes. During the session they noticed all of the lonely people who were also taking the classes. Seizing the moment, they selected people and danced with them. Rather than stopping with the music, they also tried to build relationships as friends and saw the new friendships as providing the context in which a witness of faith could be made. Their early success led them to pursue the idea. Then, in one incident (that of a man called Arthur), the relationship with Maria moved in a more intimate direction. Father David encouraged her to see what would happen if she allowed their friendship to lead to a sexual relationship. Again the results were positive, and Father David decided to conduct a more ambitious experiment.[8]

Meanwhile, at the beginning of 1974 Father David shared the results of the early flirty fishing with the movement as a whole in a Mo Letter, *Flirty Little Fishy*.[9] He urged his female readers to express their abundant love by flirting with lonely men, even to the point of some physical contact (kissing), and allowing the men to fall in love with them. Thus would they establish a context for witnessing God's love for the fish (as the men were called). At this point nothing had been said to the larger membership about Maria's relationship to Arthur, however, in March 1974, Maria and Father David moved to Tenerife, a tourist spot in the Canary Islands. Here he gathered a group of older trusted members, mostly females, and quietly launched the more challenging experiment. Accompanied by the men, the women frequented the bars and dance clubs to meet, befriend, and witness to the men they encountered. Subsequently, when the situation suggested it, they would have sex with the men they encountered in an attempt to set a better context for witnessing. There was some attempt to have men practice flirty fishing, but for much the same reason that the great majority of prostitutes were women, the success of the technique depended upon the women.[10] The Mo Letters on the subject also assumed that it was basically a female ministry.

Women's unique role in flirty fishing also followed logically from Father David's idealization of the female body. As early as 1973, in *Revolutionary Women*, he noted that God has made women beautiful as part of the natural order. "God's created beauty is a thing He's made very attractive to the human eye, which is why He made them that way, so that women would appeal to us more, and we would want to have them."[11] This idealized view was reiterated in a variety of comments in other letters, and culminated in two letters in the summer of 1978. The first, *You Are the Love of God!* asserted, "THE ULTIMATE PICTURE OF GOD'S CREATIVE LOVE TO MAN IS A BEAUTIFUL WOMAN!. . . So it's not wrong for me to love your body and to adore you, because you are the love of God!" The fish "can't understand crucifixion, they can't understand Jesus. But they can understand the ultimate creation of God, a woman. Picking up the crucifixion images from the earlier flirty fishing letter, he concluded, "Everyone of you girls who spreads out your arms and your legs on the bed for those men are just like Jesus, exactly like Jesus!"[12]

The Introduction of the Law of Love

While the experiment was proceeding in Tenerife, Father David's thoughts on sexual ethics and theology coalesced in the concept of the Law of Love, and he began to expound the new doctrine to the larger movement. He had, of course, earlier appropriated the idea of a law of love from the Bible and made use of it in his 1973 epistles on sexuality, but he now offered it as the broad new foundation of the Children's code of conduct.[13] The Children of God constituted the Church of the last generation of humankind. As such it has been given the same total freedom as the church of the first generation. God had given the Children of God the "complete freedom from the bondage of the law" and the "complete freedom of life and liberty through love." The question of the hour was, "Can you handle this new toy safely so as to bring joy and pleasure to yourself and others around you without endangering anyone or harming anyone or infringing on anyone else's freedom and others rights?"[14] If the Children cannot handle the freedom, God will take it away.

According to the original statements concerning the Law of Love's practical application to sexual relationships, Father David continued to assume the norm of monogamous marriage. However, the Law held out the possibility of some extra-marital sexual activity, though there must be a strong and compelling reason for such activity. To determine if an extra-marital sexual contact was correct, the person contemplating such an encounter must first be able to answer in the affirmative a number of questions. For example, does such activity promote the Children's evangelistic mission? Is it good for COG? It is good for the individual? Does it assist you or your partner in the service of God? Should the answer to all of these questions be yes, in addition, the individual considering an extra-marital liaison must seek and obtain the consent of all concerned parties, including their spouse, those with whom they live communally, and their immediate leaders. For Father David, motivation was all important. Any extra-marital sex must be done for love's sake, in a spirit of self-sacrifice. It should not be the occasion of simply indulging one's lustful urges. Thus, at this stage, while the Law of Love offered the possibility of legitimate extra-marital sex, in fact, the only acceptable occasion was in the conduct of flirty fishing, and the only people engaged in flirty fishing were the small group in the Canaries.

After two years of what seemed to be a successful experiment, in 1976 Berg introduced the complete plan he had in mind when he first opened the subject in 1974. Through 1976 over 50 Mo Letters were issued which detailed the sexual aspects of flirty fishing. Leading the way were 23 letters with a collective title, *King Arthur's Nights*. The letters told the story of "Arthur," the man wooed by Maria in bed who eventually joined the Children of God and married one of Father David's close disciples. The first of the letters talked of "A Dangerous New Ministry," and Arthur's story became the Children of God's *Arabian Nights*. Through weekly installments Arthur's story, complete with instructions on flirty fishing, was gradually unfolded. Subsequent letters detailed the experience of some of the other women in Tenerife. The letters encouraged women (and, to a lesser extent, men) to begin this new ministry in their community, and were surprising candid in their discussion of problems from failed efforts to the consumption of alcohol to venereal diseases. There is also consideration of the alternate possibilities of fish attempting rape the women or their falling in love and wanting to marry the woman who lured them.[15]

With the practice of flirty fishing firmly in place as an evangelistic tool, in 1977/78, in several Mo Letters, Father David further developed his thinking on the Law of Love.[16] While the earlier reflections on the Law of Love opened the door for flirty fishing, these latter ones presented the fully developed theoretical underpinning of the Children's (and The Family's) life together and action toward the world (their neighbors). The Law of Love was identical with the theological/ethical position traditionally termed antinomianism, the position that God's grace in Jesus superseded the Old Testament Laws, including the moral law as summarized in the Ten Commandments. The more general and positive aspects of the Law of Love were presented in a widely distributed Mo Letter, *Our Declaration of Love*, subtitled "A New Apostle's Creed—All you Need Is Love!. The letter affirmed that Jesus' first and great commandment was to love (Matthew 22:36-4). In the Parable of the Good Samaritan, he taught how love or compassion must be put into action. The greatest manifestation of love is the sharing of the self and personal service given to others. It closed with the statement, "Love Is God!—God Is Love!"

In *Love vs. Law*, the full antinomian position is delineated. It begins, "First of all, we know that *all Mosaic laws* are *null* and *void* as far as we are concerned. *Christ* was the *end* of the *law*." Yes, on occasion, Jesus quoted the Mosaic code, but Father David argued, He only quoted the law for the purpose of exposing the hypocrisy of the law-abiding people to whom he was then talking. The particular issue before the Children was, of course, adultery, a "law" some members were regularly breaking with flirty fishing. In response, Father David asserted, "So far as *we're* concerned and as far as the Bible says, for *us* there is no such thing as *adultery*! There is no such thing anymore as a Biblical law against adultery, as long as it is done in Love, because the "*Law* of *Love*" supersedes *all* other laws."[17]

Meanwhile, in the face of Father David's bold antinomian statements, it might appear that the Law of Love had given the Children of God carte blanche to do whatever they pleased, sexually or otherwise. That has always been the complaint of those who opposed antinomianism and there have always been some who are willing to use the Law of Love, or its equivalent, as an excuse for their indulging their own otherwise illegal desires. However, in all fairness to Father David, there was at this time no attempt to destroy or even challenge the monogamous marriages of the members of the Children of God. On the other hand, the spread of flirty fishing created numerous tensions within the nuclear family structures which threatened the stability of the Children's life and provided the crucible by which the Law of Love would initially be tested.

Father David contrasted the Law of Love to the Mosaic Law and argued that while the Law of Love proclaimed freedom from the Law, it in fact required a stricter standard of conduct from those who accepted it. Quoting Jesus and other New Testament verses, he noted that it was impossible to keep the Law. "For all fall short." Jesus pointed out that, for example, a man who looks on a woman with lust has already committed adultery. Jesus, argued Father David, was making the point that the law was impossible. Every man looked upon women lustfully. No one was good enough to keep the law. Jesus was the fulfillment, i.e., the end, of the law. On the other hand, when a husband gave his wife to another in order to bring him the message of the gospel, the Law of Love judged him according to the love he had shown. In like measure, if he stopped his wife from sharing the gospel with another, he would in like measure be judged by the Law of Love.

Through 1977/78 Mo Letters provided the examination of numerous incidents in light of the Law of Love. For example, *Love vs. Law* included a discussion of the neglect of husbands by wives engaged in flirty fishing. Ideally, husbands should consent to their wives flirty fishing activity, in the same sacrificial spirit. However, it occasionally occurred that participation in flirty fishing caused a wife to become alienated from her husband, and to deny him his "sexual needs." In such a case she had transgressed the Law of Love (I Corinthians 7: 3-5). Should she take an additional step and leave him, he is justified in divorcing her. But should she return, the Law of Love suggested that forgiveness and the restoration of the family unit was the better way. The Law of Love was, argued Father David, more strict than the Mosaic law.

What Is Love?

The effective operation of the Law of Love assumed that those who agreed to live by it also shared the same definition of love. However, the meaning of "love" was not always self-evident and its lack of definition allowed a wide variety of content to be poured into it by anyone. At times, for example, long passages of the Mo Letters could be read without any mention of the content of the word love, but in fact, a fairly clear idea emerged from a reading of the relevant texts.

To begin with, in the publicly released *Our Declaration of Love!*, love was defined by reference to the Great Commandment (Matthew 22:36-40) and the Parable of the Good Samaritan (Luke 10:25-37). It concluded that love was compassion put into action. Love was demonstrated by its visible manifestation. Love might be manifest in the sharing of material goods, but the sharing of the self and personal service to others was the greatest manifestation of love. It was assumed that God created humans to be in relation with Him, and that the goal of the race was to love God and enjoy Him forever. Therefore, the great manifestation of love was to direct another to God's love in Christ. That belief undergirded the primacy placed upon evangelism in the Children of God, the constant all-encompassing daily priority of members.

As to human relationships, love was not to be seen in relationship to a set of laws which regulated objective behavior, just as morality was not to be measured by conformity to or lack of conformity to various rules. Love began in personal intent and was manifest in action based on a set of virtues which gave content to the intention. Thus love was kind and was demonstrated in kind actions toward another. In like measure love was expressed in the negative by avoidance of an opposite set of vices. Thus love was to be shown by refusing to be dishonest in personal relationships. In *The Law of Love*, for example, unselfishness and sacrifice were positive virtues tied to love while carnal lust, harming others, and infringing upon another's freedom were condemned. Great pains are taken to contrast love and lust. "Lust is merely to gratify your own greedy selfish appetite, like eating a meal. You may need it, but if you're stealing it from someone else and taking the food out of their mouth to stuff your own, this is selfish lust, not love! But if you are taking the food out of your own mouth and giving your own meal to satisfy and feed another who is hungry and starving for love and needs it desperately and might not survive without it, then this is real love."[18]

In spite of Father David's rhetorical flourishes, he had no intention of creating a promiscuous anything-goes situation. Behavior was no longer bound by law, but it was directed by the substance of love. Actions under the Law of Love were compassionate and unselfish. Such actions must not override the other's freedom (and hence by clear implication rape was incompatible with love). In like measure, love did not hurt other people. Thus, strictly applied, the law of love required a regular inventory of motivations for every action toward another person.

In connection with his discussion of love, Father David made explicit an idea which seems to be implicit through his earlier writing, that humans had a sexual need that needed to be met. It becomes an expression of love to become the instrument by which someone can have his/her sexual needs fulfilled. Thus a husband should see his wife as doing the loving thing when she shares her body with a fish in order to show him love by filling his sexual lack. In like measure, for a wife to deny her husband her body is not a loving act. As single members came into the Children, older members would be concerned that they have their sexual needs met.[19]

II. The 1978 Revolution

By the summer of 1978 the theoretical (i.e., theological) statement of the Law of Love which has remained central to the belief of the Children of God and its successor organizations to the present was in place.[20] The practice of flirty fishing had spread through the Children's communities and many (but by no means all) of the women were participating in it. Contemporaneously with these developments a new organizational structure was imposed upon COG. The "New Revolution" of 1975 established what was termed the Chain of Cooperation, a leadership structure comparable to a chain of command in the Army. A pyramid of leaders from colony shepherds to district, regional, national and international leaders was appointed all the way to the Children's leadership at Father David's headquarters. As with any authoritarian structure, the Chain of Cooperation made for efficiency, but offered numerous possibilities for abuse by the young inexperienced untrained leaders operating virtually without checks within their assigned territories. And by the end of 1977, there were too many reports of power abuse to ignore.[21] Among the complaints was the reluctance of some leaders to give more than a few women permission to engage in flirty fishing.

Thus in January 1978, by fiat, Father David launched the Reorganization Nationalization Revolution (RNR) and fired all of the leaders from the lowest colony shepherds right up to the top. This action not only removed the new leaders appointed in 1975, but all of the older leadership which had been in place since the early days of the Children of God. A few leaders were returned to office in February 1978 when the various homes (as the colonies had been renamed) elected new home shepherds, but most were simply cut off. At the same time the large communal living situations were down sized. The ideal home was to have less than twelve members. Threatened with complete organizational disintegration, Father David created two new positions, visiting servant

(VS) and king's/queen's counsellors (KQC's) shepherd. The former visited the homes and offered guidance and inspiration, but had no authority to interfere with what people were doing. King's and queen's shepherds took charge of publishing and distributing the movement's literature and had some minimal oversight of the visiting shepherd's. The RNR led into the Nationalize Reorganize Securitywise (NRS) Revolution, the effect of which was the further destruction of the Children's organization. The last of the large homes were broken up, and many of the members established a single nuclear family household. Some lived out of campers and scratched out a living selling literature. Most members returned to the country of their birth, and thus (for a brief time) the Children were once again present in the United States in force. Assuming a low profile, they were little noticed. Many sought secular employment, and thus took themselves and their literature off the street. There, as yet, being no internal educational structure, Father David suggested that the children be placed in public schools, and to compensate for the compromise with the "System," he urged that school events be used for witnessing whenever possible. Assisting their blending into their environment was the dropping of the name Children of God. They began to call themselves the Family of Love, a name used by the flirty fishing corps at Tenerife, and officially adopted by the movement in 1978.

Through the late 1970s and into the early 1980s, at the very time that the practice of flirty fishing was being touted by Father David and the movement's leaders, and the Law of Love was being established as a basic ethical perspective, the Children of God/Family of Love experienced its time of least organizational stability. The New Revolution established a strong hierarchial organization. Suddenly, with the firing of the leadership, its guidance disappeared over night. Nothing replaced it. What little leadership remained above the level of the individual centers had its hands full just getting the literature out. Thus, no one was present to enforce and, more importantly, interpret the ideas of the Mo Letters. This situation became more serious with the NRS Revolution. Not only were most of the homes broken up, but many of the families relocated internationally. Friendship ties were broken between the members and contact with headquarters was the weakest ever. Simultaneously, members were being told, in a theological level, that they were God's free people. On a practical level, they were being instructed to find their own way in the world and were provided with a number of options for ministry.

Sexual Ethics During the RNR and NRS

At the same time that the Children of God was being dissolved, its members scattered into their family units, and the slow transition to becoming The Family initiated, a host of new problems arose. Heading the list, children were now present in significant numbers. There had been a steady stream of new babies since the formation of COG simply because of the policy against birth control. However, now, an additional number of new infants, termed Jesus babies,[22] were arriving as a result of flirty fishing. Concurrently, a sizable number of the children, the babies born to COG members in the early 1970s, had reached school age and their care and education had become a major new concern on The Family's agenda for which neither the leadership nor the membership were yet equipped. There were as yet few teenagers.

As part of his attempt to fill the gap left by the dissolved leadership and establish direct contact with the members, in January 1978 Father David asked each full-time member to fill out a lengthy personal questionnaire. These questionnaires served a number of purposes. They gave Father David, Maria, and his personal staff, a snapshot picture of the movement. It provided the members a chance to ask questions and to present their gripes about life in the colonies. These became the basis for many of the changes Father David soon initiated. The questionnaires also included a number of items relating to the members' sex life. The questionnaires, along with additional questions from the field during 1978, led to the production of a fresh set of Mo Letters on sexual behavior. They spoke to a broad set of problems which The Family now faced because of the variant practices of flirty fishing in different countries, the first appearance of venereal disease, and the needs of the older children. Answers to old questions were revisited for those new members who either were not around when they were previously answered or lacked access to the older letters.

The new set of letters, the most important being a three-part series, *Sex Questions and Answers*,[23] provided the opportunity to reiterate the positive perspective on sex so integral to The Family. The continuity of The Family's position was emphasized in the transcription and circulation in 1980 of a 1970 talk as a Mo Letter, *Sex in Heaven*.[24] In the spirit of the new freedoms, the answers to many of the questions assumed the tone of advice and commentary but left considerable room for individuals to make decisions on their personal behavior based upon the situation in which they found themselves. Also, in the face of the disintegrating Family organization Father David never missed an opportunity to reaffirm the oneness of The Family. Possibly the most important advice concerned the comments on the raising of children. Of some interest, amid that advice he began to comment on the development of children and sexuality.

The new dialogue on children and sexuality was initiated by Father David in an autobiographical treatment of his own developing sex life. Using himself as an example, in *My Childhood Sex!—Doing What Comes Naturally*,[25] he made the point that pre-pubescent children should as a whole be left alone and allowed to discover and experience sex naturally. He contrasted the several experiences in which his mother chastised him for his own sexual explorations with his hopes for a happier life for The Family's offspring. Particularly traumatizing to him was his mother threatening to cut off his sex organ after she had caught him masturbating. He encouraged the parents in The Family to allow children to explore their natural sexuality, so that by the time they hit puberty they would have a natural transition to their teen years. By that time, he argued, "If you were already accustomed to it, there wouldn't be any big deal about it, nothing new!—It's only natural! Father David also described his early experience of having his penis manipulated by his Mexican baby sitter as a means of getting him to take his nap (a widespread practice in Latin countries).[26]

The question of childhood sexuality was raised in the first part of *Sex Questions & Answers*, issued in 1979. Again, he reiterated what he had said earlier. Children should be taught that their body is a beautiful creation of God and their sexual functions and feelings are as normal as eating. He then adds in no uncertain terms that "our bodies in no respect must ever be abused or mis-used or over-used, or exposed or used in such a way as to offend or hurt others." Allowed, even encouraged, behavior included nude mixed bathing, nude mixed play, self-sexual examination, experimentation and/or interplay when playing or sleeping together. Allowing children to watch adults engage in sexual intercourse is allowable, but each case must be judged on its own merits according to the child's reaction. He cited an acceptable and an unacceptable case on each side.[27] Very much in line with the instructions on childhood sexuality were the passing references to it in the otherwise lengthy treatment of child raising issues in *The Story of Davidito*, a book written about a Jesus baby born to Maria as a result of her flirty fishing.[28]

Father David also raised the question of marriage for the youth. While the question seemed to be of interest to some members, it should be noted that the discussion was largely academic as there was not at this time many youth in the movement, even fewer who lived close to each other. The overwhelming majority of the minors in the movement were less than ten years old. He suggested, theoretically, that there seemed little reason to delay marriage much beyond puberty (a common practice in human society until recent centuries). However, in the end, present societal custom must reign supreme. While all things (in this case, the marriage of teens in their early years) are lawful, not all things are expedient. He returned to this theme the following year in *Child Brides*,[29] He considered at some length on the possible marriage of teens in the years from 13 to 15. Again drawing most of his argument from his own life experience, he suggested that those teens who wanted to should be allowed to marry.[30] Since society would probably not allow such marriages, minors might be allowed to pair off as lovers and even have children (remembering that The Family discouraged any use of contraceptives).[31]

A second theme which was further developed at this time was that of sexual contact among the adult members of The Family. While most of the writing about sex had concerned flirty fishing, i.e., sexual contact carried on in the process of witnessing to a non-Family-member, members of the colonies/homes had been allowed a certain amount of freedom to enjoy sexual contacts (apart from the several forbidden varieties) among themselves. This practice was (and is) termed sharing. In a 1980 letter, *The Devil Hates Sex!—But God Loves It!*,[32] Father David stated what is possibly his most radical position regarding life among Family members, "AS FAR AS GOD'S CONCERNED THERE ARE NO MORE SEXUAL PROHIBITIONS HARDLY OF ANY KIND. . . . God's only Law Is Love."[33] The Devil hated sex, and society, the system, had aligned itself with the Devil, by making all kinds of anti-sex prohibitions. Particular targets were forced vasectomies, public nudity, and sex between those just above and just below the age of adulthood.[34]

The Fellowship Revolution

By the beginning of 1981 Father David attempted to reverse the chaos into which the former Children of God had fallen through what he called the Fellowship Revolution. He reached back into his background in the Christian and Missionary Alliance to suggest that those people still related to the Family of Love begin to establish new fellowship links. Each home that wanted to be in fellowship was to meet together weekly with those two or three homes closest to it. Thus was established a Local Area fellowship. Several Local Area Fellowships met monthly and formed a District Area Fellowship. Several District Area Fellowship would meet together quarterly and form a Greater Area fellowship. All of the Greater Area Fellowships in a country would meet together annually as the National Area Fellowship. As each level was formed and leadership elected, a new hierarchy arose. This differed from the old one in that it was elected at every level by the members rather than being appointed from the top down. This new organization represented a compromise between both the abusive hierarchy and the chaotic freedom which had preceded it, and it has remained in place to the present. The cumulative changes which followed the Fellowship Revolution marked a watershed in the Family's life. A shifting perspective was marked by a self-conscious need to develop mature leadership. The most illustrative break with their own past came with the banishing of the outward signs of hippiedom

Above and beyond the obvious new level of fellowship and oneness and the welcome guidance of the new leadership, the Fellowship Revolution nurtured the development of new ministries. Among the most important for the long-term development of The Family was the video ministry. Even before the Fellowship Revolution, with The Family scattered as never before, two members in Europe, Paul and Marianne, hit upon the idea of making home videos. In 1980 they began visiting the various homes and making videos of the members. In this manner, the separated members could communicate their joys and concerns. They could give their testimonies and show the videos to potential converts. After some hesitancy, Father David recognized the value that the videos could have both in reuniting The Family and as an evangelistic aid. Through 1980 he encouraged the making of home movies to circulate within The Family.[35]

It was also at this same time that a problem developed. It seemed to have emerged during the flirty fishing activity in the Philippines. Some of the men who were being fished were addicted to pornographic movies. In their attempt to meet the fish on their own level, the women occasionally watched the movies with the fish. By that process, such movies were introduced into The Family. Given The Family's stance on nudity and sexuality, it was difficult for some members to articulate a rationale against them. A prominent member of The Family even suggested that Father David would enjoy watching them. Upon hearing this, Father David's response was blunt:

I THINK IT'S UGLY & UNCLEAN AND I THINK IT'S WICKED: If it's something beautiful & right & clean & decent, including artistic & romantic scenes, sex that is beautiful & pretty, artistic & romantic, I think that's fine. But I don't like ugly porno photography. . . .

IN FACT, UNTIL I SAW SOME PORNO MOVIES, I NEVER REALIZED SEX COULD BE SO UGLY & SO SICKENING & SO PERVERTED AND SO HORRIBLE!

He advised The Family members to get rid of the movies and not to watch them even with the fish. They were garbage and should be dumped in the sewer.

Meanwhile, Father David began to speculate about the potential of the new video ministry for handing the pornography problem. At the beginning of 1981, in the midst of some detailed instructions of a purely technical nature (lighting, camera techniques, backgrounds shots, etc.), he made a passing suggestion that along with the other videos that some be made featuring female members, including shots of their dancing in the nude.[36] Suggestions on how to do the nude dancing movies followed a short time later. Here he made his most radical suggestion. "MAYBE YOU COULD SLIP IN A NICE MALE HERO IN THERE ON THE SCENE, in some of those scenes perhaps, a little love-making, artistic & beautiful like some of the show dances perhaps you've seen in some of the clubs, some of those *simulated* sex acts. Not hard porn but soft, beautiful & pretty with some lovely dancing combined with some of that gorgeous love music of yours, folks."[37]

Beginning in 1981, in response to these suggestions, several cameramen, primarily in Family homes in Greece and in Brazil, made dance videos. Adult female members of The Family were invited to dance to their favorite music. The dance videos followed a very stylized format, following suggestions from Father David, with a single woman dancing in the nude usually with a piece of gauze-like see through material as a prop.[38] In a few cases, at the home in Greece, minors, both teens and preteens, were allowed to participate in making a video. There were also several love videos made in Greece. Love videos differed from the dance videos in that they involved two or more people on camera in various erotic situations.[39] Copies of the videos were sent to headquarters and circulated to those homes which had televisions and VCRs during the early 1980s. The dance videos continued to be used into the mid-1980s before they were discontinued in 1987.[40] The love videos, however, quickly proved unacceptable and were, after only a few months discontinued.[41] Thus the love videos were never circulated widely in The Family, and the majority of the members never saw them.[42] The other video work, of course, continued and developed into the professional enterprise it is today.

The Fellowship Revolution proved very important for the circulation of the videos. The quarterly and annual meetings proved a time when members who lived at homes without televisions or VCRs could watch The Family's growing number of videos, including the dance videos. It should be noted that at this time, in those videos made in

Brazil, a brief dance video was often placed at the beginning of videos on another subject. Father David emphasized that the dances were to glorify God and to glorify sex, which The Family believed was good.[43] They were seen as possibly leading to sexual arousal in those who watched them. They were also seen as an attempt to promote a wholesome sexuality in a loving context, and as an alternative to pornography which promoted lustfulness. Members gave the videos mixed reactions. Some liked them, others found them boring and even comical (in those cases where the dancer did not conform to current standards of beauty).[44]

Sexual Behavior During the Fellowship Revolution

A description of life in The Family during the period of the RNR must be put together somewhat like a jigsaw puzzle. Members actually took to heart the message of freedom and as they moved out into nuclear family units adopted practices as they were led and as they felt able. They received the letters and followed them, however, their putting the admonitions into practice was very much limited by (1) their understanding of them, (2) their agreement with what was being said, and (3) their financial resources. If they had trouble accepting what they understood they were being asked to do, they often rationalized that the directions did not apply to their particular national situation. From reading through the literature produced in this period and from interviews with members, it is obvious that a wide variance of behavior was operative, a fact most clearly observable from the many complaints in the letters. In regard to sexual behavior, on one end of the spectrum were nuclear families with children who launched family witnessing ventures. These proved the most conservative. Some were conservative from simple lack of options. Others had chosen to launch family ministries in order to avoid behavior that they felt unable to adopt. While in these nuclear family situations, many had to take secular jobs to provide for basic necessities and used their spare time for witnessing. While working and living basically with nonmembers, they had to conform, at least outwardly, to the "system's" mores.

On the other end of the spectrum were some communal establishments, most notably Greece and Brazil, which worked together in a very active witnessing program. Their communal life allowed for communal child care thus freeing parents for witnessing activity. Given the amount of time in caring for the growing number of children, even in these centers, the amount of time given to FFing was slowly cut back and largely limited to single females.[45] The organization in places such as Greece, Brazil, and Manila, coincided with the most liberal of sexual attitudes. An attitude of open sexuality pervaded the homes, and sexual sharing between adult members was frequent, with multiple partners ofttimes the rule.[46] The majority of family centers seem to have been somewhere in the middle of this liberal conservative spectrum. Through the RNR, the NRS, and the Fellowship Revolution, The Family entered its freest phase as regards sexual behavior. Prior to 1978, only a small minority of the members were involved with flirty fishing. Many more became involved beginning in 1979 and into the period of the Fellowship Revolution. Sharing, i.e., sexual contact among the adult members (including the few teenagers as young as 15 years) became more common, though the opportunity of such contact was countered by the movement of the majority of members into nuclear family living arrangements. The movement into the nuclear units was led by those members who assumed the most conservative interpretation of the sexual teachings of the group. Such living arrangements made it almost impossible for women to do flirty fishing and the lack of contact with other family members prevented sexual relations with other family adults.

The amount of sexual contact between the adults rose dramatically after the Fellowship Revolution when members began to live in communal homes again and as homes began to gather regularly for weekend fellowship meetings. Thus while the Fellowship Revolution brought some organizational sanity to The Family, it also shifted the membership to the more liberal end of the behavioral spectrum as the new fellowship meetings became occasions for sharing with people who lived in other locations. Without a doubt 1981 and 1982 were the years in which most of the events for which the Family has been criticized occurred. It was the era of the first dance videos, its was a time in which adult-teen age sex was allowed (though it was never the norm), and it was the period in which the widest range and the most sensitive issues of sexual conduct was discussed by Father David in the literature. For example, he discussed the pleasurable feeling he received from his mother's maid manipulating his genitals during his pre-school years. This practice was again discussed in *The Story of Davidito*. Though no one was ever told to do it, its free discussion was seen by some (though never the majority) as an encouragement to begin doing it.

However, the free life of many in The Family was countered by a number of trends. For example, the sudden burst of flirty fishing activity beginning in 1978 was countered in the early 1980s by the increased need for parents to stay home and care for their children. The proclamation of the end of the law as regards sexual activity, which led many into a era of unbridled sex, did not change the sexual behavior of many who claimed their freedom not to engage in unwelcome sexual activity. The free sexual life of some that reached its peak in 1981 and 1982 also led to numerous problems and criticism throughout the movement of the group's behavior.

III. The *Ban the Bomb!* Era

The Fellowships Revolution set in place a new national and international leadership with the ability to recognize and handle the many problems which became visible in the Family. And problems, such as the need for educating children and alcoholism, quickly presented themselves. Included were problems on the sexual front.

Among the first problem to assert itself (as reflected in the literature) was venereal disease. Some recent converts to The Family and some women who had been FFing had contracted a venereal disease, primarily herpes. As sharing expanded in the fellowship meetings, the disease began to spread through the fellowship. As early as August 1982 this was recognized as a problem in the Mo Letters and procedures on cleanliness and sex hygiene were instituted.[47] The problem did not go away which led Father David to complain, ". . . some people are just too carnal & too selfish & too inconsiderate! Others don't want to be branded as selfish for not sharing & and some don't want to admit that they do have a disease."[48] Unable to deal with the problem with lesser measures, in March 1983, Father David issued what is possibly the most important policy change in The Family on sexuality to date: *Ban the Bomb!* Simply put, *Ban the Bomb!* ordered that sexual sharing at the fellowship meetings stop altogether. Sharing was to be limited to the home fellowship in which one resided.

On a second level, however, *Ban the Bomb!* set a precedence for action. As problems of sexual behavior arose they would be handled informally, on a case by case basis, but if they persisted and appeared at geographically separate locations, Family-wide policies would be articulated. The cumulative effect of those policies would be the development of a mature sexual ethic which would address the variety of patterns of sexual behavior that will emerge in almost any large population.

As members accepted the "*Ban the Bomb!*" policies a second problem emerged. It appeared that some male members were assigning themselves the duty of supplying the sexual needs of new female members immediately after their formally joining The Family. As a result, a number of the new members began to express feelings that they were being sexually exploited. Several had become pregnant very soon after coming into The Family and soon left. Again informal handling of the situation failed. Leaders did not understand how the problem could be handled in light of the sexual teachings of the group. Finally, Maria, Father David's wife, who gradually assumed some of the leadership role along with him, offered the new policy. In December 1984 she ordered that new members refrain from any sexual participation in the home for their first six months in The Family. During that time they could gain some first hand perspective on The Family's sexual mores and make some well-thought out decisions as to how they would participate.

By far the most significant time-consuming problem which had to be addressed through the 1980s was that of teenage sexuality and behavior. During the days of the RNR (as noted above) discussion of teen sex was opened at a time when, for all practical purposes, there were no teens in The Family. However, by the time that *Ban the Bomb!* was issued, teens were emerging in significant numbers, and a new crop appeared annually. Father David had begun to consider a position on teen sex and marriage as early as 1977. He released his initial ruminations to the membership in 1980. In the meantime, as the movement bounced back from its period of organizational chaos, and the more immediate problems were solved, the problem of the growing number of teenagers, several hundred of which were fast approaching age 15, rose to the top of the list of priority concerns. Prior to that time, parents had only the guidance from *Child Brides* (1980), which discussed a range of issues related to sex, marriage and the younger teens. While *Child Brides* highlighted Father David's opinion about the way things ideally should be, it gave little specific direction. Now the need for that direction was acute.

In the mid 1980s, The Family initiated teen training camps, at which teens from around the world were brought together. Among other activities, the attendees and the leaders engaged in a rather frank discussion on sexual issues. In 1985, in anticipation of the first set of camps, teens were invited to submit questions ahead of time so that a considered and authoritative response could be prepared to be delivered by the camp leaders.[49] In September 1986, some of the more important ones were compiled by the Teen Training Center staff. About the same time, Father David issued an important policy statement on "Teen Sex."[50] From the letters, it is obvious that a few teens had paired off and were into heavy petting short of actual intercourse. They were more concerned with the wide range of questions common to all teenagers about their emerging sex life.

As to consideration of actual sexual intercourse with the additional possibility that pregnancy might result, Father David reached for some middle ground between the ideal he had articulated in *Child*

Brides! and what was possible, given the laws and the dominant policies in the many countries in which Family members lived. Thus he decreed that young teens were to avoid intercourse until after their fifteenth birthday. Marriage, a still more serious step, was not to occur until after their sixteenth birthday. These limiting guidelines do not reveal the extent to which the teens were engaging in sex. (It is obvious that while some teens began having sexual relationships as soon as they were allowed, the majority, for various reasons, did not.) These articles were republished as chapters in the *Basic Training Handbook* (1987) that is still used today, though these two chapters have been expunged.

Each year the teens grew older and a larger percentage of The Family fell into that age group. The constant pressure they put upon The Family has caused what has amounted to an ongoing policy discussion which periodically led to policy revisions. In 1989, for example, new policy was articulated. Father David decreed that teens should wait until their sixteenth birthday before beginning any sexual relationships. Also by this time teens were opting for marriage, thus adding a new element to considerations. Thus the rule concerning serious courtship was expanded. Most young people who were proposing marriage did not live in the same household. Therefore, when they were allowed to marry, a serious step in The Family, they were first to move into the same house and work together for six months, during part of which they were to refrain from sex contact and concentrate on getting to know each other on a daily basis. If they had not satisfied their elders that they were ready, that period could be extended.[51] By this time, The Family had developed both a marriage manual and a course to assist teens who were moving into marriage to understand what they were heading into.

The emergence of so many older teens in the late 1980s also brought to the fore another problem which had largely heretofore been handled quietly on a case-by-case basis, the problem of sex between minors and adults. During a decade of writing on child and youth sexuality, the problem under consideration was always the sexual life of children in the assumption that any sexual contact involving children or youth was between people of approximately the same age. Earlier incidents of adults having sex with children (there were no youth) brought strong reprimands. They were plainly wrong.[52] By 1989, however, a new situation had presented itself. Women in their late teens approaching adulthood were allowed to have sexual relations (with their peers) but were also being placed in close working relationships with older men. In such situations, older men are attracted to younger women and will often see in younger women a delightful conquest. In return younger women are both attracted to older men and on occasion might attempt to use their attractiveness as an entre into power. Thus in October 1989, Maria issued a policy letter warning both parties in such a potential relationship to refrain, and excommunication was threatened to those who violated this rule.

By 1991, the ongoing debate over teen sex was strongly affected by charges of child abuse which began to be hurled at The Family by some former members. The charges added further urgency to the discussion which already demanded a considerable part of the leadership's time and energy. One result, in August 1991, was the issuance of an even stricter policy on teenage sexual activity. The leadership advised the teenagers that it felt it was time "to enforce a strict *'no sex'* policy for all of you Teens who are not yet 18 years old. (—Unless you're in a country that legally permits under-18's to marry, & you're married or have been engaged for over three months.)" This position remains Family policy to the present.[53] It suggests that any further policy changes will be in the conservative rather than the liberal direction.

While this paper is concerned with patterns of sexual behavior, one cannot help but notice that the discussion on child and teen sexuality within The Family has been carried out, on the one hand, within the context of the overall experiment in positive sexuality, and on the other hand, as part of a response to the presence of children and the need to train new parents, many of whom had had little or no experience in raising a family and who were cut off geographically or emotionally from their physical families. In relation to the sexual experimentation, The Family discovered many of the reasons for societal rules outlawing various kinds of sexual behavior. In any large social setting, people, if allowed, will give in to lust as they will give in to gluttony or alcohol abuse. On the other hand, it takes more than love to raise children, it requires some knowledge and a lot of effort. The changing policy statements represented the wisdom of a growing experience imposing itself on the social order of The Family and a reasoned response to the quickly changing situation as the children aged. A long-range goal, to which constant reference was made in the literature, was the development of a society in which young mothers would have the immediate presence of their parents and grandparents with whom to share the experience of raising children. *It would be a distortion of history to see each new policy decision on sexuality as if it were being made in a vacuum or purely for reasons of expediency*, though often some immediate concern would push a particular decision to the fore. In most societies, laws are not made until a situation demands it. Handling questions of sexuality emerged out of a growing body of experience in being parents and the increasing level of maturity in the leadership. And at every stage it seems to have reflected an attempt to do what was best for the children.

Other Changes

Besides the changes in policy concerning teen sexual behavior, The Family continued to adjust its overall policies concerning adult members. These changes were made in the midst of having to deal with all of the personal issues which members had with spouses, jealousy problems, differing sexual needs, and the same host of marriage problems encountered in any groups of families. The Family members had their own set of problems due to their open sexual arrangements.

Some new trends were also evident in FFing. First, with the number of new children in the group constantly growing, a steady decline in FFing was noticed. It was becoming more and more the domain of the relatively small number of unmarried younger female adults. Some of these had taken jobs in escort agencies which provided them with a different set of clientele than they could meet in bars and other more public situations. Among the women participating, however, it has also been noticed that there were a group of overly enthusiastic FFers, women who seemed to concentrate more on the monetary and sexual aspect of their ministry than the evangelistic. A problem had also been spotted with the fish. Many had converted to Christianity and were continuing a relationship to the women who initially led them to their new faith. However, they were receiving very little training in the spiritual life.

In light of the ongoing critique of FFing, in the mid 1980s, a pilot project was undertaken, much like the one on Tenerife, in an isolated location. FFing was reoriented around a less sexualized approach in which beautiful women allured, but then moved to their message of Jesus and salvation as soon as possible. The results were that far more men were converted, a minimal number were involved in any sexual relationships, and thus few developed entangling emotional problems with the women. Given the success of the experiment, in 1987, Father David and Maria announced *The FFing/DFing Revolution!*[54] While affirming the value of FFing, the letter emphasized use of the "Word" in the witnessing process and the need of strengthening converts in the faith through DFing, the use of a series of inspirational and devotional booklets produced at that time for new converts, entitled *Daily Food*. The use of the *Daily Food* booklets gave the FFers a means to immediately involve people who had converted, most without any sexual involvement. The thrust of the message in the letter was to de-emphasize sexual sharing and to place greater emphasis on communicating love (apart from sex) and using the *Daily Food* series.

During the period of planning and announcing the FFing/DFing Revolution, The Family's leadership became existentially aware of AIDS. Over the summer of 1987, intensive consideration of its implications for The Family began to alter policies. In the experimental situation where the FFing/DFing Revolution was tested, a new policy was initiated. All sex with outsiders was to include use of a condom, and other sexual activity, such as oral sex, which might spread disease, was curtailed. In August and September of that year, a whole set of new regulations and precautions against disease were instituted. The most far-reaching one, besides the new condom rule, was the stopping of any FFing which involved sexual contact altogether. Sexual contact with any outsiders was limited to a few close "friends" with whom the FFers had already established longstanding relationships.[55]

Presently, The Family is also experiencing the arrival at adulthood of the first children born into the movement and the integration of these young adults into the movement's adult roles. From this point forward, for the foreseeable future, there will also be a steady stream of new adults joining The Family from its youthful ranks. A major response to the new adults was the "Personal Encouragement Revolution (or "PER!") announced in 1993.[56] Following extensive give-and-take with the young adults, a new policy was initiated by which the young adults were assigned a variety of adult responsibilities and granted a larger degree of freedom. The "PER!" welcomed them into leadership positions at local homes and in a few cases on the national level, though the international leadership still rests in the hands of the older adults.

Conclusion

To summarize, in regard to its teachings and behavior regarding sex, the Family has passed through three essential stages. The first, lasting approximately from 1970 to 1978 was one in which the doctrinal position on the Law of Love, their doctrine of positive sexuality, was developed. It was given a practical application through the practice of flirty fishing. The second phase, based upon the most radical understanding of the Law of Love, was one of radical freedom in which extramarital sexual contact between adults within the family became common. While many people took a more conservative interpretation of the Law of Love, others felt at liberty to have relatively unlimited sexual contact with members of the opposite sex. The unbridled sexual conduct of many Family members generated numerous problems, the most important being venereal disease. Thus in 1983 a major set of restraints was placed on sexual activity. beginning with the *Ban the Bomb!* letter, the leadership of the group has placed new rules one after another upon the membership. These rules have now limited sexual contacts to consenting adults who have the approval of the leadership in their home. The newest rules carry an extreme penalty for those who do not heed their admonitions, excommunication from the organization.

The movement of the group from their antinomian situation at the beginning of the 1980s to their relatively conservative stance at present was initiated by the spread of venereal disease (consistently a powerful argument against sexual promiscuity). However, it was given added impetus by the changing situation—the emergence of a large number of children into their teen years, the aging of the leadership, a growing sensitivity to the situations of women and children, the need to conform to the laws of the many different lands, and, by no means the least, the desire by many members to re-enter mainstream society and re-establish relationships with previously estranged parents and family members.

J. Gordon Melton is Director of the Institute for the Study of American Religion and Specialist in Religion at the University of California, Santa Barbara. The author of such standard reference works as the *Encyclopedia of American Religions* (1987-1992) and the *Encyclopedic Handbook of Cults in America* (1992). Dr. Melton is widely recognized as a leading authority on non-mainstream religions.

Chapter 7

Keeping the Faith and Leaving the Army: TRF Supporters of the Lord's Endtime Family

Charlotte Hardman
University of Newcastle

> He drew a circle that shut me out. But I drew a circle that brought him
> in! ("Other Sheep" Mo Letter, No. 167/1972)

The Family are an international group of Fundamentalist Christian
missionaries, better known under their old name, the Children of God.
In the last few years they have had to confront an intensive anti-Family
campaign. Since 1990, this campaign has culminated in charges of child
sexual abuse being filed against them in Spain, Australia, Argentina, and
France. In each case they have been acquitted; no evidence of abuse
could be found.

Since 1991 I have been carrying out research on the Family as part
of a more general research project looking at children in new religious
movements.[1] I became interested in the group of "TRF Supporters" after
being invited to one of their big fellowship meetings in London in 1993.
I was excited when I realized that here was a lay congregation of Family

supporters who shared beliefs and goals with the Family, yet chose to live a different lifestyle. This group offered children in the Family an important possibility of experimenting with an alternative to remaining in the full-time missionary Family, without having to leave the movement completely. As with many other new religious movements, the options prior to the introduction of TSers had been a clear-cut IN or OUT. For some second generation members, safe experimentation with the outside world was what they wanted, in order to help them make up their own minds about leaving or staying with the Family. TSers offer Family children a half-way house.

To explain the terminology, "TRF Supporters" (also known as TSers) is a term introduced to the Family in 1989 to describe "saved" ex-missionaries of the Family, ex-disciples of the Army of the Lord's Endtime Family, who continue to keep the faith and support their work in witnessing and saving souls but no longer live in "disciple only homes." The term TRF (Tithing Report Forms) is used by the Family to refer to the forms filled in by all "disciple only homes" and hence also came to mean "full-time member."[2] TRF Supporters now live independently, without Shepherds, deciding themselves the extent to which they adopt Family culture and rules. They continue to send their monthly tithing report and 10% of their income to World Services. The following paper looks at who the TRF supporters are, their status within the Family and how this is linked to the historical situation in which they emerged as a category in the Family, what they offer children in the way of an alternative, and what they reflect about Family values and beliefs.

Historical Background to the TRF Supporter Classification

The new classification was introduced at a time when a large number of Family members were returning to the US and Europe after intensive missionary work in the East. By the end of 1989, according to Family statistics, the Family population in Europe had increased by 25% and in North America by 38%. This was the result of the new restrictive visa policies in India and the leader Moses (Mo or Dad) Berg's positive reaction to everyone returning to their home countries—to their home fields. "Even though we're now having to leave some of the foreign Eastern fields and having to go home to the West, the Lord is blessing us with a new harvest in the West." The Homes at this stage had become much larger. Whereas in 1988 there had been 701 communities, by 1989 this had been reduced to 388—and with a population of 12,419, the average Home size was now 38. With larger Homes there was a need for close cooperative living in a way that had not been demanded of members since about 1979.

The stream of missionaries from the East and the larger size of Homes strengthened "the Army of the Lord," and at the same time highlighted both the problems some people were facing in, for example, keeping up with the pace of working at 100% demanded of disciples, and the inability of some members to stick to Family regulations. Given the growing number of teens as well as the returning missionaries, there were now more than enough people in the Army. It was also apparent that some disciples were handing over "Disciples Only" literature to anti-cultists, who were using the material against the Family, and this was further reason for tightening the Family. The diminishing loyalty of a few members was mentioned in an advisory from World Services:

> . . . there are a number of weak folks who continue to receive DO mailings simply because they tithe and supposedly remain reasonably loyal . . . a number of these weak people spend much of their time sitting around drinking beer, smoking, criticizing the Family and murmuring.
>
> Now that we have discovered that our internal publications and inside info is being leaked to our enemies and the anticult network, the Lord is spotlighting these home fields, and many of these weak or independent supposed Family members are being brought into question. ("Tightening up our Family," 1989)

The focus of the Family in 1989 was, then, to raise the standard of behavior of its members, to totally eliminate from the Family those who would not obey Family rules, and to keep as a supportive group those who were still loyal but needed a different style of life. Every Home was visited and every adult interviewed by their National Shepherd. The news bulletin that was sent out at the time went as follows:

> For any individual TRFers or Homes who are not reinstated to full D.O. mailings after their Home is visited, we would like to announce the establishment of a new reporting status. With the understanding that individuals of Homes who are not fully reinstated would still want to continue to tithe to the Lord's Work and would want to receive Family mailings, this new concentric circle of TRF disciples is being established.—"TRF Supporters."

TSers would receive much of the Family literature but not all Mo letters, Good News or directional literature and they were no longer held by Family regulations, communal lifestyle or the high standards of dedication required; they could be independent, pursue their own goals, live as they wished with their own families without having to answer to Family leaders. "TRF Supporter" status was given to those who might benefit from a different lifestyle and to give independence to those who clearly wanted more independence than the Family Army could offer. Disciples were expected to work for the common goal and give up personal ambitions.

There were several reasons for the introduction of the TS programme; one was tightening up the Army; another was bringing policy into line with practice. There were Family members already living in a style more like that of TRF Supporters than disciples; there was clearly a demand for a support group of people who did not have to be part of the "front line troops." Members of the Family themselves constantly use the military image to describe their roles. They talk about the "main fighting force" and the TSers as the "reserves" who want to be in the battle.

After RNR (1978-1981) there was a lot of coming and going. The Family had not been a "community" in the way that it is now—they had all been "doing their own thing," earning their own living and living mostly in units of couples and children. There were people who wanted to maintain this way of life. "The TS programme was the answer. Before it had been a black or white/all or nothing situation." After RNR when the Family was trying to live in communities again, there were rules and some members felt they were struggling to "make the grade" yet didn't want to leave the movement. At the time there was a contradiction in supporting the Family and its goals whilst questioning the degree of commitment required. "All the little rules and we found it hard to apply them all the time." Some wanted to leave but didn't want their children to leave; they felt they couldn't themselves give the kind of education and training the Family can offer. Communal living was a struggle for others:

> It's against human nature to take other people into your home & share everything. It was our own weakness that we couldn't live with others. I simply had a battle with communal living.

Others missed the comforts of life. "The Family has a simple lifestyle and we found it hard to live so frugally." As one TSer put it:

> Now, it's up to us how far we want to go. We're still Christians and we want to help the Family. But we're more individuals—we have freedom and choice to do what we want. In the Family as DO it's 100% commitment. Even people who want to join can't unless they have gone through 6 months of waiting and trying it out.

Other adults were faced with teens who did not want to live their lives as disciples serving the Lord in the Family and the Family had to find a way of dealing with them.

The emergence of the TS-ers is seen as having helped the group understand, define and satisfy an already existing demand, given the wide variety of people brought together in the movement. Deciding whether someone should be DO or TSer

> involved discernment of the Holy Spirit. If someone has real commitment then maybe they should be disciple and not TRF Supporter, whereas for some maybe it's best for them to have a job and become a TSer. If people don't want to surrender some of their autonomy and work for the common purpose or they get fed up with the schedules and the rules then they will probably be happier as TSer.

The TSer classification was a solution, after two previous and unsatisfactory strategies, to the problem of those who, though loyal, detract from the evangelical fervour, smooth running and exciting pace of the fight to save souls. The Army of Family disciples have to work 100%, accepting schedules and rules. In the past discipline and authoritarianism and then extreme tolerance were both tried. In the Chain of Cooperation, for example, the method of dealing with problems was, I gather, at times heavy-handed and dogmatic, to try and overcome the slackness that had come about as a result of the RNR period in which people had operated "according to their own faith."

> You just cannot have everybody running loose or you're going to have some key bad conduct . . . we're no longer a bunch of harem-scarem, wild and woolly-headed hippies! . . . We're going to have to start excommunicating people who don't set a good example and are not good samples of our Family, lest the community thinks that's us! (The Future is here—And Needs Leaders, ML 1200, 1982)

In contrast to any over zealous and ruthless handling of problems, the Fellowship Revolution of 1981 emphasized cooperation and fellowship, and communities were encouraged to tolerate people who were perhaps not suited to the kind of rigorous life demanded of a Family disciple. To ask members themselves to be realistic about the kind of life they want to lead and to offer them the alternative as a TS-er reflects the generally more mature and tolerant attitude of the Family.

Berg wrote a significant letter in 1972 called "Other Sheep." It is still a key letter today, relevant to the introduction of the TRF Supporter Program. The letter reminds members of the Family that there are Christians outside of the Family, that they don't have to be in the Family to be Christians, that the Family had been extreme in the past in order to prove their ideal works, and that "Other Sheep," including ex-disciples, should be included somehow into the flock.

I HAVE ALREADY SAID THAT WE NEED TO ACCEPT MANY
OUTSIDERS AS ASSOCIATES AND FRIENDS. May I suggest that
we do the same for Jesus People who are interested in us: Welcome
their fellowship, share our literature . . . Ban doctrinal arguments,
condemnation and accusations! Love never fails . . .

WE USED TO HAVE THREE GRADES . . . IF AFTER
COMPLETING ANY ONE OF THESE . . . A STUDENT DID NOT
WISH TO CONTINUE IN OUR SCHOOL OR WAS NOT EVEN
SUITABLE or capable of continuing to a higher level of leadership, and
wanted to go home, we didn't call him a "Backslider" . . . we called him
a "Graduate" . . . with a Graduation Certificate and our blessing to show
he'd done the best he could, and we hoped he'd be a better Christian
and a good witness for the Lord . . . even though he didn't qualify for all-
out, full-time service.

AS A RESULT, WE KEPT MANY OF OUR "GRADUATES" AS
FRIENDS and co-workers, who continued to fellowship with us, pray for
us, root for us, and even help to support us for years afterward, some of
them even returning to go on with the Lord later.

WHY CAN'T WE HAVE: (1) DISCIPLES—Full-time members of our
Colonies, the 100 percenters who have taken our training and are serving
the Lord full time with us. (2) GRADUATES—Those who have gone
as far as they feel able, but don't feel suited to our type of life or
ministry, and hopefully go back home to serve the Lord as best they can.
(3) ASSOCIATES—Those who do not feel able to forsake all and join
us, but love us, like to fellowship with us and help us all they can.

DISCIPLES WERE NOT THE ONLY CHRISTIANS! . . . we should be
as merciful and patient as possible with those who are following as far
and as fast as they can, even though they may seem far behind us. (ML
"Other Sheep," No 167, 1972)

The letter ends with the recollection of and comment on the line of a
poem (quoted at the beginning of this article), "'He drew a circle that
shut me out. But I drew a circle that brought him in!' Beloved, can't we
do this with the Lord's 'Other Sheep'?" The introduction of TSers does
this; it brings ex-disciples closer to the main army than any other
category, such as "Catacombers," "Live-outs," and DFers. Catacombers
are usually young people who want to become full-time disciples but are
not considered ready, either because they are too young (i.e., under 18),
have not finished their studies, or have other commitments outside the
Family. Live-outs are older people with families and jobs whose
commitments have never allowed them to become full-time disciples.
DFers are those who receive the publication "Daily Food"—lay people
who have received Jesus into their hearts and want to remain in

Fellowship with the Family without ever wanting to be missionaries or disciples. Members of these categories have never been disciples as is the case with the TSers.

Status of TSers

In spite of the "Other Sheep" letter and the demand for something like a TS programme, most TRF Supporters nevertheless feel they have low status in relation to the disciples. None of the TS teens I spoke to felt they could talk about TSers and DOs as being equal but different. More common was the following feeling: "We feel embarrassed if we bump into DOs. What they're doing is exciting; we're just stuck with being TS because of our family." Several factors contribute to the lower status of TSers. Firstly, TSers do not receive all the literature that Family disciples do; they are therefore excluded from the most recent policies and orientations of the Family. "We don't have Good News or the Stuff from Dad, so we don't hear the latest, what the different revolutions are; we only hear about them through the grapevine." Second, inevitably the fact that the programme began as part of a process of "Tightening the Army" to make it more efficient has also contributed to the low status. As we have seen, at the time when the TS classification was first introduced some members were considered to be "the weak folks" who were sinning and committing offenses, unlike the "very dedicated folks," and these "weak" ones were asked to leave the Family or become TS. The people who were chosen to remain in the Family Army were the "folks we can count on." The letter "D.O. is for Doers of the Word" issued at the same time as the bulletin about the new TS programme made clear what behaviour was considered as offenses, sins or weaknesses, and whether people were to be demoted, reclassified or excommunicated. Behavior for which people would be excommunicated included bootlegging D.O. literature, sex with outsiders, sex with minors, violent behaviour, sex with new adult disciples in the Family less than six months, sex with outsiders, sex with minors (anyone under 21). The less serious offenses which were nevertheless still considered to be "offenses" included unbelief in the Letters, being critical of Father David, the Family or the Letters, persistent murmurers, troublemakers and "bad apples"; failure to obey Family rules or leadership, smoking, excessive drinking, excessive reading of worldly books, continual listening to System rock music etc. People who had been struggling with such "weaknesses," and for whom even many years of prayer and counselling within the group made no difference, were asked to become TRF Supporters. It was felt that if the weaknesses had been disruptive of the community over a considerable time and no improvements had been made, then it was only fair that the individuals should be asked to sort out the problem themselves.

In the years subsequent to the Chain of Cooperation (when some leaders had abused their power and use of discipline) there was a general concern to have a truly compassionate and loving style of shepherding. There was a definite emphasis on understanding problems that disciples had in their ministries and their relations with other members; on trying to inspire rather than condemn. Nevertheless, the Family has standards, it has rules and regulations. "Try and run an Army without them," I was told.

In order to maintain standards, the Family has adopted a general emphasis on overcoming personal weaknesses and cultivating Christian virtues in everyone in the Family. They believe that the ability to act unselfishly and sacrificially depends upon spiritual strength and maturity, and that once people are saved they have the potential to live the Law of Love by which people know how to act rightfully and lovingly. Nevertheless, I was repeatedly told, everyone has NWOs "Needs to Work On"—the Family term for weaknesses and bad habits. It is believed these can be worked on with prayer, counselling and renewed inspiration to "get the victory." Everyone was expected to adopt "Prayerfulness," "teamworking" and "loving interactions with others." It was only when people could not achieve the changes necessary that they might be offered TS status. One man explained TS as:

> Some people joined the Family for Jesus. They saw something about the way it was being done had the right results. Like joining a political party you stick with it through thick and thin if you believe the principles are right. Some weren't so sure. They liked what we did but they wanted to do it their way. If the way they wanted to do it was fairly close to our way then they become TS. If further away then they become one of the "Other Sheep."

According to Family members the general attitude is that TSers, however, are definitely not "backsliders"—a traditional Christian term used to describe people who relapse into sin or error, returning to old ways. As one member said:

> We can't consider them as backsliders—they're our brothers and sisters. It depends on what they do, what they did when they left. We wouldn't condemn them. One woman was asked to become a TSer because she found it difficult to concentrate on her children, which meant they were a handful. One girl was constantly screaming and being naughty to the other kids. We tried to help her, tried to work with her about how to discipline them. She was very permissive with them saying, "They'll learn eventually." She was so dependent on other people doing the childcare

work for her. It was more helpful for her to be a TSer. It was affecting
the other kids. We had to pray about what was best for the Home and
what was best for the individual. We expect a certain standard in the
Family . . . She's much better now . . . Very often it helps if people
become TSer and they can spend more time with their own children. The
1989 "Tighten the Family" letter talked about people not putting their
whole hearts into being disciples. Some couldn't.

Some TSers were defined as having a "difficulty," like naughty
children, and this meant it was eventually considered better for them and
the Home they lived in for them to leave. Not surprisingly, this carried
with it some negativity and contributed to the status of the category as
a whole, however much it is now emphasized that the shift to TS status
was a matter of optimising options.

To give an idea of figures, about 2000 people dropped away from
the status of "disciple only" and life in a D.O. communal Home in 1989.
There are no Family statistics relating to the number who became TS.

From the TS adults and the children's point of view the main
reason being a DO has higher status is that disciples are serving the Lord
100%—some say 110%! The TS teens declare that "because of what
they know about being a disciple when their parents were disciples they
would still like to be DO." And to stress how little she appreciated being
TS one girl added, "Some who leave the Family say they would rather be
completely 'OUT' than be a TSer!" Another expressed her desire to
become DO, wistfully sighing, "You can only try DO when you are 16
but we are all trying to think of ways of getting in earlier."

One of the attractions of being a DO is the training and learning
from others in a Family Home—at Nelly's knee—rather than going to
school. They said it was partly the enthusiasm of the group which carries
you through. "In the Family if you are a good cook you teach others to
cook; if you're a good teacher you teach others to teach. After 'school'
we (4 jets and 4 teens) were each allowed to learn what we wanted, using
our talents. I chose kitchen; some wanted to learn to type."

Life as a DO is seen as living with a standard, an ideal, something
to work towards and something to do all the time which feels
worthwhile. Life as a disciple is seen as a good training ground for life.
As one man said, "Dale Carnegie, Vincent Pearl and James Dobson—
they all say that the building of character is more determining of success
than formal education, and that's what you get in the Family." One
mother explained the teens' reluctance to pursue higher studies:

> When I became a disciple I had to put all my university education in the
> garbage. I learnt more in my time with the Family than I did learning
> philosophy at University. At their age they want to learn, but their

curiosity is different: they're at an age when music is important, things
that are exciting ... and they want to do things that will be needed as a
missionary—like childcare. They know what skills are needed when there
are 30 kids and 12 adults in a home and that's what they want.

Though missionary life may have higher status, many of the adults
describe the shift from DO to TS as "a blessing" whereas for their
children "it's a let down." Sara summed up the extent to which the
adults shift gear: as a TRF Supporter she had been determined to put
aside several hours each day to learn the guitar, learn to type, do healthy
exercises—things she had not had time to do as a disciple. She is still
trying to find the time.

The following are examples of reasons given to me by TS adults for
leaving full-time missionary life with the Family and becoming a TSer:

1. Working too much and too fast; I have a slow rhythm. The rhythm in
    The Family is very fast. Everyone is giving their ALL. I needed to slow
    down.
2. I had some lessons to learn. I needed to slow down and learn what I
    needed to.
3. We had teenagers who want as much of the world as they can get; they
    want to leave the Family. They want to be able to watch as much TV as
    possible, wear the clothes they want, drink and smoke.
4. I felt I could be a better mother without people telling me how to do
    things. "I actually wanted to teach my own kids."
5. We had a lot to find out for ourselves.
6. We felt rebellious—had joined the Family when we were 18 and 19, so
    we had 18 years and 21 years in respectively. We needed a change.
7. The Family has changed. It became a lot stricter and tougher and more
    disciplined. There was a general standard and every aspect of life was
    covered with certain rules. We began to think we didn't agree and
    couldn't see the importance of all the little rules. Now I can, but I had
    to have my own conviction.
8. Not being able to sustain the sacrificial role of "learning to be a humble
    person who will fit in and do the job that has to be done rather than
    what you want to do."

The TS group highlights the intensity with which the DO's live, the
extent to which they have religious fervour and sacrifice their own
desires for the sake of the group as a whole.

To be in the Family you must *know* that's what you want. There is
pressure living within the community. We try to make everyone happy
and we have counsels (once a week). If someone is having a hard time
we try to work it out. If you are outside the group you are more likely
to be able to do what you want when you want to. Here you have to
plan it more: you have to take the larger family into account. If you

take the whole "home" as your "family," the other children "as your own" then it comes naturally and other mums do it for you too.

In the life of the TSer the locus of control shifts from the community to the individual. TSers themselves find it difficult to describe the shift, though the main emphasis is on learning how to live individually rather than learning how to live in harmony with others in community; they live with more freedom of choice, more time to reflect on options, time to reflect about themselves and about how to act, increased responsibility, learning to make new friends, the challenge of having to take the initiative.

How TSers Live

TRF Supporters no longer live at the core centre. They live on the periphery as lay members yet they share the culture of the Family, dominated by their religion, their dependence on the Bible, belief in the "Endtime," witnessing and serving the Lord. They can continue their dedication to saving souls, loving others and living lives led by prayer. They can make their own rules, decide their own routines and boundaries.

Given the freedom one might imagine that TSers would find a new meaning system for their lives or that at least the followers would change. The sources of coherence, however, for their new setting, and the ideology for their everyday lives remain very much the same. Serving the Lord 100% is still the ideal.

How is it that the TSers can let go of the high standards required by the Army of the Family and at the same time keep their faith in those standards? This has to do with the ideology itself. As we have seen, the admission of weaknesses and mistakes is part of the Family ideology. Everyone has "NWOs" (Needs Work On), everyone can be selfish, jealous, self-righteous, lacking in love. Admitting them is part of spiritual growth. It is acceptable to make mistakes—man is weak. The gap between reality and the ideology is explained. The belief is that everyone can work for the higher standards and they are to be found in the Word—that the Scriptures are:

> ... the divinely appointed standard and guide to our faith and practice. Holding fast this truth, that "all Scripture is given by the inspiration of God, and is profitable for doctrine, for reproof, for correction, for instruction in righteousness" (2 Timothy 3:16), we strive to study, memorize and obey it, that we may grow in faith, wisdom and spiritual strength. (From Family Statement of Faith)

In addition, change and experimentation are believed to be part of the process to perfection:

TO STAY ALIVE, EVERYONE MUST HAVE MOVE-MENT! There must be change,movement, motion . . .

IF WE DON'T BREAK OUT OF THAT OLD OVER-STRETCHED BOTTLE WE'LL FIND OURSELVES IN A BOTTLENECK . . .

I'VE GOT MORE FAITH FOR THE GUYS WITH ENOUGH GUMPTION TO BREAK OUT OF THAT OLD-BOTTLE mold of nothing but colony life. (ML "Old Bottles" No 242 1973)

TSers have seen the Family pass through many different stages and changes, Revolutions and New Eras (RNR, Chain of Cooperation, FF-ing, being sent home to families, mobile era, Fellow Revolution, etc.) (see Richardson and Davis, 1983). They have seen the Family through many experiments, and to some degree to be a TSer is just another experiment doing whatever is needed in "the Last Days," in a way that is more constructive for them as individuals and for the Family as a whole.

The extent to which TSers still live "by faith" is exemplified by the way they still pray before doing anything—going in a car, crossing a road, doing some work—either silently or openly . . . and still seek to have their needs met by prayer. When they have needs many TSers will, for example, "work on them making a needs list, praying on them, saving for them, looking in a car boot sales, or 'provisioning' (asking someone in the 'system')." They believe "the Lord will provide" but this does not entail just sitting back and waiting; they actively set the goal before them in a way that many "self-improvement" courses would applaud. When the goal is achieved it is interpreted as a "blessing" and sometimes a "miracle." Children are taught to go to the Lord themselves if they have needs: "They that shall preach of the Gospel shall live of the Gospel"—i.e., if you're working for God he'll give you a salary. This kind of goal-oriented attitude encourages effective positive thinking which may also contribute to the particular enthusiasm for sticking to Family ideology.

The Children

The second generation of The Family are seen as God-given for His glory—to love and praise Him; they are the future of The Family. The children of TRF Supporters are also viewed as gifts from God but whereas in The Family there are strong directives from the leadership, as in the Discipleship Training Revolution (DTR) of 1991, TS parents must decide for themselves how to raise their children and the extent to which they encourage them to serve the Lord. For some TSers the chance to focus on their own children, without having to look after all the children of a Family Home, was a major reason for becoming a TSer; for others TS status brings with it "loss of a kind of training for my kids I can never give them myself." "There's a lot of care and energy poured into the kids but as a TSer it's all on your shoulders. You pray and the Lord provides. He still does miracles but you have all the responsibility."

Inevitably, TSers reveal different individual notions about how children should be raised. Many, however, feel they are still finding out what works best without the rules of the Family to guide them. In terms of younger children TSers still use the manual *Raise 'em Right*, a collection of condensations of books on how to raise happy, healthy and secure children. One parent described TS parents as facing a new situation in which they are only just beginning to find out what the problems are that arise, let alone the solutions. Their teens expect some advantages from being TSers. In principle, they think they can now dip into the youth culture of the "system" whenever they want to, listen to rock as much as they want. The parents know that their teens "want something exciting and strong," but how far should they let them go? She said:

> At first we didn't want them to listen to any heavy rock music—the kind of music many of us used to listen to before joining The Family when we took acid. But of course they need music. And then we realized it was better to let them listen to rock but we said no to the black stuff, that kind of satanic music that talks about depressing feelings and suicide.

TSers have had to balance bringing up their children within the faith without lowering standards at the same time as allowing them the freedom they want—letting them wear the clothes they want, watch TV, drink alcohol, make the friends they want, go to State schools. They want to know what it is they will be giving up if they do become disciples.

Most TSers live in single family units although there are a few who have joined forces with one other family. Some have a son or daughter who has remained as a disciple in the Family. Children of TSers who were over 15 and who wanted to remain core members were allowed to remain as "DO" (Disciples only), spending some days a week with their parents but working primarily as missionaries.

Children of disciples who are over 15 and think they want to leave the Family may be given the opportunity of staying with a TS family for a few months, though I was told "they often want to keep the door open so they can go back to DO" if they decide not to leave. The age of decision is between the ages of 14 and 16, and some decide as early as 12. Members I talked to emphasized that teens themselves have to decide what they want to do. "There are teens that leave, about 10% at a guess, and some of those come back." Many of these will live with TSers for a while to see what it feels like to live outside the Family to take a paid job, to be independent, to have a "system" boy/girl-friend, to go out by themselves. Teens I spoke to said they might find it difficult to make a final commitment to the Family without knowing what it was like "on the other side." Living with a TSer family gives them this opportunity.

Only a minority of DO teens experiment with TS life. Conversely, children of TSers describe the life of the DO in positive terms, if not superlatives. The Family has brought excitement to the life of their DO teens with various projects, the latest in London being The Coffee Shop, an outreach organized and run by teens with as little supervision as possible from adults. It should be said that there are plans to incorporate some of the TS teens. The song and dance routines of The Family teens have become an increasingly significant part of their outreach as talents have been professionalized on videos and tapes. TSer teens have not failed to notice the kind of training that is now being given DO teens, as the future of the Family. The life of a disciple appears to the TS teen "as a big responsibility and as challenging." Although they can participate in the "system's" youth culture to the degree that their parents allow them, many consider there is even more excitement in the life of the DO teen.

When the children of TRF Supporters have reached the age of 16 and if they want to become full disciples, they have to find themselves what is termed a "guardian." They have to express in writing why they want to become disciples and their parents have to agree. These requests are sent to the World Services in Geneva where the likelihood of commitment is given full consideration before acceptance is finalized. At the time of my research there were three TS children in London old enough to become disciples, but all three had decided to remain TRF Supporters or join the "System." One was going to an aunt and uncle, ex-members in the US. None of them was against the Family: they simply "wanted to do their own thing." One TS girl, nearly old enough to become a disciple, wisely explained, "Sometimes you just want to do what your parent doesn't agree with at all. You want to be outrageous. Sometimes you just want to be bad, to break the rules." Others who could become disciples in a year or two were anxious to see if they could find ways to join earlier.

In Conclusion

The TRF Supporters reflect the degree to which the children in the Family are offered a choice to remain as a disciple, to try out the wider society by joining a TS family, or to leave the group completely. Several mothers expressed the view that they would be surprised if all their children wanted to remain as missionaries for the rest of their lives, and that the best way to test out uncertainty is to try TS life. Horton (1967) argues that people from a closed system cannot have consciousness of their own system. Similarly it is assumed that totalism produces highly committed followers (Balch in Robbins, 1979). The children in the Family have clear insights into their own "system" with a clear capacity to reflect about their lives and whether it is what they want. They look at their own life in comparison to others—the lives of those they witness to, those in the mass media, and those of TSers or disciples.

The TS-ers are also an attempt to solve several inherent problems of The Family. Firstly, the tension between loving fellowship, charity, the law of love and at the same time the view of the Family as an army fighting a very tough battle "we are God's elite troops" . . . "we are warriors & must keep moving & fighting & dying for Jesus." (ML 1033.81)

> Love is the Answer—The whole World's problems—political, economic, social, religious and physical could be solved through the love of God and each other! That's what we teach and preach, and that's our message, our life, our goal, our love, our everything: To love God, and our neighbours as ourselves. (ML, 633, 1981)

alongside:

> We have to go into all the World & Preach the Gospel & we can't do it very well if we're dragged down by a bunch of time-taking, energy-draining, spirit-depressing, retarded and handicapped people. . . . this is an army and we're fighting a very tough battle. (ML 1033, 1981)

or

> We'll just tell them flat out that we want to eliminate all of the weak links, people who aren't really willing to pay the price. . . . I'm sick of these backsliders and traitors and sickening betrayers and lazy sitters instead of soldiers. . . . We still want quality, not mere quantity!—A determined Gideon's band of dedicated disciples and workers for the Lord!—not a bunch of do-nothing sitters! (ML 2527, 1989)

These apparently conflicting attitudes in The Family reflected in the Mo letters and the problem of how to deal with people who hold up the main goals, the other sheep who have their own ideas, and who do not change after years of loving encouragement have been given a solution by freeing them from the Army. Can we see TSers as part of a more general shift in the Family from totalism to an acceptance of individual needs and differences?

Charlotte Hardman is a Professor of Religious Studies at the University of Newcastle. She was formerly a director of INFORM, Great Britain's highly respected information center on alternative religions.

Chapter 8

The Children of God and The Family in Italy

Massimo Introvigne
Center for Studies on New Religions

The Children of God and The Family have had their share of controversy in Italy, but less so than in other countries. They have also been involved in fewer controversies in Italy than have other minority religious movements, old or new. Both the secular anti-cult movement and the religious counter-cult movement in Italy have regarded the Church of Scientology and Jehovah's Witnesses as their primary targets, recently placing the New Age movement at the top of their list of priorities. The Children of God were the subject of a strongly-worded press campaign in Winter 1978. An offshoot of this controversy, a Court case begun in Rome in 1979, was not decided until 1991. This is minimal compared to the hostile press Court cases involving the Jehovah's Witnesses and Scientology, particularly when one considers the controversy surrounding the Children of God and later The Family in other countries, including nearby France.

1. The Origins of the Children of God in Italy, 1972-1978

David Berg visited Italy in 1971 and seemed to have placed high hopes on a future missionary activity there. On March 19, 1972, a small missionary team headed by Faith, Berg's daughter, arrived in Rome in a van from Germany. They started witnessing to tourists and hippies on the steps of Piazza di Spagna and other favourite tourist locations. One of the first Italian converts was Emanuele Canevaro, scion of a noble family from Florence, who later was referred to as "our Italian king" in one of David Berg's visions,[1] and who put his Bassetto farm in Poggio Secco near Florence at the group's disposal. Canevaro's farm was later the home of the first Montessori school of the Children of God in Italy (Canevaro is no longer a member of The Family).

On Easter Sunday, April 22, 1972, Faith and her group gathered with the crowd in St. Peter's Square to hear Pope Paul VI. They tried to attract the attention of the crowd with signs in English and Italian reading, "The Love of Jesus is not Religion!—But Reality!" Although at the time the Children of God had only six members in Italy, they attracted the attention of a group of Little Sisters of Jesus, a female Roman Catholic order of nuns devoted to radical poverty and already active with the hippies. One of them, Sister Magedlena, proved a long-standing friend of the group, and rendered to the Children of God a number of important services in the following years.

Prospects seemed reasonably bright, and Faith went back to the England to report to her father. He was enthusiastic enough about Italy to write one of the MO Letters, *Arrivederci Roma,* in which he reported a vision of a river—God's will—coming down from Northern Europe to Italy, avoiding hostile France. "The current of the river is like God's will: you just flow with it." He went on to comment that the Children of God were "now beginning to invade the Catholic countries" where they would have to show themselves to be "pro-Catholic," to the point of honoring the Pope ("kiss the Pope's foot, if necessary") and attend Catholic mass. Rome thus became a critically important city: "All roads lead to Rome, they say, but we are going to find, God Willing, that all roads lead from Rome and through Rome!" Berg mentioned Emanuele and Sister Magedlena in the letter, and gave it the title *Arrivederci Roma* from a famous Italian song he fondly remembered, sung by one of his favorite performers, Mario Lanza ("it was," Berg noted, "the last song he sang in the last movie he made before he died," and in his vision he even "saw a big piazza and Mario Lanza with his arms outstretched over Rome").[2]

MO's Letter *Arrivederci Roma* was printed in September 1972 and brought by Faith to Rome in October, where understandably it was received with considerable excitement. Although some of the suggestions to behave like good Catholics in Italy may simply sound like public relations strategies, Berg was at that time engaged in a re-evaluation of Roman Catholicism, and in another letter of September 1972—published under the title *Are the Children of God Catholics or Protestants?*—he concluded that "surely we Children of God have more in common with the Catholics than with the Protestants."[3]

On October 4, 1972, Sister Magedlena accompanied Faith and six other Children of God (small children included) to Pope Paul VI's general audience. At the end of his speech the Pope passed through the crowded hall and gave to the assembled faithful, including Sister Maddalena and Faith, his hands to kiss. An excited Faith reported in a MO Letter dated October 1972 that the Pope put his hand on her head twice and said to her (in Italian) "God bless you," and the Letter carried photographs of the Pope placing his hand on the head of a little baby from the group (today a grown-up member of The Family) and blessing a group including Faith, and of Faith playing guitar with a smiling Sister Magedlena. It is probable that most Children of God outside Italy did not realize that attending a general audience with the Pope was not an exceptional occurrence (in fact, thousands of people every year attend such audiences), but Faith's enthusiasm sounds genuine.[4]

A small coffee house was opened in the center of Rome where the Children of God tried to attract young people from the hippie subculture. In 1974 they added a disco in Via della Farnesina in an old warehouse (the place has now been converted to an Italian public television's storehouse), later called by different names, including the O.K. Club. With the disco came real success for the Italian Children of God (who in 1974 had also started distributing MO Letters in the streets). The disco became popular and was attended by hundreds of young people; the success enabled the Children of God to expand their missionary activities all over Italy and to open a second coffee house in Via Melzo in Milan. When the press campaign against the movement began in 1978 there were around 300 Italian Children of God (including foreigners living in Italy), and some Italian members had started missionary activities in other countries.

2. The Campaign Against The Family of Love, 1978-1991

The consequences of the "reorganization" of February 1978, which disbanded the Children of God, dismissed a number of leaders, and initiated The Family of Love period, where felt in Italy as they were everywhere else. Flirty fishing and an emphasis on sexual freedom reached Italy through the movement's international literature, although according to later Court enquiries flirty fishing was more talked about than actually practised in Italy.[5] Even an ex-member who appeared on Italian public TV to expose the evil of the Children of God declared that she was acquainted with flirty fishing and sexual "revolutionary" practices through reading internal and external literature rather than through direct experience.[6]

A campaign centered on flirty fishing (labelled as "prostitution") and free love was, however, started in the Winter of 1978 by Rina Goren, a reporter for the Rome daily newspaper *Il Messaggero* (Goren, then a young reporter, was propelled by the campaign into a successful career of investigative journalism, later mostly in politics). Goren, under the assumed name of "Sara," started attending the movement's Rome disco. As the subsequent police investigation declared, she gathered very little evidence of unorthodox sexual practices,[7] although she did collect rumours (mostly from youngsters who were not considered members of the movement because of their minor age—they were called "catacombs" in the group's jargon—and who were apparently inclined to gossip), and of course evidence of unorthodox *theories* on sex was not hard to gather from The Family of Love at that time. Goren, however, decided to go on with her story, relying mostly on information supplied ultimately by anti-cult movements in the United States and Europe, which had previously appeared in the German magazine *Stern*. The story had a number of follow-ups by Goren herself in *Il Messaggero,* and was picked up by most of the major Italian newspapers. 142 articles and 4 TV stories appeared within one month. Since, however, little few evidence from Italy surfaced, and because most of the stories concerned The Family of Love abroad, interest died out quite soon, and by early 1979 the campaign had, in fact, come to an end.

The press campaign had, however, set in motion the sluggish machinery of the police. In January 1979, the Rome disco was raided and fifteen persons were identified as members of a "cult," possibly operating a "prostitution ring." On March 17, 1979, the Public Prosecutor of Rome indicted thirteen people, including Emanuele Canevaro, his wife Barbara, the manager of the disco, Angelo Giardinelli—and David Berg himself. He also ordered the arrest of these four people, although in fact only the Canevaros were arrested, and released immediately after their deposition. Berg obviously could not been reached by the Italian police, and Giardinelli was in Greece. In fact, he was busy with the production of the international missionary music show *Music with Meaning*. He had worked in the international team which had produced the show, and from Greece he helped produce national versions for several European countries, including Italy.

By 1980 the Family of Love took advantage of the new freedom of establishing private radios in Italy (where only a public radio had been allowed for decades), and the Italian version, *Musica con Messaggio,* was aired by dozens of small radios. Although the name Family of Love was occasionally avoided for being too controversial, by 1980 the controversy had largely been forgotten. What was not easily forgotten, however, was the Court action. Giardinelli was arrested in Greece in 1981 on the basis of an international warrant, and spent three and a half months in jail there before a Greek Court decided (and the Greek Supreme Court later confirmed) that the evidence offered by Italy was too weak to justify an extradiction. Italy, however, did not abandon its claim on Giardinelli and, when he returned to his native country in 1987 (and, unsuspectingly, made himself known to the authorities by applying for a new passport), the police again attempted to arrest him through an unsuccessful raid at his parents' home. At this stage, Giardinelli finally consulted with a friendly lawyer, who obtained the annulment of the warrant for arrest pending the group's commitment to trial.

Italian Courts are notoriously slow, but the fact that a case started in 1979 went to trial only after twelve years in 1991 also shows that the press and political pressure on the prosecutor was not very high. In the meantime, most of the original Italian members of the Children of God who had joined The Family of Love had spent some years in faraway missions (in the Far East or South America) and, because of visa restrictions in the mission countries and other strategical considerations, had participated in the return home of most European members in 1988. Flirty fishing had been stopped in 1987, together with many of the unorthodox sexual practices of the 1970s and early 1980s, and the literature on these subjects (including the very controversial letters suggesting that sexual initiation for children at an early age was permissible) was being eliminated. The former Children of God had come of age, and had opened their main new centers near Rome and Perugia. They were busy distributing their new attractive posters, music cassettes, and Kiddy Viddy videos for children, and above all organizing home schools for their children that were consistent with their doctrines.

Italian anti-cult literature was remarkable for, if anything, the minimal attention it paid to the Children of God/The Family of Love. Only professor Michele Del Re, a lawyer and law professor operating an anti-cult organization called Studio dei Culti Emergenti in Rome, devoted a significant portion of one of his books to flirty fishing, authoritian power structures, sex between and with minors, and brainwashing in the Children of God movement. His material for this 1988 book was, however, admittedly derived from American and German anti-cult sources, with very few references to Italy.[8] This volume was intended for a popular audience. In a 1991 scholarly study of the legal aspects of brainwashing, Del Re was careful to introduce more sensationalistic accusations derived from ex-members of the Children of God with the caveat, "their accusers relate . . ."[9]

Overall—although anti-cultists at times mentioned flirty fishing and other practices as a graphic example of how bad some "cults" could be— The Family of Love was largely a non-issue among critics of new religious movements in 1991. That the old case went to trial in 1991 was, in a sense, anachronistic. The Roman judges, however, made a reasonably careful assessment of the case. They concluded that Berg had indeed written the MO Letters found during the police investigation, but that none of them were outside the limits of what is legally permissible in Italy. The judges also regarded as "probable" that Berg was the final recipient of the ten percent of the group's revenues sent to Zurich and other foreign destinations, but there was no evidence that this was done by breaching any Italian law. They found "not the slightest evidence of fraud" in the group's dealings with actual and would-be members.

Their analysis of flirty fishing is particularly interesting. The judges concluded that it was only in "the last months of 1977 Berg started counseling the members that it was permissible for proselyting reasons to offer sexual contacts and services to perspective members, the more so when the latter were potentially good financial contributors to the cult." However, not only the young members, but also the older ones and even the leaders, were at the same time exponents and "victims" of this rather bizarre vision of sex and proselytism. In order to find someone guilty of the crime of causing or exploiting the prostitution of another person (prostitution per se is not illegal in Italy), the objective element of suggesting that someone offers his or her own body to an unknown partner for a fee or another reward is not enough. It is also necessary to show that the parties involved did in fact understand their activities as prostitution in the legal sense of the term. Among the Children of God, the judges argued, flirty fishing was not understood as prostitution but "as a personal contribution to the humanitarian aims that the sect always claimed to pursue."

This important conclusion shows the reluctance of Italian Courts to accept the distinction between deeds and creeds that has become a trademark of the anti-cult movement internationally. The same deeds—if carried out in the name of different creeds—are in fact subject to a different legal evaluation. If offering one's body for a reward is motivated by greed, only the action is prostitution, and causing this action to be performed by another is a crime under Italian law; if the same deed is motivated by "humanitarian aims" (perhaps The Family of Love would have preferred a more theological definition) there is no crime, although the material facts are the same. Besides, the judges added, there were only rumors that such activities occurred in Italy, the evidence showing only that sometime in 1977-1978 flirty fishing was regarded as theoretically permissible by the group's literature.[10] The Court could have easily added that, by 1991, flirty fishing had been abandoned and a movement very different from the one active in 1977-1978 was now entering a new stage of its history in Italy.

3. The Family Goes Public, 1992-1993

By 1991 a new name, The Family, had replaced The Family of Love. Italian members were excited to contribute to the new missionary expansion of the movement in Eastern Europe, and in fact the first missions in the former Yugoslavian countries, Russia, Bulgaria and Albania were organized by Italians or were from Italy, with Italians also contributing to the missions in Romania and Hungary. The distribution of videos and other materials was meeting with considerable success, and the group's children's choir was the frequent guest of schools and other public and private institutions. The Italian Family—now reduced to some 250 members, most of them having never been members of the original Children of God—was living a quiet and peaceable life.

The Family, however, was not feeling safe. Events in Australia, Spain, and later in France and Argentina troubled the lives of Italian members in the 1990s. Nothing similar, so far, has been threatened in Italy, and Italian anti-cult groups are still comparatively uninterested in The Family. Incidents involving former members are minor, particularly when compared with what has occurred in other countries (one of them, Gabriella Valpondi, appeared on the national public TV in 1991, and another was interviewed by a couple of newspapers in Tuscany in 1992). In fact, it seems that international anti-cult organizations did try to recruit Italian ex-members for their international crusade against The Family, but with little success.

As in other countries, Italian leaders of The Family have decided to go public, and to initiate a campaign of contacts with scholars, officers of the Roman Catholic Church, reporters, and even leaders of Italian anti-cult and counter-cult groups. They have admitted (although at times downplayed) their early involvement with flirty fishing, and they recognize that their position on sexual initiation of minors was "questionable" and some of their attitudes "immature." They have, however, insisted that in the second half of the 1980s these practices have been not only abandoned, but have been strictly forbidden under penalty of excommunication.[11] Perhaps an even stronger repudiation of past doctrines and practices would be in order. On the other hand, it is difficult to ask from any religious movement more than a certain amount of self-criticism. It is a paradox—and, in some countries, it has been a tragedy—that at the very moment when The Family seems ready to repudiate the most objectionable features of its past, the ghosts of this same past are evoked by anti-cultists before the press, the police and the Courts of justice. Serious scholarship has a responsibility to help prevent the potentially tragic confusion of The Family's past radicalism with its present lifestyle.

Dr. Massimo Introvigne is Director of the Center for Studies on New Religions (CESNUR), Italy's highly respected information center on alternative religions. He is also the author of many important scholarly works on magical religions and new religious movements.

Chapter 9

From "Children of God" to "The Family": Movement Adaptation and Survival

Stuart A. Wright
Lamar University

At the same time that the touted "global village" moves closer to realization through satellite communications and advanced computer technologies, fragmentation and conflict across ethnic, religious and political lines remain firmly ensconced both within and between societies. One only has to point to a few recent episodes around the globe to be reminded of this fact—the "ethnic cleansing" taking place in Bosnia, the World Trade Center bombing by Muslim extremists, the growing disenfranchisement of Christian fundamentalists in the U.S. and the ensuing "culture wars" (Hunter, 1991). As a sociologist of religion, I am always concerned about the role religion plays in such conflicts. It is known that religion can be a powerful source of unification, cohesion or solidarity. Durkheim's (1915/1965) work on religion largely reflects this functional perspective. On the other hand, Marx (1964) and others suggest that religion may contribute to conflicts, promoting in-group solidarity while encouraging adversarial relations with out-groups (heretics, infidels, heathen). Predisposition to conflict may be heightened by absolutist religious ideologies that are intolerant of other traditions and practices.

Some of the new religious movements that have appeared in the second half of the twentieth century, while sharing characteristics of historical sects (Wilson, 1970), may demonstrate some innovative and even evolutionary *adaptations* to the social environment. Here I refer to a kind of globalization process which, in the context of a changing world order, links pluralism, diversity and toleration to movement adaptability and strength (Wuthnow, 1978, 1980). Wuthnow suggests that the transitional condition of the world order, characterized by political instability and uncertainty, lends itself to the proliferation of new religious movements that seek to fill the void by constructing overarching, universal religious ideologies. As governments fail, national boundaries are redrawn and new alliances formed, the perception of a world crisis may help to legitimate the claims of religious movements as harbingers of a new world harmony and peace. Movements that are able to adapt to international audiences and diverse cultural needs are more likely to be successful in voicing such claims.

The characteristics of such movements suggest a religious response to a perceived world crisis—international political unrest, shifts in world economic markets, fragmentation of the normative order—that work to forge unification based on an alternate worldview, a profound ideological reformation. With the increased mobility and communications of the modern world, these movements are distinctly less culture-bound, provincial and territorial. In-group/out-group differences are much less likely to be drawn along the lines of race, ethnicity or class. They tend to be more syncretistic, eclectic and universalistic with regard to religious beliefs and cultural values. They draw their members from all over the world and incorporate features from these different cultures as they develop and expand. New religious movements may reveal varying degrees of globalization, but some that exhibit these characteristics would include Elizabeth Clare Prophet and the Church Universal and Triumphant, the Unification Church, ECKANKAR, Transcendental Meditation (TM), and a host of New Age movements (see Melton, 1992). One movement that has borne many of these features over its short life-span, though it has rigid fundamentalist roots, is The Family, formerly called the Children of God.

The Family

The Family is now a world-wide movement with approximately 250 communities in over 50 countries and 9,000 members. The movement originated in Huntington Beach, California in the late 1960s as a countercultural, Jesus Movement group. In the early 1970s, the movement's leader, Moses David Berg, instructed his followers to leave the U.S. after predicting God's judgement on America. The initial prophecy contained warnings of the comet Kohoutek striking the nation and inducing calamity and chaos in the U.S., marking the Great Tribulation as recorded in the Book of Revelation. Subsequently, Berg revised the prophecy suggesting that the more figurative language in his prophecy was not to be taken literally. In the following years, adherents travelled the world establishing communities and recruiting converts in foreign countries. As the ratio of American converts to foreign nationals changed, the movement also changed. The influences of indigenous cultures and new converts began to transform the movement from a California-based, hippie, fundamentalist group, rigidly and centrally structured under the authority of Moses David Berg to a more eclectic, multi-ethnic, decentralized missionary movement of relatively independent communities dispersed all over the globe. Indeed, the movement of today bears only a few organizational semblances with the movement founded over twenty-five years ago. It may be argued that the ability of the Children of God/The Family to adapt to change over time has contributed significantly to its survival into the 1990s. It is suggested here that adaptation to change through cross-cultural expansion, leading to marked increases in pluralism and diversity, is a critical reason why the movement has survived.

Pluralism, Adaptation and Survival

With the dispersion of the Children of God (COG) in the mid 1970s into Europe and Asia, the American core of the movement was soon faced with the repercussions of its own success. New converts, of course, brought with them their own cultural baggage. But more importantly, movement recruiters were also faced with learning the language and customs of the countries in which they resided. Members were encouraged to blend in and cultivate a rapport with local residents in order to bring them salvation, and achieve what Roy Wallis has called a "favorable ecology" (1987:86). The thrust of this initiative culminated in the "Re-Organisation Nationalization Revolution" (RNR), a concerted strategy to integrate with native cultures in order to better train leaders and eventually transfer independent responsibility for the missionary work to nationals. In a 1978 letter outlining the RNR strategy, Moses David announced that "Just as Jesus had to leave his disciples so they could go on to greater works, . . . so our N. American leadership is going to have to step down and out of the picture and push forward the nationals in order to integrate and nationalize the many countries we're in" ("The Re-Organisation Nationalization Revolution," #659, January 1978). He instructed followers to make "(a) genuine endeavor of identification with the people, . . . including their language, adopting their customs and dress, eating the food they eat, sometimes even assuming their citizenship, . . . to actually become one of them like Jesus did" (#659, 1978).

Later in this same letter, Moses David described the failure of typical American missionary efforts when nationals were not brought into the organizational structure. "If we can't get enough converts . . . to run their own colonies and their own country," Berg cautioned, "then I will be highly disappointed, because then we are not missionaries, we haven't established anything native and we're just a foreign colonial empire." Berg recounted "horror stories" about missionary efforts that languished and collapsed because they had not "prepared the nationals to take over." When the Americans were forced to leave or kicked out of a country, he argued, there was no "native church" left behind.

Of course, the RNR initiative was not without substantial costs to the movement, largely in terms of defections. It is estimated that as much as one-third of the membership were lost in this reorganization. Veteran or high-ranking movement leaders were replaced, new converts and friends were lost, conflicts over policy and lines of authority arose, incomes declined and COG homes ran into financial debt (Wallis, 1982:92-93). But the RNR plan probably helped to secure the long-term survival ability of the movement, even though there were serious short-term costs.

The first wave of American COG members who settled in Europe faced immediate challenges to their own cultural beliefs and predispositions. Van Zandt (1991:41) notes that the "anti-system" message carried by American converts played less well to European youth because "it was no great revelation to them that American society was far from perfect." The Americans were required to make a number of adjustments to European culture in order to fit in and be successful in their witnessing. Some of these adjustments included the formation of Poorboy clubs or discos, the upgrading of dress and lifestyle of members, the refocusing of recruitment efforts aimed at middle-class individuals rather than social dropouts, and the softening of the COG's worldview (Richardson and Davis, 1983; Van Zandt, 1991; Wallis, 1982, 1987). Van Zandt writes,

> Instead of society's dropouts and young radicals, the COG pursued those who were employed or in school. The COG found that such people were more receptive to the message, made better long-term members, and required less time to be spent dealing with their problems. Potential members also tended to be somewhat younger than before, a fact which led to the creation of a new status, "catacomb member," to account for members

who, for reasons of age or legal condition, were unable to live in colonies as full-time members. This innovation, of course, reflected the COG's growing flexibility in dealing with the System (1991:45).

Sexual unions through proselytization ("flirty fishing") and marriages with indigenous nationals, almost all of which produced children, tied them inexorably to these foreign cultures. What mere recruitment, litnessing or preaching couldn't accomplish because of formidable cultural barriers, intermarriage and familial ties could. Indeed, the marriages of the American core of members to foreign nationals was strongly encouraged by Moses David as a part of the RNR plan.

> In those colonies established for two years or more, all colony servants (leaders) must be national or integrated with a national and speak the language. ...So a capable American woman could marry a native husband and train him, or a capable American man could marry a native wife and train her (#659, 1978).

By converting and marrying the nationals, the message of salvation was no longer tied exclusively to the Americans but allowed to spread along kinship and relational lines of family members. When COG members finally did pick up and leave, they often had established a native work that continued after their departure. Occasionally, adult children would even remain behind in these countries to assist the indigenous missionary efforts and to sustain familial ties and communication.

According to Van Zandt, flirty fishing was adopted as a strategy specifically aimed at Third World countries. As the movement "left more affluent parts of the world, its normal recruiting pool of young and unattached people started to dry up. Flirty fishing brought the Family into contact with people who tended to have more status and responsiblity in the local community" (1991:29). It also "dictated better clothing, more concern for cleanliness, and even the use of makeup to facilitate members' participation in the nightclub and discotheque scene" (1991:29). Wallis makes a similar observation, noting that after the introduction of flirty fishing, the movement shifted its target of potential converts: "Thenceforth, a movement which had seen its purpose as proselytizing among the alienated of society, the hippies and dropouts, would begin to direct itself more to the respectable and influential" (Wallis, 1982:80).

Aside from the effective strategy of nationalization, the increasing pluralism of the movement had a distinct appeal to certain segments of the wider population, particularly the young and the humanitarian-oriented. The text and the substance of biblical preachments in conventional churches frequently emphasize the universality of the Christian faith ("In Christ there is neither male nor female, Jew nor

Greek . . ."). However, rarely does this amount to anything more than sentimental rhetoric and platitudes. On the other hand, the actualization of this message as embodied in a religious movement that offered living "proof," so to speak, by virtue of a highly heterogenous membership certainly presented a marked advantage over other churches or sects in attempting to convince potential converts of the "truth" value of the message. It suggested consistency to a worldly, skeptical audience that is all too often cognizant of the numerous inconsistencies between religious belief and practice. Numerous converts to The Family that I interviewed expressed just such an opinion, indicating that they were more willing to listen to proselytizers and take their message seriously because the group's universal emphasis on "love" was expressed by members of such diverse nationalities.

The Miami Community

I was struck by this ethnic diversity upon first visiting the Miami community in the summer of 1993. My previous research on the Children of God (Wright, 1983, 1984, 1986, 1987) was conducted in the late 1970s and early 1980s, before the RNR initiative had produced any notable results. During the decade of the eighties, there were few communities in North America, so monitoring of the movement became difficult. Only recently, since The Family has begun to resettle communities in the U.S. has this aspect of the movement come to the attention of scholars.

A major task in the data collection during the Miami visit was to conduct a census of The Family's community there. At the time of the study, there were six nuclear family clusters and a separate group or cluster of Family Teens. Family Teens are mid-to-late adolescents who have expressed in interest in training and preparation for leadership. The Family encourages young teens to achieve independence from their parents so that they can serve the Lord more fully. Family Teens essentially function as young missionaries, travelling in small groups, and are assigned to specific communities. Not all teens aspire to be independent missionaries and separate from families.

Out of a total of 49 members of The Family's community in Miami, 11 are adults, 22 teenagers, and 16 children. These 49 members represent 22 different countries, as measured by their origin of birth. All of the adult members had lived in at least three different countries and were conversational in three or four languages. The most common languages spoken were Spanish and English. Five of the six nuclear family clusters in the community represented four different nationalities each. Predictably, the adult members were most likely to be North American (8 of 11, 73%). However, the children and teens were more likely to be native-born Puerto Rican (5) or Chilean (5). In fact, of the

38 children and teens in the community, only 6 were native-born North American (16%). Most were born in Spanish-speaking countries of the Carribean, Central and South America. The full impact of this rich, ethnic amalgam could be seen in the clear leverage and ease of access to Miami's minority communities enjoyed by The Family. The dramatic population shifts in the Miami area in recent years posed few problems for members of The Family. Not only were they conversant with Spanish-speaking residents, they were well-suited to the highly pluralistic composition of the city. Indeed, they seemed more than comfortable with it. Their own community served as a microcosm of Miami's own ethnic and cultural diversity. The Family's experience in Third World nations made them familiar with many Hispanic and Latin customs, insulated them from culture shock, allowed them to avoid the pitfalls of American ethnocentrism or xenophobia, and gave them a degree of "street-wise" knowledge and demeanor in their interaction with low-income, minority groups.

The Family Teens moved freely within and between these communities, even at night, witnessing on the streets and challenging minority youth with their salvation message in local hangouts, places where few suburban, middle-class white youth would venture. Though they took certain precautions to safeguard themselves from harm, such as always travelling in groups, one sensed that their mastery of the diverse cultural landscape gave them substantial confidence and courage.

Conclusion

Is it suggested here that the adaptation of this new religious movement to cultural pluralism and diversity through global expansion, spawned by changes in the world order, can be linked to movement strength and survival. It seems unlikely that the same COG movement that originated in the countercultural sixties in California could survive as an international movement today. Indeed, many of the key leaders and members out of that period were lost to the movement during organizational shifts or changes in policy and leadership, epitomized in the RNR plan. But these same shifts underscore both the difficulty and the significance of adaptation. Difficult because the inummerable obstacles to change—the inertia of institutionalization, the resistance of entrenched leaders to relinquish authority, the anomie and turmoil of reorganization—involved painful choices and actions. Significant because the survival of COG and its success in foreign cultures, it seems safe to say, was contigent upon this pluralistic thrust. Such adaptation will likely fare well for the Family's success in the future, both here and abroad, as societies become more pluralistic and each continues to chart a new course in the shifting political structures and boundaries of the new world order.

Stuart A. Wright is Associate Professor of Sociology at Lamar University in Beaumont, Texas. He holds a Ph.D. in Sociology from the University of Connecticut and is the former recipient of an NIMH Research Fellowship at Yale University to study the social and psychological effects of cult involvement among former members. Dr. Wright has published a book entitled *Leaving Cults: The Dynamics of Defection* (1987), as well as numerous journal articles and book chapters in edited volumes on this controversial topic.

Chapter 10

New Religions and Child Custody Cases: Comparisons Between the American and European Experience

Michael W. Homer
Salt Lake City, Utah

The stand off and subsequent clash in Waco, Texas between the Federal Bureau of Investigation (FBI), Bureau of Alcohol, Tobacco and Firearms (ATF) and the Branch Davidians (an offshoot of a schism of the Seventh-day Adventists Church) in Waco, Texas is not the first clash between a religious group [led by a charismatic, messianic leader who advances teachings which include communal living, millennialism, military preparedness and polygamy], and civil authorities in the midst of an otherwise peaceful community. In the United States, where new religious movements are as American as mom, apple pie, the girl next door and free speech,[1] there is a long history of such standoffs involving polygamous groups. Some of these standoffs could no doubt have been avoided and accomplished absolutely nothing since they were predicated upon false assumptions and bad judgment by the police and local civil authorities. Others were probably unavoidable. Before the March disaster in Waco (and a previous incident in 1988) the Branch Davidians (or groups with other names from which they originated) had co-existed with the local community for more than fifty years. In fact, the longer the standoff continued, and as now confirmed by the Justice Department investigation, the disaster was precipitated not only by the rhetoric of David Koresh and his violation of United States firearms laws but also by disinformation disseminated by the local press and anti-cult organizations, including a deprogrammer, and rivalry which developed between the FBI and the local police. The unfortunate result was preventable bloodshed.

Other standoffs involving polygamist groups and several authorities have been dealt with more successfully. For the most part, Mormonism's forty year battle with the federal government, including the so called Utah war in 1858, avoided bloodshed and was resolved peacefully in 1890 when the Mormons abandoned polygamy,[2] even though it has since been shown that they actually continued the practice outside the United States until 1904 where they believed it remained legal.[3] Following Mormonism's abandonment of polygamy, various splinter groups were organized by those who taught that when Church authorities ceased to teach polygamy they began to violate a law of God.[4] Various polygamist communities were thereafter established in Salt Lake City and in rural areas, where they continued the practice of polygamy. Although these fundamentalist Mormons consider themselves to be faithful to the Church organized by Joseph Smith, the Mormon Church, which now numbers more than eight million members worldwide, does not consider them to be members, and, in fact, fundamentalist Mormons who advocate or practice polygamy are excommunicated. Nevertheless, most fundamentalist churches premise their cultural and religious practices on the Mormon experience. These twentieth century fundamentalist offshoots have experienced both peaceful and violent standoffs. Arizona's raid on the polygamous community of Short Creek in 1953 was peaceful, whereas, standoffs between the Singers and the State of Utah in 1979 and 1988, and the 1988 LeBaron murders ended in bloodshed.[5]

Although these and other polygamous groups have been the subject of debate in the United States for more than one hundred forty years[6] the discussion emerging in Europe regarding polygamy, the status of children of polygamist parents and whether such children should be removed and placed in foster homes is comparatively new.[7] Just as new religious movements not associated with the Branch Davidians leader, David Koresh, including the Church Universal and Triumphant,[8] the Davidian Seventh-day Adventists Association,[9] and the Seventh-day Adventists Church itself, have pleaded with the American press to discontinue any suggestion that they are comparable to the Branch

Davidians, it seems appropriate to both compare and contrast the experiences of polygamous religious groups in the United States with the situation developing between multi-wife systems and the governments in Europe and elsewhere. Perhaps the most well known movement rumored to be polygamist in Europe, other than Muslims, includes the adherents of the Fellowship of Independent Missionary Communities, commonly referred to as The Family (formerly Children of God).[10] This movement, like the Branch Davidians (and unlike the Mormons) has been accused not only of keeping children in polygamous colonies but of inducing them to have sexual relations with adults at an early age. The Family's current leaders in Europe admit that some radical sexual experiments took place in their "colonies" in the 1970s but insist that such practices were discontinued between 1978 and 1987. Now, they insist, sexual contact with minors is a ground for excommunication for the adult members of the movement. Their position on polygamy is somewhat more ambiguous. Although they "do not encourage it among our members" it is apparently only prohibited "in any country or culture that specifically disallows it." Ironically, it encourages its members "to respect the laws and customs of the countries they live in."[11] Other groups, such as Damanhur, an Italian communal group, do not practice the textbook definition of polygamy but do teach an unconventional family arrangement in which marriages are contracted for limited periods of time, sexual activity is allowed between spouses—one at a time—in a manner which is strictly controlled by the community, and children are communally educated.

Although each of these groups has its own brand of marriage, each has been, and will continue to be, accused of illegally practicing polygamy. There is also a common thread in proposals made by opponents of these movements and, in the case of The Family, one that has been attempted by authorities in some countries, and has been seriously proposed by anti-cultists in the case of Damanhur. That thread is that children should be forcibly removed from religious communities which "teach" unconventional lifestyles or sexual behavior. According to this view, it is better to separate these children from their families and to arrange for their placement in foster homes regardless of whether there is any evidence of sexual abuse of minors.

A similar solution was attempted with respect to the children of Mormon fundamentalist groups in the 1950s, even though these groups were, and rarely are accused of child abuse. On the morning of Sunday, July 26, 1953, a force of one hundred twenty Arizona peace officers, together with one hundred news reporters, drove across unpaved roads to the fundamentalist community of Short Creek, Arizona to arrest thirty-six men, eighty-six women, and pick up two hundred sixty-three children. It was a sneak attack and was compared by one Associated Press reporter to "a military assault on an enemy position." The fundamentalists were clearly out numbered as there were two officers for every home in the community. Although the element of surprise was not completely successful, the officers arrested most of the targeted men and women and the Arizona Governor announced on the radio that the purpose of the raid was "to protect the lives and futures of two hundred sixty-three children" and that the religious community was "the foulest conspiracy you could imagine" which was "dedicated to the production of white slaves."[12] Apparently, some officials in the Mormon Church (which had only abandoned polygamy itself fifty years earlier) not only applauded the raid, but may also have provided relevant information to the police and other civil authorities. This has fueled suspicions among many of the fundamentalists that the Mormon Church not only participated in, but may have also helped instigate the raid.

Shortly after the raid, the mothers and children were bussed to Phoenix where they were initially kept in a crowded rest home and were told they would remain there for up to a month before being placed in permanent foster homes. Eventually, juvenile hearings were held in Arizona State Courts which resulted in the placement of most of the children in foster homes around Arizona, often accompanied by their mothers. For reasons which are beyond the scope of this paper, an Arizona Superior Court Judge ordered in March, 1955 that all of the children be restored to their families, which brought an end to Arizona's efforts to segregate children from fundamentalist parents.

Similar efforts to segregate children from polygamous parents were also made in Utah, especially in communities in the southern part of the state which bordered Arizona and which were also part of the "raid." The most prominent case involved the seven children of Vera Black, who were removed from their home, accompanied by Mrs. Black, and were ordered to be placed into non-polygamous homes. When the Blacks challenged the State's authority to take these actions, the Utah Supreme Court held that parents who enter into polygamous marriages may be deprived of their right to control and custody of their children.[13] When it became certain that the Black's would lose custody of their children, they agreed to sign pledges to "obey the law of the land," including the law of monogamous marriage and, by virtue of this pledge, the children were returned to their custody. However, subsequent to the family's return to their polygamist settlement in southern Utah, the Blacks continued to practice "plural marriage." Despite this, no further action was taken against the Blacks, or any other polygamists, and no further efforts have been made since that time to remove children from any polygamist community in Arizona or Utah. The community of Short Creek has since been renamed Colorado City, in Arizona, and Hilldale, in Utah. These communities now have more than two thousand polygamists, a high school, and plans are now being discussed to established a university. These plans are supported by many members of the Utah community, including a number of respected historians and sociologists. There are, however, occasional outcries for the punishment of polygamists and the removal of children from their homes.[14] Nevertheless, even though there are now an estimated 20,000 polygamists living in the western United States, anti-polygamy laws are not, for the most part, enforced. On August 5, 1991 the Utah Attorney General in Utah was quoted as stating:

> Unless it's associated with child abuse, welfare fraud or any other illegal act, polygamy for its own sake has not been a crime susceptible of successful prosecution and uses up an awful lot of resources.

He further observed that although the Utah Constitution forbids polygamy, the state's laws do not specifically bar the practice.[15] In fact, even if the practice of polygamy is still technically illegal under Federal Statute passed in 1862 and the Utah State Constitution, the Utah Supreme Court has protected the civil rights of polygamists,[16] including the right, under limited circumstances, to adopt children.[17]

One of the primary reasons the "raid" on Mormon fundamentalist communities and the subsequent efforts of Arizona and Utah officials to separate polygamist parents from their children failed, was because state officials eventually recognized that polygamist family ties were so strong that all attempts to punish the practice of polygamous marriage, perpetuated by the parents, through their children, would be counter productive, and that it would not be in the best interests of the children to be separated from their parents, since there was no evidence of child molestation or deviant sexual activities involving the children. Cases involving the legitimacy of polygamy in Europe may well be determined much differently than in the United States. In 1972, the House of Commons effectively struck down an 1866 ruling by the Divorce Court in the United Kingdom which refused to recognize a Mormon polygamous marriage, because of the new realities of Muslim marriage relationships in that country.[18] Similar challenges to laws against bigamy in countries which follow laws derived from the Napoleonic Civil Code, including Italy, are also being made.[19] It is likely that countries besides the U.K., will eventually recognize polygamous marriages, (not because of new religious movements, but because of Islam) and when this occurs it will be virtually impossible to prosecute polygamists in new religious movements without some evidence of aberrant sexual behavior, even if particular movements have reputations for such behavior. For example, even if graphic depictions of the joys of the "sexual revolution for Jesus" in the Children of God's old booklets (that they claim are no longer circulated) will not appease suspicions of illicit sexual activity,[20] their actual practices have been assessed in different ways by observers.[21] Furthermore, various scholars believe that journalistic accounts of sexual mores in Damanhur are extremely exaggerated.[22] Even the Mormon fundamentalists who were raided in 1953 were accused of "profligacy" by the Governor of Arizona, and continue to be the subject of rumors of this nature which are spread by anti-cultists. Nevertheless, virtually all scholars who have observed the fundamentalists have concluded that these rumors have no factual basis.

Thus, Mormon fundamentalist cases offer a significant precedent for the current debate in Europe and elsewhere regarding the placement of children of polygamists and other non-conventional religious groups in foster homes. Raids, similar to those in Utah, have taken place during the past four years in Australia, Argentina, Spain and France on communities of The Family. Other forms of intimidation have also been alleged to have occurred in the United Kingdom. According to The Family's own literature these raids were undertaken to remove children from these communities because of allegations of child abuse. In those cases where children were removed, no evidence was put forward to support such allegations and the children were eventually returned to their families.[23] Based on these experiences, and the history of the Mormon raids, it appears that indiscriminate raids on groups that may practice polygamy, but with no evidence that sexual abuse has taken place, will not be supported by public opinion. Although states regulating family relations should always consider accusations of incest and abuse, such accusations should be strictly proven in an open forum which permits all groups (cults, anti-cultists, civil authorities and professional experts) to examine all of the evidence if the public is expected to sustain the removal of children from the households. Legal mechanisms providing for these persons to participate in dialogue, at least as a preliminary step, is preferable to undercover raids which may lead to bloodshed and ultimately a determination that the children should be returned to their families. Improved communications and dialogue between mainline and new religious groups, similar to the approach favored by CESNUR, and other groups, would allow monitoring of possible cases of child abuse and would help avoid confrontations like those in Waco, where firearms violations may have occurred, but where it is still unclear whether rumors of child abuse or mass suicide have any basis in fact.

Michael W. Homer is a practicing attorney in Salt Lake City, an authority on legal issues involving new religious movements, and an Arthur Conan Doyle scholar.

Chapter 11

Today's Jackboots: The Inquisition Revisited

Moorman Oliver, Jr.
Santa Barbara Sheriff's Department

Somebody tell me that I'm dreaming, that it's all just a horrible nightmare. Tell me that I'll wake in a moment and everything will be as it should be. No doors being smashed open in the night. No children being awakened with the prodding of a machine gun barrel. No families being terrorized and torn apart because of their religious beliefs. Tell me that I am dreaming and I'll know that, at the very best, *you* are dreaming, or, at the worst, you're lying to yourself.

The Nazi-jackboots are alive and well. Alive in France, Spain, England, Argentina, and even in the United States of America. Alive, well and very active, all over the world. Kidnapping and assaulting those who have a different religion, a different view of God.

We thought the Inquisitions of the Dark Ages, the Salem witch hunts of early America, Hitler's Nazis and Stalin's Communism were long behind us—memories, brought back only in history books. New Inquisitors, aided by corrupt, ignorant governmental officials, relying upon deceitful criminals as their tools, show this to be only wishful thinking. Thoughtlessly causing untold pain, misery, and even death, they collect their "thirty pieces of silver" and move on to the next victim.

Christian, Jew, Muslim, Buddhist, Pagan, Hindu or any one of the myriad of religions, none are immune to the terror of the closed minds that spew forth lies and twisted half-truths under the label "*cult*"*!* If they can make this label stick to your church, then you do not have the proverbial snowball's chance in Hell of opposing the tide of negative publicity.

February 28 - April 19, 1993 in Waco, Texas, proved to be very successful for the mental midgets whose fusillade of biased untruths contributed heavily to the fiery deaths of almost a hundred men, women and children. Why? Because a small minority religion called "Branch Davidians" had successfully been branded a "cult." This was in the United States of America, where the Constitution supposedly protects against religious persecution. "Successes" like this one only encouraged the Inquisitors' fervent passion to assault other minority religions like The Family.

The United Nations has several human rights Declarations and Conventions to which "civilized" nations, including those listed above, have agreed and pledged to uphold. For example, Resolution 260 (III), adopted December 9, 1948; "The Convention on the Prevention and Punishment of the Crime of Genocide":

> Article 2: In the present Convention, genocide means any of the following acts committed with *intent to destroy, in whole or in part*, a national, ethnic, racial, *or religious group*, as such:
>
> (c) *Deliberately inflicting on the group conditions of life calculated to bring about its physical destruction in whole or in part;*
>
> (e) *Forcibly transferring children of the group to another group.*

Article 4 of Resolution 260 (III) says that people committing an act of genocide shall be punished, "whether they are constitutionally responsible rulers, public officials or private individuals."

Another example is the United Nations "Universal Declaration of Human Rights," adopted December 10, 1948:

> Article 18: Everyone has the right to freedom of *thought, conscience and religion*; this right includes the freedom to *change his religion or belief*, and freedom, either alone or in community with others, and in public and private, *to manifest his religion or belief in teaching, practice, worship and observance.*

The Bill of Rights was added to the American Constitution specifying certain inalienable rights. If any single amendment can be said to be the cornerstone of a free country, it is the First Amendment. It is appropriate that the First Amendment dealt with religion, and reads: "Congress shall make *no law respecting an establishment of religion, or prohibiting the free exercise thereof*; or abridging the freedom of speech, or of the press; or the right of the people to peaceably assemble, and to petition the Government for redress of grievances." The U.S. Supreme Court has upheld and expounded upon this remarkable Amendment.

I do not know of any "Free" country that does not include some similar form of protection from religious persecution in its Constitution. In several of these "Free" countries, a small Christian sect, called "The Family," has been targeted by "cult watchers." These bigoted and often godless *vultures,* with the aid of inept or corrupt officials, have shredded the rights of The Family and other minority religions, with members being assaulted, criminalized, brutalized, and their children terrorized.

The founder of The Family was born into a family of Evangelists. As an adult, David Brandt Berg, better known to current followers as "Father David," was traveling the evangelical circuit with his wife and children. Their "home" base was a small ranch in Texas, where they operated an evangelical venture called the "Texas Soul Clinic."

From the outset, the Berg ministry reached out to the lowest of the lost—those in prison, on drugs and alcoholics—as well as to so-called "normal" people. Their traveling evangelism was known under the name "Teens for Christ," and radio programs such as the "Church in the Home." The center of Berg's ministries was his gifted children: Linda (a.k.a. Deberah), Paul (a.k.a. Aaron), Jonathan (a.k.a. Hosea or Ho), and Faith.

At the insistence of his mother, living in Huntington Beach, California, who was an evangelist in her own right, David Berg and his children sold everything in Texas and moved west. Berg's mother wanted him to carry the Word to the "lost generation," the "drop-out generation," the "drug generation," better known as the "Hippies." Berg and his family (an expanded family, because they had several followers by then) arrived in Huntington Beach on December 24, 1967.

A "mainline" Christian church was running a coffee house in Huntington Beach that was open Monday through Friday called the "Light Club." Father David and his family persuaded the church to allow his small group to keep the "Light Club" open on the weekends. Soon there were more people coming to the "Light Club" on weekends than at any other time to hear Father David preaching the "Jesus Revolution." This didn't set too well with the church, but he didn't stop with preaching at the "Light Club."

Father David, his children and their followers took their messages into places where Angels really did fear to tread, where mainline religion shuddered at the thought of endangering themselves for those "druggies." Most of the mainline churches turned their backs on those "already condemned to Hell."

How were they able to reach those who had fallen so low? They got out of their suits and dresses, dressed as those to whom they witnessed, and sang their hearts out about the *love* of God. They reached out into the vomit-strewn and blood-smeared back alleys, often at the risk of their very lives, where the real lost souls were found. They travelled to the many drug and protest events like "Woodstock." This kind of radical outreach work often upset mainline churches. As they spread the Word their following grew, and the "Children of God" was born in the Jesus Revolution.

This was a time of great upheaval, civil unrest and social chaos. Our country was engaged in a very unpopular war, a "Policing Action" called "Vietnam." The whole world seemed to be in conflict; it was a time of sexual experimention, a time of deep soul searching, a time when the saying "God is dead" became popular. Most people had their own idea of what "hippies" were, and they weren't in the mood to listen to some hippies preach about a God that may or may not be dead. But something was happening.

Soon, those who were once high on drugs were no longer using drugs. Instead they were getting a higher high on the love of God. The very idea that a hippie could find God and be saved was alien to many devoted Church goers. "They just have to be doing something illegal."

The Children of God weren't doing anything illegal, just different than readily acceptable by the prevailing social consensus. They took up communal living, as had the first followers of Christ. They believed that sex between adults was meant to be pleasurable as well as procreative, not hidden in secret behind closed bedroom doors. They believed that everyone should be loved and that love should be freely given. By the late seventies they had begun to express their love openly when witnessing, a practice referred to as "flirty fishing."

Flirty fishing may have been controversial, but it was effective. Unfortunately, many of their detractors, through envy and ignorance, construed flirty fishing as prostitution, open and casual sex, evil and sinful, and rushed to label the Children of God a "sex cult" and "hookers for Jesus." "Of course," their critics claimed, "with such free and open sex, they must be abusing the children in this *cult*." Instead of being sexually abused, the children were being educated about sexuality and the responsibility that goes along with the sex act. The Family's current policy is that adult sex with a minor results in immediate expulsion.

Some of those expelled for these reasons are among the most fervent antagonists of The Family today.

During the formative years, there were certainly many incidents that the current followers of Father David would prefer not to have occurred. For example, as the Children of God grew, some authority had to be delegated to others within the various communes. Some of those who in positions of power became abusive in the exercise of their authority. The Family's detractors found it easy to attribute many of these deviations to the Children of God as a whole, and to Father David in particular because of his revolutionary thinking.

Reports of serious misconduct by many of the established leaders caused Father David to dismiss (fire) over 300 leaders and declare the general dissolution of the movement. The Children of God as an organizational entity ceased to exist in February 1978. Some of these leaders, including Father David's own daughter, Deborah (Linda) Davis and her husband, Bill Davis, have since launched a bitter campaign against Father David.

A third (2,600) of the total members at the time of dissolution decided to return to secular lives or remain independent missionaries with no further ties to Father David. The members who remained chose to form a new fellowship of autonomous communities called "The Family of Love," later shortened to "The Family," with Father David as their "Prophet" and spiritual head. Most of the dismissed leaders and the majority of the members who left at that time bear no ill will toward The Family of today.

The sexual aspects of The Family began to change and evolve. In March 1983, sexual relationships between members living in different communities were stopped. A bit later, in December of 1984, sexual relations with new members of less than six months was made an excommunicable offense. With the rising threat of AIDS, all flirty fishing was officially banned in September 1987.

With the evolving of The Family's sexual attitude, many materials that reflected previous sexual concepts, such as "dance videos" which portrayed female members in various stages of undress dancing to music, were ordered removed from all remaining Family communities. However, a small number of such videos were overlooked in trunks at a storage facility near the Family home in Manila, Philippines.

In October, 1992, two ex-members, Ed Priebe and Dan Welsh made an illegal incursion into a Family community in Manila. They were aided by others who would later "edit and doctor" some of the stolen documents and videos, and disseminate false versions to The Family's detractors throughout the world. According to official documents in the

Philippines, They posed as Family officials and stole $25,000 cash and several trunks containing video and audio tape masters valued at $3,000,000. While there, they tried to forcibly "deprogram" (a politically correct term for brainwashing by terrorist means) members of The Family. They were subsequently arrested, but fled with the stolen property before trial. Warrants were issued for their arrest by the Philippine government.

The stolen video depicting members of the defunct Children of God was edited so as to support the detractor's slanted views, and disseminated to the international news media. The sensational news media hype that followed precipitated witch hunts against The Family that can only be termed religious persecution.

In November, 1993, Family homes in Southern California began to be harassed by their detractors. After The Family obtained restraining orders against them, reports of child abuse were made against The Family. Some of these reports were by "anonymous phone tips." Not satisfied with making false reports to a single responsible agency, the detractors made several false reports to numerous local government agencies. From May 6 through June 10, 1993, local officials, which included the Sheriff's Office, Department of Children's Services, Department of Health, Building Inspectors, Environmental Services Department and even the City Council were descending on Family homes.

According to The Family, the investigating agencies began antagonistically, but soon became less hostile and even friendly after they discovered the allegations to be untrue. However, I have lingering doubts and questions about the accusers. Documents given to Los Angeles officials show that two of the accusers were wanted criminals, one using an alias (Daniel Welsh a.k.a. Pat Price and Edward Priebe). Samuel Ajemian and Asa Matian, according to documents given to the FBI by The Family, had been involved in the fraud and theft by fraud that followed the thefts in the Philippines.

Why were these people allowed to get away with making false reports of non-existent crimes? To knowingly make a false report of a crime is in itself a criminal act. Why were the Philippine warrants not recognized? Why has the FBI not acted on the obvious interstate/ international transportation of stolen property?

The U.S. and the Philippines were not the only countries in which the detractors chose to attack The Family. In Spain, two ex-members in cooperation with CROAS and "ProJuventud" (two vehement Spanish anti-cult groups in Spain) and the Barcelona Bishop's conference, goaded the Catalonian police into action against The Family with spurious charges of child abuse. The Catalonian police carried out a 24-hour surveillance of The Family in Barcelona with hidden cameras and tapped phone lines for four months before their July 8, 1990, raid, and should have known that there was no truth in the allegations. Fifty Catalan police smashed into the Barcelona Family home, dragging out 10 adults and 22 children, aged 11 months to 14 years. The adults were soon released, but the children were kept in institutions for the next 11 months. During the illegal imprisonment of these terrified children, they were plagued with phony Psychiatrists (Dr. Jose M. Jansa, posing as a psychiatrist, is a *skin doctor* by profession, but is also a "deprogrammer" from ProJuventud) who attempted to break the children's faith, and submitted phony psychiatric reports against the children and their parents.

While the children were illegally incarcerated, they were often neglected and/or mistreated by social workers, which resulted in numerous serious injuries. Non-Family Spanish citizens who were neighbors that supported and/or were friendly with The Family were visited by the police, who attempted to intimidate those friends. However, this tactic failed and the friends showed up and testified for The Family in the Spanish courts.

A final hearing in the Civil case to remove the children from their parents was held on May 22, 1992. The presiding judge, Adolfo Fernando Oubiña, implied that the actions by the Catalonian government was "reminiscent of the Spanish Inquisitions" (a comparison not lightly made in Spain), and compared their incarceration with the "concentration camps of those former empires that ceased to be when human dignity brought down the Berlin Wall."

The judge further noted the lengths the detractors were willing to go, declaring that The Family was an "attacked group." He further decried the so-called care the children received while in state custody, saying, "They were put in the hands of a group of psychologists who, in a language the children did not understand, psychoanalyzed them for prolonged periods, and issued reports cast in esoteric language designed rather to justify the operation (the seizure of the children by the authorities) than to describe any intellectual anomalies, which are completely nonexistent."

In June the Catalonian DA, Teresa Lema, seeing the civil case disintegrating about her, pressed for a criminal case against The Family. She accused them of such crimes that, had they actually been convicted, the 10 Family adults would have been sentenced to a collective time in prison of 200 years. But in this criminal case, the judge wrote a strongly worded 42 page verdict which, as in the civil case, cleared The Family of *any* wrong doing.

Diario de Barcelona reported, "The Courthouse compares the official action in the Children of God case with the Inquisition . . . . The Judge believes that the confinement of the minors at the [social services] center is comparable to a Soviet concentration camp." The national paper, *La Vanguardia,* wrote, "The magistrates affirm that the operation of the Catalonian Police of July 1990 was a mistake and that the [Family] community was assaulted."

One of the questions was, "were the children abused"? The answer was YES: They were abused by ProJuventud, CROAS, England's Cult Information Center and the Spanish officials. Another question is, "were the children brainwashed"? Again the answer is YES: They were brainwashed by the "deprogrammers" who were in the pay of those same cult-watchers with the collusion of certain Spanish officials. It is clear that the only criminal acts were those of the participating cult-watchers and public officials in their terrorist activities against The Family.

The Family has not been free from oppression in England, either, where in January, 1991, they were accused of child abuse and pornography. Police, acting on information provided by the cult-watch groups Cult Information Center (CIC) and Family Action Information Center (FAIR), and armed with search warrants, raided two Family communities. Naturally, the press had been advised of the "nasty sex-cult," and were tagging along to get their juicy stories.

At one home, a police Sergeant kicked in a glass panel of the front door to enter. When members of the community attempted to call their lawyer, the officer ripped out the phone. The officer was later reprimanded for his actions. No one was arrested, and none of the children were removed.

The homes were searched for better than six hours, but the searches revealed no evidence of child abuse, nor of any pornography. The children were examined for abuse and were found to be in perfect health. The officials apologized for the raid, and said they must have been given "misinformation." (No kidding!!) Why were charges of providing false information not filed against those responsible?

The most questionable raid on Family communities in London came in February, 1992. A grandmother, after receiving false information from CIC and FAIR, filed a charge of child abuse against one of the members and sought custody of the child. In two communities, the police searched for the mother and child in the most unlikely places, such as through clothing, freezers, pantries and cupboards. Did the police think The Family kept their children in their pockets, or maybe in pickle jars?

There were no arrests and no charges were brought against anyone. The police apologized and left. The child custody case, however, is still ongoing.

Toward the end of 1990, The sole Family community in Norway came under investigation as a result of a negative media campaign. The media attack was due to a disgruntled ex-member and reports from outside the country. The investigations were carried out by the Child Protective Agency (CPA) and a specialist from the Youth Psychiatric Center, who were fair in their visits and dealings with The Family. Although at the initial contact the officials were rather antagonistic, they became quite friendly towards the end of the investigation.

After a six month investigation, the case was closed in favor of The Family, with official approval of their home schooling. Then, finally, The Family began to receive nationwide coverage in the media that was favorable and factual. Wouldn't it be nice if the officials and news media in other countries could act as responsibly as those in Norway?

Unbelievable as it may sound, Gestapo-like raids, in the pre-dawn hours of May 15, 1992, were launched against six Family communities in Sidney and Melbourne, Australia. Australia is a constitutionally free nation, very similar to the United States, that has provisions in its Constitution for the protection of religious beliefs. The raids were violent, and brutally carried out by 20-25 police and 30-40 people from the State Department of Community Services (DOCS) at each of the six Family communities, removing 142 children, ages two through sixteen, and hauling them off to undisclosed locations.

A week of terror for the children followed. They were held as virtual prisoners of a government agency gone berserk. The DOCS refused to allow the parents to even know of their children's whereabouts. When the children sought the right to contact legal counsel, they were rebuffed. The police took it upon themselves to visit friends and supporters of The Family, in an attempt to intimidate them into halting any assistance they were providing.

Again, as in other countries, the press was in on the raid from the very first moment, to see "the poor children being *rescued*" from the "dangerous cult." But after six days of intensive questioning, examinations and evaluations, Australian officials were unable to bring a single criminal charge against the family, and the courts, in both Sidney and Melbourne, ordered the children returned to their parents.

Many freedom-loving Australians became concerned about the callousness and excessiveness of the raid and the manner in which the children were abducted, and a large number of lawyers in both cities volunteered their services. The opposition political party decried the raids as "oppressive, excessive and heavy handed," and called for a government inquiry into the entire affair. The *Sidney Morning Herald* wrote, "We are witnessing a department of State, for the first time in decades, using its processes and powers for direct religious persecutions." However, all of this uproar did not halt the involved agencies. They went into over-drive, trying to come up with some charge to justify their raids.

After almost four months of fruitless investigations, the DOCS still could not justify their actions and the Government wanted out. A mediated settlement was agreed to on October 31, 1992. On November 1, 1992, banner headlines read, "The Family Sect Case Collapses," "Most Outrageous Prosecution in Memory" and "Demand for Inquiry into 'Soweto-like' Police Raid".

Crimes were certainly committed in Sidney and Melbourne, heinous crimes against the parents and the children of The Family, crimes of terrorism by government agencies sworn to uphold the rights of those they were terrorizing. How far did those government inquires go? Were they effective? Did the inquires halt the religious persecution in Australia? As of this writing (November 1993), the Australian communities of The Family are *again* having to defend themselves!

French justice was trampled June 9, 1993. Another early morning (dawn) raid of two Family communities in Lyon and Marseille, France, as well as several private homes of Family associates. At 6:00 AM, over 200 French police, many in combat fatigues, brandishing fully automatic weapons and some wielding axes, smashed into the dwellings of peaceful families. Doors that were not even locked were kicked down. Unsuspecting victims, awakened to what "sounded like some insane killers were breaking everything and killing everybody." Fifty non-resisting adults and ninety horrified children were hauled out of bed at gun point.

Terrified, unarmed parents were dragged down the stairs in full view of their children, women handcuffed and thrown to the floor. One handcuffed mother was dragged by the hair, losing a handful of hair in the process. Other parents were dragged across a gravel driveway, bruised and bleeding. Young adolescent girls were forced to dress under the watchful view of sniggering, smirking male officers. One fifteen year old girl was handcuffed for hours, wearing only her underwear. A seventeen year old boy had a muscle in his left arm torn and wrists ripped by the cuffs from the violence of the officer.

The next 48 hours were pure terror for the parents from the two communities. Under continuous interrogation, the men *and women* were screamed at, struck in the face, lied to, threatened with physical violence and told that they would never see their children again. The police Chief told them that he had three goals:

1) to dismantle The Children of God
2) to take your children away
3) to put you in jail.

The children were treated no better. No one would tell the children why they were being attacked and separated from their parents. The detention centers the children were taken to were like dungeons.

One group of children were taken to what seemed to be an old abandoned building. Taken straight from their beds without breakfast, they were given nothing to eat until almost noon. They had only one cup to drink from for 32 kids. When the children answered "no" to questions of abuse and sexual relations with their parents, the inquisitors would slap and pound the table, shouting that the children were lying.

Many of the children were unable to completely understand the questions because they were not conversant in French and, when they asked for interpreters, they were rudely turned down. An 18 year old girl was *forced* to sign a statement written in French that she was unable to read. A doll was ripped from the hand of a three year old child. The examining doctors were no better than the police. One psychiatrist, Jean-Marie Abragall, appointed by the court to evaluate the children, was discovered to be an associate of ADFI, the very group that instigated the raids.

At the goading of the Association for the Defense of the Family and Individual (ADFI), the police were trying to make a case of child abuse, prostitution and other related charges against The Family. With no evidence to support any of the allegations, and ample evidence and psychiatric reports favorable to The Family, the case folded. Now The Family, adults and children alike, must struggle to recover from the extreme trauma they needlessly suffered at the hands of bigots and callous officials.

Since 1987, The Family has undergone 10 separate investigations in Argentina. The latest, occurring on September 1, 1993, is still ongoing. Prior to this most recent episode, Argentine authorities had physically and psychologically examined 173 Family children and had not found a single instance of any kind of abuse. Moreover, in each of the prior cases, The Family had been acquitted of all charges. World wide, court-appointed officials have altogether examined over 600 children of The Family, and not a single instance of abuse has been found. Members of The Family have been exonerated in every case.

In the cold morning hours (approximately 2:00AM) of September 1, 1993, the police raided five Family communities in Buenos Aires, Argentina. As in every other case around the world, the media was dragged along to show what terrible people were in these evil and abusive "sex-cults." Although knowing from all previous investigations that Family communities were unarmed and non-violent, police smashed into five Family communities brandishing fully automatic weapons. The police deny any forced entries, but in at least one home the door was kicked down without any prior knocking.

Not only were the adults assaulted in the most brutal and cruel manner, but the children were terrorized and awakened by being jabbed with the barrels of the machine guns. The police claimed to have search warrants (not arrest warrants), but refused to show the warrants to anyone at any of The Family homes. Adults and children alike were threatened. A female officer screamed at an *eleven year old child* who brushed against her, "If you touch me again, I'm going to kill you! Do you understand? I'm going to kill you!" In all, 39 adults and 137 children were rounded up and dragged off to jail. Not one of The Family members were allowed to contact legal representation per the orders of the federal judge, or so the police told The Family.

Before any hearing was held, the federal judge who ordered the raids, Roberto Marquevich, publicly prejudged The Family, proclaiming them "guilty." Even before the raid was completed, Judge Marquevich claimed to the world news media that the raids had turned up "huge amounts" of evidence showing child abuse, incest, kidnapping, prostitution and a host of other crimes. The impatient media, *Reuters, The Associated Press, United Press International* and even the *British Broadcasting System,* reported the ridiculous and unsubstantiated stories from Marquevich around the world as if they were gospel truth.

International media quoted Police Commissioner Juan Carlos Rebollo as saying that when the children were awakened by the police at two and three o'clock in the morning, they "were like zombies, with sad eyes and a lost look as though they were someplace else." I don't doubt that in the least. I feel and act like a zombie myself almost every morning until my first cup of coffee. Any child, anywhere in the world, would look the same way if awakened in the middle of the night out of a sound sleep by screaming madmen who were prodding them with machine gun barrels. There is no question that the children must have been terrified. It's a wonder they didn't go into shock!

The panel of 20 court appointed doctors who examined the children declared that there were no signs of abuse present whatsoever. Despite the testimony of the 20 forensic experts, several days later Judge

Marquevich declared that nine of the 137 seized children bore "sexual wounds." The doctors immediately and publicly disputed the judge's claims. Judge Marquevich was furious and ordered a second set of examinations for the children. According to several of the children who suffered through these examinations, "the second examination was morbid and much worse than the first one."

An eleven year old girl was treated so viciously that she screamed in pain. An optical device was thrust into her without regard for the damage and pain it was causing. There were five doctors present, and only one, the woman, had gloves. Two of the men forcefully held her down and one covered her mouth while the others checked her without gloves. It was so painful that she vomited at the end of the examination. Another man, believed not to be a doctor, was also present with a camera, photographing the exam.

It is interesting to note that some of the "evidence" allegedly found in The Family's homes, were out-takes from videos which were produced in the late '70s and early '80s, and have long been banned and removed from all Family communities. These video tapes had been long-forgotten in a storage facility in the Philippines, from which they were stolen by Ed Priebe in 1992. Detractors of the Family who were involved in the Argentina raids with Priebe have admitted that copies of these videos were *planted* in the Family homes by corrupt Argentine officials during the raids. During the physical examinations, some of the children were photographed while being examined by the doctors. Are these photographs now part of the so-called "evidence" of sexual misconduct?

"A source close to the prosecution had said," reported *Reuter's*, "'...[of the children] there appears to be a serious trend of mental and psychological degeneration. They're very backward and closed to the outside world.'" Now I personally know that to be a lie, having met a good many of The Family's children myself. I also know many of the scholars who have lived with and studied The Family for extended periods of time who claim just the opposite. Children of The Family *were* abused, brutalized and traumatized—*not* by The Family, but by the officials who were sworn to protect them.

Judge Marquevich appointed Dr. Maria Lourdes as the psychologist to evaluate the children. However, The Family claims to have evidence that Dr. Lourdes is a professional "faith-breaker" who works for SPES, an organization which advocates forcible deprogramming and publicly campaigns for the outlawing of any New Religious Movements not of the Roman Catholic Church, such as The Family. There was no way the children could expect an impartial evaluation by Dr. Lourdes. It is obvious that The Family members and children who were incarcerated were victims of state-sponsored deprogramming in Argentina.

Judge Roberto Marquevich has been denounced to the Minister of Justice and the Argentine Congress by the President of the BAR Association, Carlos Cichellos. Cichellos requested an investigation to determine the extent of the judge's responsibility for the inhumane conditions to which The Family was subjected. The BAR Association extended its request to the Argentine Congress, the Law School of San Isidro, and the Commission of Human Rights and Guarantees of the Argentine Senate.

Argentina has been a struggling democracy for a little more than ten years, after having been under a repressive military dictatorship. It will be interesting to see whether they continue to strengthen their new-found freedoms, or sink back into the death and destruction of the still-strong Fascists who are attempting to regain their strangle-hold on the country. It will be a difficult struggle, especially since those who would suppress those freedoms are being aided and encouraged by U.S. Ambassadors and the U.S. State Department. (The U.S. Council, Nicholas Ricciuti, offered his assistance only to those who would leave The Family.)

Many of the "star witnesses" against The Family are themselves criminals, and one has spent time in mental institutions. Richard Dupuy, for instance, is a self-admitted child abuser, and Ed Priebe is a thief with a warrant out for his arrest. TV networks like NBC who eagerly relied upon the likes of Dupuy and Priebe should be aware of the character of these people. Utilizing Priebe's stolen and "doctored" videos makes NBC a party to several crimes. Tabloid reporting is, however, nothing new to NBC—remember, this is the network that faked trucks bursting into flames when they crashed by setting off explosives during the crash.

Many crimes have been committed, not *by* The Family, but *against* The Family as well as other "Minority Religions." Crimes by alliances of bigots, aided by corrupt police and government officials, perpetuated and fueled by tabloid media and "yellow journalism."

The human rights violations against The Family by Argentine officials during the September 1, 1993, raid is the grossest example of violations against a religious community in the modern era, exceeded only by the extermination of the Branch Davidians in Waco, Texas, earlier in the same year. Why this comparison of raids on two diverse religious communities? Two very good reasons. First, because the U.S. State Department has been surreptitiously cooperating with Argentine officials in this persecution and, secondly, because both raids were instigated by a worldwide network of cult-watch groups.

It is past the time for responsible governments, including the U.S., to investigate the unholy alliances between the various "anti-cult/anti-religion" groups around the world. Responsible governments also need to investigate the numerous criminal conspiracies between those alliances and certain corrupt officials in the various countries where religious persecution and human rights violations are being perpetrated against The Family and other minority religions. How many more massacres of falsely accused men, women and children have to occur before this travesty is brought to a screeching halt?

Detective Moorman Oliver, Jr., is a retired criminal investigator with the Santa Barbara Sheriff's Office. He served as his department's specialist on gangs and cults. He currently serves as Law Enforcement Consultant for the Association of World Academics for Religious Education (AWARE).

Chapter 12

Island Pond Raid Begins New Pattern

George Robertson
Maryland Bible College

In the wee hours of the early morning on June 22, 1984, the residents in the small village of Island Pond, Vermont awoke to a literal governmental invasion of their community. With no advance warning or notice, more than 150 law enforcement officers and agents from various state agencies stormed the twenty or so homes where the members of the Northeast Kingdom Community church lived, arresting more than 100 adults and 112 children.

What was so unusual about this church? How did the State of Vermont become so entangled in the controversy surrounding this community that they acted precipitously, without first conducting a thorough investigation—actions for which they were later forced to apologize? How did a typical fundamental Christian sect become a major target for such radical activities? The answers to these questions and many more reveal startling truths about a seedy underworld of kidnappers and vigilantes who stir up bigotry and prejudice in order to profit from people's emotions.

The Northeast Kingdom Community Church began in the foothills of Tennessee around 1972, when an independent fundamentalist preacher, Elbert Eugene Spriggs, built a loyal following of believers into a model New Testament community church. Spriggs called his group the Light

Brigade and he spent most of his early ministry pulling drug addicts and alcoholics off the streets of Chattanooga. Later, the name was changed to the Vine Christian Community Church and the ministry spread into surrounding communities.

The church members separated themselves from worldly pursuits and materialistic gains, supporting themselves with homegrown foods and necessities which they also sold to local area residents. One of the mainstays of financial support has been their delicatessen and take out shop, which features natural foods. The church has always attracted the attention of the local residents, but most of them accepted the group as "different, but nice folks." At first glance, the members of the church remind you of the Amish church members. The women wear kerchiefs on their heads, long dresses, little or no make-up, and the men usually wear beards, long hair, and overalls.

The Tennessee community grew to more than 400 residents and became a very successful example of the "community paradigms" which dotted the countryside during the early seventies and eighties. There was never any violence and very few confrontations with anyone outside of the community. There were a few marital disputes, but only a small number of divorces compared to a typical church of similar size. One of the few problems to surface during the Tennessee years lit the match for the attacks which have followed them for the past fifteen or more years.

Clifford Daniels, a young man with a history of personal problems, joined the community and soon rose to a leadership position managing one of the business interests of the community. Problems developed problems with the church elders when Daniels "borrowed" some of the business funds and a church vehicle without authority. When the indiscretion was discovered and he appeared before the church Board of Elders, he became violent and attempted to attack one of the leaders with a tire iron.

He was banished from the community. Seeking revenge, Daniels fell in with another former resident of the area, Ted Patrick. Patrick had migrated to Southern California, but was still active in the Tennessee foothills where his family and friends continued to live. It was the mid-seventies, and Patrick had gained some notoriety among a growing number of anti-religious activists as a "deprogrammer"—a term he coined to give credibility to his kidnapping and abductions of young people from religious groups. Borrowing from the brainwashing techniques used by the communists on the American prisoners of war, Patrick's exploits were quickly giving him wide recognition among relatives of adult children who had joined the religious versions of the hippie revolution. They were more than willing to hire him to return their adult "children" to their control.

Daniels became a good team member for Patrick. The members of Sprigg's quaint community church provided excellent potential for Patrick's deprogramming-for-hire enterprise. Daniels was an eager student, and soon became an independent deprogrammer on his own. He now kidnaps more than 20 to 30 people in any given year from a variety of local churches. Throughout his career, Daniels' favorite target has always remained the Northeast Kingdom Church. In spite of the publicity stirred up by Patrick and Daniels against the church to support their kidnapping activities, the church continued to grow and prosper.

In 1976, the church had an opportunity to move onto land they had acquired in northern Vermont. It offered the perfect haven for their lifestyle and the vision which Spriggs saw for his church. The move provided even more fuel for the anti-religion activists whose numbers had also increased significantly.

Former members that had been deprogrammed by Patrick, Daniels, and other deprogrammers had jumped on the lucrative circuit. Local anti-religious contacts throughout the country were promoting uneasy relatives to "rescue" their adult offspring with the deprogrammer's expert services, even if it meant that they returned to a life of drugs and alcohol! Many of the kidnapping incidents were perpetrated by the deprogrammers as a means to gain custody of children who were still in the church when one of the parents had left or were previously deprogrammed.

Some of these would end up in court where the non-custodial parent would seek a new custody hearing by injecting stories by deprogrammed former members about child abuse. A campaign of letters and charges to various officials continued in order to build their cases. At one point, several families were even charged with truancy for failing to send their children to a public school instead of home schooling or because their children were in the church school. The charges were always dropped for lack of evidence.

The fact that they were dropped never troubled their antagonists. The publicity surrounding the charges and the documents alleging the charges proved sufficient documentation to use for more attacks. At the height of his notoriety in the mid-seventies, Patrick traveled the country meeting with local anti-religious activists and training new converts to become deprogrammers. Long before Spriggs contemplated his move to the New England countryside, Patrick had planted his seeds of destruction.

Patrick joined forces with a local New England activist who owned a remote farm in upper New York state, and the hide-a-way provided

Patrick and other deprogrammers with a perfect "safe-house" to keep their kidnap victims while they brainwashed them into forsaking their cherished religious beliefs. Patrick eventually gathered a number of like-minded individuals together in the New England area and started the formal organizations that became the Citizens Freedom Foundation (later changing its name to the Cult Awareness Network) and American Family Foundation. All of these organizations are interlocked with overlapping board members, leaders and deprogrammers who function as conduits for the deprogramming network.

Although numerous members of these organizations have been arrested, charged, and usually convicted for crimes involving their attacks against local churches and religious groups, they have been able to maintain an air of respectability that has gleaned support for their activities. There are many sociological reasons for this phenomenon, but their best ally has always been the natural tendency of people to accept bigotry and prejudice.

The Cult Awareness Network, with the help of New England deprogrammer Galen Kelly, eagerly picked up the campaign against the church from Tennessee. Vermont is a very rural state, and the Vermonters seemed eager to accept the wild accusations and charges levied against these "strangers" from Tennessee. An article in the *Vermont Magazine* (March, 1991) makes the point very well:

> For the residents of Island Pond, it was watching out for children that proved the greatest challenge to their intolerance of newcomers. It was one thing to wake up and find a couple of hundred New Testament zealots had come to town from heaven knows where. It was another to learn that they had given up all their earthly possessions to join the church—a vow of poverty— and held all things in common, and lived, ate and worked together. It was still another that they criticized much of American culture as corrupt and all other Christian denominations as misguided. It was yet another to see that they drew members from among the young, the transient, the dissatisfied and the burned out. Worse, they looked like hippies.

Jumping on the prejudices, the deprogramming network of deprogrammers, anti-religion activists, and deprogrammed former members relentlessly pursued a campaign against the church. The campaign included town hall meetings where lurid stories of abuse and wild allegations of killing babies were proffered with vivid details. Letters of protest and allegations of abuse flooded the offices of the Department of Social Services, the Department of Education, the Congressmen, the Senators, the Governor, and every law enforcement agency that could be found. Even Immigration, the Internal Revenue

Service, and State Departments were petitioned!

The allegations and protests were peppered with supposed "atrocities" from other states which involved "similar" local churches that had to be addressed by government officials. The charges were embellished with overtones drawn from publicity surrounding the Jonestown incident. Finally, Governor Richard Snelling and Attorney General John Easton were convinced that there were enough allegations and testimonies to take serious action against the community of believers. The anti-Northeast Kingdom Community campaign was working. Kelly and company were actually invited to tag along for the raid on the community at Island Pond.

AT 6:30 AM on Friday, June 22, 1984, a caravan of state police officers, social service workers, sheriff deputies, and an assortment of other officials swooped down on the residents and arrested 110 adults and took 112 children of all ages into custody. They loaded the 222 men, women and children into separate buses, separating crying children from their distraught and bewildered parents with little or no explanations. A local resident later recalled "It was awful. It was just like Vietnam!"

While the Northeast Kingdom Community were huddled in a gymnasium which served as a makeshift detention center, the State Attorney requested a blanket detention order from the District Court in order that a full scale investigation could be conducted on the incarcerated residents. The Judge refused. The court held that "the state failed to present any specific evidence of abuse," and ordered all of the children to be released. After a thorough examination by the social service case workers, no evidence of any abuse of any kind could be found.

The event, however, served the purposes of the Cult Awareness Network. The raid made headlines in news media across the nation. As usual, the fact that the children were all returned, the parents released and no charges ever filed for lack of evidence, barely rated a back-page mention. To this day, if an inquiry about the church is made to the offices of the Cult Awareness Network today, the inquirer will receive a packet thick with articles from the raid and other stories relating similar charges. With a policy that can only be described as gross deception, the information packets do not contain even one mention of the false charges, the return of the children, or the role that the Cult Awareness Network played in instigating the ill-fated raid.

The deprogrammers are still kidnapping children as well as adults from the Northeast Kingdom Community. Some have been taken to courts in other states and custody given to the non-custodial parent and others have been returned by the courts. The deprogrammers get paid for their services either way. More deprogrammers have joined the swarm of locusts. Most notable has been the widely celebrated Rick Ross, whose consulting services helped start the similar raid on the Branch Davidians in Waco, Texas. Those allegations, which were all provided by deprogrammed former members, were later proven to be totally false.

The children at Island Pond have been investigated by every agency possible, and the church has never charged with abuse. News reporters have visited the community and found only fresh, happy, well-adjusted children who are growing up to be responsible, mature adults with deep religious convictions. The ministry of Eugene Spriggs continues to grow. Currently, there are expressions of the home base church in Vermont which are now located in areas throughout the world and in a number of cities throughout America.

The techniques and strategy developed for the raid at Island Pond, though, have proven to be very successful for the anti-religion network. They have been used with varying degrees of success against a large number of churches and religious groups throughout the world. The list includes The Family in more than a dozen countries, the Tony Alamo Foundation in Arkansas and in California, the Church of Scientology in Spain, Italy, and various American locations. The list also includes many other small local churches. The anti-religious organizations have now even published books and papers for their agents detailing the strategy for such raids. They include "Cultivating Cult Evading," "Litigating the Cult Related Child Custody Case," and "Investigating Destructive Cults."

With children's issues remaining as a major interest of today's society, and the virtually unchecked powers of the social service agencies, the problem of unwarranted and unethical raids being promoted in such a manner is likely to continue and may even increase. It is imperative that government officials and workers for the social service agencies consider the sources of allegations brought against churches and religious groups who are being attacked by the deprogramming network and investigate the charges more fully before taking such drastic actions.

Wholesale raids on religious communities like Northeast Kingdom Community, The Family, the Branch Davidians, and others simply should not be allowed to happen. There are no excuses for such agencies disregarding appropriate investigative techniques and taking precautionary measures to protect the children involved from unnecessary trauma.

Dr. George Robertson teaches at Maryland Bible College, and serves as media spokesperson for Friends of Freedom, a religious-liberty information center.

Chapter 13

Child Abuse at Waco

James R. Lewis
Center for Academic Publication

> According to Attorney General Janet Reno, nobody high up in
> government said "don't do it" as she considered the disastrous plan. But
> it is not mere hindsight to say that someone should have. On March
> 10th the *Houston Chronicle* reported that former Houston police SWAT
> commander Lieutenant Jim Gunn had advised that, considering the
> variety and firepower of weapons Koresh and his followers were alleged
> to have, "About the only thing you could do is go in there with the M-1
> tanks and start knocking down walls, and they are not going to do that
> with the children in there." And use of tear gas was not a feasible
> alternative, according to Gunn, because "tear gas can get into a child's
> lungs and cause congestion and kill them."
> — Robert W. Lee, *New American Magazine*

Lieutenant Gunn, it turned out, was terribly wrong about the authorities'
concern for the children. The tear gas used in the FBI attack—a white,
crystalline powder called CS (O-chlorobenzylidene malonitrile)—is such
an inhumane form of tear gas that it has been prohibited for military
use. It causes nausea, disorientation, dizziness, shortness of breath,
tightness in the chest, burning of the skin, intense tearing, coughing, and
vomiting. In January of 1993, the United States and 130 other nations

signed the Chemical Weapons Convention agreement banning CS gas. This treaty does not, however, cover internal uses, such as quelling domestic disturbances.

On April 23, 1993, Benjamin C. Garrett, director of the Chemical and Biological Arms Control Institute in Alexandria, Virginia, was quoted in the *Washington Times* as saying that CS gas would have had the greatest impact on the children at Mt. Carmel. "The reaction would have intensified for the children," Garrett said, because "the smaller you are, the sooner you would feel response." According to the FBI, the anticipated scenario was that mothers, in an effort to protect their children, would leave the building with their offspring when the gas saturated the insides of the building. White House spokesman George Stephanopoulos, speaking at a news conference, was unwilling (or unable) to account for why such a deadly form of tear gas—one that temporarily blinds and disables a person—was selected over other possibilities.

Also, despite claims by the FBI that the community had not tried to save its children during the final fire, a May 14 report issued by the Associated Press revealed that, "Most of the children were found huddled in the concrete bunker, enveloped in the protective embraces of their mothers," in what had clearly been an attempt to avoid the flames. These and many other particulars that could be cited indicate both that the Davidians were not planning a mass suicide, and that they were not child abusers.

About the fortieth day of the Mt. Carmel siege, David Koresh informed his besiegers that the community's babies and children had run out of milk. A number of different efforts to respond to this call for aid were repulsed by authorities. (While it was O.K. to provide humanitarian aid to Contras, U.S. citizens are clearly a different matter.) Linda Thompson, an attorney from Indiana who drove to Waco in a vain but admirable attempt to head off the holocaust, tried to deliver baby food and baby supplies on April third and fourth. She and her husband were detained for questioning, and then turned back. At FBI headquarters, she posed the question, "Has it come to this? Does the United States government want babies to starve to death?" The answer she received was, "Yes." Exasperated, they finally placed the food alongside the road block at the press entrance with a sign that read, "Please take this food to the Mt. Carmel babies. The FBI says, 'Let them starve.'" Moments later, an ATF agent drove up in a pick up truck, and stole the food.

A man named Gary Spaulding and another person from South Bend, Indiana, were arrested the following week for attempting to take food to the Mt. Carmel children. Gary pointedly suggested to the arresting officer that he should perhaps "check with his high command to be sure that the officer was doing what the high command wanted." The response he received was, "I can assure you that I speak for high command when I say that food is not going to those babies."

Although child abuse is technically the jurisdiction of the state rather than the federal government, concern that the Davidian children were being abused has been one of the principal reasons cited by authorities as justification for both the initial ATF attack and for the concluding FBI assault. On April 21, White House spokesperson George Stephanopoulos, defending the holocaust, asserted that there "is absolutely no question that there's overwhelming evidence of child abuse in the Waco compound." This was a very odd line of defense, as if the assertion that the Davidians practiced such abuse justified gassing and incinerating the entire community.

However, on the very day Stephanopoulos was putting his foot in his mouth, the Justice Department publicly acknowledged that they had no solid evidence of child abuse—only *speculation* by mental health professions who had been studying Koresh from a distance. On the same day, 1,100 pages of unsealed documents relevant to the case were released. These included only two allegations of child abuse by disgruntled former members. Otherwise nothing else was reported, certainly nothing like credible evidence.

Certainly during the seige itself, the FBI showed little regard for the children. The weird light and sound show, which included recordings of dentists' drills and dying rabbits, would hardly have promoted any child's sense of well-being. Deteriorating sanitary conditions, caused by decaying bodies and the buildup of sewage, were also given as a justification for attacking Mt. Carmel on April 19. The Attorney General told Larry King on national television that she feared that "if I delayed, without sanitation or toilets there . . . I could go in there in two months and find children dead from any number of things." Yet if this had truly been an overriding consideration, Why didn't the FBI restore the water and utilites it had shut off in March?

The Texas Department of Human Services had investigated Mt. Carmel on child abuse allegations on at least three different occasions. No credible evidence for such accusations was found. The same can be said for the twenty-one children released from Mt. Carmel between the ATF raid and the FBI assault—no hard evidence of child abuse. On March fifth, Janice Caldwell, director of the Texas Department of Protective and Regulatory Services, stated that, "They're in remarkably good shape considering what they have been through. No signs of physical abuse have been found." The March sixth edition of the *Houston Post* noted that "all the youths appear to be in good condition psychologically and physically." In the same article, a social worker asserted that "the children are remarkably well-educated and they're fascinated by the books in the residence where they're staying."

The only other relevant accusation of child abuse originated with the chief of psychiatry at a Texas medical school in Texas who examined several of the children released between February 28 and April 19. In the words of psychologist Lawrence Lilliston, a widely recognized expert on children in non-traditonal religions:

> This psychiatrist's conclusions were widely reported in the media, including a lengthy article in the *New York Times*. He concluded that the children had been abused, and cited as evidence marks on their bodies. These physical marks, described as round red marks on the skin of several children, comprised the only specific evidence reported. The psychiatrist otherwise described the children as being friendly, happy, and likable, and as having good interpersonal skills and being open to others. They were also described as generally being bright and above average on cognitive and educational tasks. This picture is clearly not consistent with expectations for children who have been abused.

The lack of any solid evidence for Davidian child abuse probably explains the reason why the Attorney General and the FBI dropped this explanation as soon as reporters began to raise questions about specific evidence for abuse. But, as Prof. Lilliston further points out, there *was* child abuse in Waco:

> Consider the following. Knowing that there were many children inside, federal agents conducted a raid on the compound, firing a fusillade of bullets through windows and walls, killing one child and surely terrifying the others. Knowing that there were many children inside, federal agents cut off electricity and other utilities necessary to the maintenance of health and safety standards for these children, and then, incredibly, criticized the adults because children had to perform elimination functions in buckets. Knowing that there were many children inside, federal agents bombarded the building with spotlights twenty four hours a day in an admitted attempt to disrupt sleep and rest. Knowing that there were many children inside, federal agents incessantly assaulted the building with loud music and bizarre sounds, such as rabbits being killed. Knowing that there were many children inside, federal agents used tanks as battering rams, crashing into the building and punching holes in the walls even though they were aware that the building was a potential tinder box and that the people inside were using lanterns which could easily be knocked over. Knowing that there were many children inside,

federal agents pumped in tear gas—tear gas of such strength and capacity for producing pain, it has been banned by international law—and they did this, knowing that there were no gas masks inside small enough to protect children. Certainly these children's last living moments must have been filled with unbelievable horror and agony.

Who, considering these facts, could dispute the charge of child abuse in Waco? If firing bullets at them, disregarding and disturbing their health and tranquility, destroying their home while placing them in clear danger, and intentionally inflicting intense pain on them is not abusive to children, what is?

   — Lawrence Lilliston, "Who Committed Child Abuse at Waco?"

In short, it seems clear that the charge of child abuse leveled against the Davidians was little more than a pretext that legitimated the drastic actions of April 19, 1993.

Child abuse is one of those issues like AIDS and the plight of the homeless which has been uppermost in the public consciousness during the last decade or so. As a consequence, accusations of child abuse are more effective at attracting attention than other kinds of charges, particularly if the media can be persuaded to pick up the story. Although one of the principles of our legal system is that a person is innocent until proven guilty, the mass media presents its information so that merely reporting sensationalistic accusations is often sufficient to convict the accused in the mind of the general public. If it later turns out that the accused was innocent, this item of corrective information rarely gets reported, and the public is usually left with the impression that the accused is guilty.

The mass media is not, of course, motivated primarily by the quest for truth. Instead, the mainstream media is driven by market forces and by the necessity of competing with other newspapers, other TV news shows, and so forth. This is not to say that reporters necessarily lie or fabricate their stories. Rather, in the case of non-traditional religions, news people tend to accentuate those facets of "cults" that seem to be strange, exploitative, dangerous, totalitarian, sensational, and the like because such portrayals titillate consumers of news. This kind of reporting contributes to the perpetuation of the cult stereotype. Another important factor is the marked tendency of the mass media to report on a phenomenon only when it results in conflicts and problems.

What this means for non-traditional religions accused of child abuse is that such groups lose their chance for a fair hearing as soon as the media labels them "cults." Cults are, by definition, abusive, so that to attempt assert that such-and-such a "cult group" is *non*-abusive sounds like a contradiction in terms. Thus simply succeeding in getting the cult label to stick to any given religious community—whether the community be the Branch Davidians, the Northeast Kingdom Community, or The Family—is to succeed in "demonizing" the group. Once effectively demonized, the enforcement agencies of the state are free to undertake otherwise unthinkably repressive actions against the target group, even, as in the case of the Davidians, incinerating an entire community with scarcely a peep of protest from the American public.

James R. Lewis is academic director of the Association of World Academics for Religious Education and senior editor of the Center for Academic Publishing. He has published extensively in the field of new religious movements, editing such important works as *From the Ashes: Making Sense of Waco*, a scholarly compilation on the Branch Davidian tragedy.

Chapter 14

Scholarly Studies on the Children of God/The Family: A Comprehensive Survey[1]

John A. Saliba
University of Detroit, Mercy

There is little doubt that the Children of God/The Family[2] has been one of the most controversial new religious groups since its appearance in the late 1960's. The rise of the anticult movement can be directly related to its activities (see Beckford 1985). The first deprogramming efforts, led by Ted Patrick (1976), were directed against The Family's members. By 1974 the movement's activities were under legal scrutiny.[3] For over a decade The Family assumed a low profile in Western countries and concentrated its evangelizing programs largely to Third World countries. Now, it would seem, its members are renewing their missionary efforts both in Europe and the United States. Their presence and their residences are no longer difficult to trace. They have already aroused social opposition in several continents and are being forced to defend themselves against legal suits.

During the 1970's and early 1980's the Children of God (COG) were the object of study of several social scientists who were intrigued by their revolutionary lifestyle and sexual mores, constantly changing organizational patterns, and religious ideology. The body of scholarly literature, however, has remained rather thin. The secretive stance which the movement adopted since 1983 has meant that, for a whole decade, little has been published to reveal what further changes have taken place in a rather volatile movement and to explore ways of understanding its members' behavioral patterns.

The Current Research Status on the Children of God/The Family

In surveying the literature on the Children of God one must stress that it covers only 12 to 15 years (1968-1983) of the movement's history. Because of the many changes in COG's organization and behavioral patterns that have taken place over the last decade, much of the ethnographic material upon which scholars had based their sociological speculations no longer reflects the current scene. This does not mean that this early research is insignificant or unimportant. On the contrary, one cannot understand The Family unless one begins with the research on the initial phases of COG. Two major reasons make these studies crucial for contemporary scholars. The first is historical. The Family is rooted in its past and has maintained some religious ideology and practice over the years, in spite of the many changes that have occurred. The second is sociological. In order to understand the mechanisms of cultural change, the processes that characterize an evolving ideology, lifestyle, and organization, and the very nature of charismatic leadership, sociologists must take into consideration the early literature on COG.

The most complete bibliography on The Family is that of Pritchett (1985). It is still an indispensable tool for scholars even though, as Wallis (1985, pp. 35-36) observed, it omitted many of the then available primary sources and was already out of date by the time it was published. One of its better qualities is that it brings together a variety of publications on the Children of God, thus enabling the researcher to view this movement from different perspectives, namely ethnographic, sociological, religious, legal, and popular. It contains abundant sources for research on the early history of COG.

Pritchett begins with a lengthy introduction and then goes on to list 1728 items which, notwithstanding the title of his book, are not annotated. After dealing with the MO-Letters and other COG Publications, which occupy about three-fourths of the book, he then moves on to secondary materials that are divided under 7 headings: 1) scholarly, 2) religious publications, 3) journalistic material, 4) newspaper articles, 5) government investigations, 6) anti-COG material, and 7) audio (cassette tapes). The list of 34 references under scholarly works reveals how little serious work had been done on the Children of God, even before the movement went underground. Fewer than a third of these references would qualify as studies on the movement; the rest are books and/or articles that contain very short allusions to the movement's activities, usually cited to buttress the individual author's understanding of current religiosity. Further, Pritchett's distinction between the various types of secondary materials on COG is not always clear, to say the least. Thus, for example, he lists Drakeford's (1972) book (Pritchett 1985, p. 145, item 1507) with the religious material. Drakeford's work, however, contains descriptive records of the movement that were obtained by first-hand contact with the members of various communes. Unlike the works of, for example, Enroth (1977) and Martin (1980), Drakeford's account does not attempt a theological evaluation of the movement. And contrary to the commentaries of so many Christian apologists, his book does not attack the movement's ideology and practices. In fact he provides a favorable sketch of its early phases.

Though both scholarly and religious writings contain a lot of first-hand information on the COG, there is only one published ethnographic monograph on the movement. Van Zandt's (1991) book stands in a class by itself, even though it is rather dated, since it is essentially his 1985 dissertation which was based on his research carried out in the late 1970's.[4]

Short reliable accounts on the Children of God appear in many books on new religions (e.g., Bromley and Shupe 1981; Barker 1989), but these are, as a rule, rather short and repetitive. Probably the best and most reliable overviews of COG are found in Melton's authoritative *Encyclopedia of American Religions* (1978, 1987, 1989, 1993) and *Encyclopedic Handbook of Cults in America* (1986, 1992). In the handbook, he divides the chapter on COG into several useful sections dealing with its 1) founder and early history, 2) beliefs and practices, 3) organization, 4) current status, and 5) controversial status. A very short bibliography of primary and secondary sources is appended.

Though Melton's works are the standard reference tools for the study of new religious movements, his latest editions (1992, 1993) confirm Wallis's view (1985) that statements on the COG are bound to be dated by the time they appear in print. Since his latest volumes were already in print before contact was made with COG members in early 1993,[5] they seem to assume that the movement is still living in its secretive stages and that its official name is "The Family of Love." They make no reference to the recent legal controversies in several countries, which include Italy, England, France, Argentina, and the Philippines. Van Zandt's work is not listed at all.[6]

For sociological analyses of the movement the most valuable materials remain those of Wallis (1976, 1977, 1978a, 1978b, 1979, 1981, 1982a, 1982b, 1985, 1986, 1987), who lost contact with the COG early in 1983 (Wallis 1985, p. 36).[7] Enroth et al. (1972), Hopkins (1977, 1980a, 1980b), Ellwood (1973), Davis and Richardson (1976), Richardson and Davis (1983), and Wangerin (1984a, 1984b) supply the reader with data and/or sociological reflections. Wright (1987) has contributed one of the major studies on defections from several new religions, including the Children of God. But like most works on COG, his data belongs to the early phases of the movement. Works like those of Deborah Davis (1984) and Ruth Gordon (1988) contain more recent information, but they are written by disillusioned ex-COG members and are excessively colored by their negative stance against the movement.

The History of The Family

The story of the origin of The Family has been amply recorded. Probably one of the better accounts is Ellwood's (1973). Though his section on the movement is limited to one short chapter (pp. 97-111), Ellwood contributes to the understanding of its emergence by placing it within the commune tradition and in the context of the Jesus Movement of the mid-1960's.[8] He also states that "there is no way that Children of God can be evaluated except on religious grounds" (p. 111). In what way and to what degree the Christian fundamentalist background of the Children of God contributes to our understanding of the movement today are not easy questions. This initial stage is so different from various later developments that the historian many experience some difficulty in pinpointing the constant elements that might characterize the movement.

The scholar intent on writing a history of The Family/COG faces innumerable problems, largely because the movement seems to be in continual flux. Wallis (1985, p. 36) states that "understanding the Children of God is a demanding enterprise which defeats all but the most tenacious." He himself had the determination and persistence to attempt the first outline of the movement's early historical stages. In an overview of the "natural history" of COG (Wallis 1976, pp. 823-825), Wallis distinguished four stages in the early period of COG's history:

1. *COG as a prophetic gathering.* This first stage started with the foundation of the Teens for Christ and included the wandering unsettled period till the settlement in Texas (1968 till the end of 1969).

2. *The New Nation and Subsistence Communitarianism.* This period covered the commune's settlement at the Texas Soul Clinic under Jordan's patronage. The group maintained it opposition to established religion and

society ("The System") and adopted a religious stance not much different from Christian fundamentalism. COG was structured after the tribes of Israel and the gypsies. This period lasted for about 2 years (1970-1971).

3. *Evangelical millennialism.* Following their ejection from the Texas ranch, a phase of dispersion followed. Small colonies were founded throughout North America and Europe. Through increased evangelization the number of recruits grew. It was also during this period (1971-1972) that the movement experienced the beginnings of negative reactions from anticult groups.

4 *Colportage and routine proselytization.* The next phase (1973-1974) saw the movement stress the need to raise money and to distribute literature on a large scale. Wallis labels this period as one of "functional rationality."

A different kind of fourfold division of the movement's history is given by Davis and Richardson (1976, pp. 322-327), who describe 1) the early days of the movement, 2) the period when David Berg[9] began to direct his followers through correspondence (the "MO Letters"), 3) the time when the Children of God moved out of the United States and started forming colonies in Europe and Latin America, and finally 4) the leadership crisis in 1975. Like that of Wallis, this outline is dated, and is not clear about what factors contributed to the continuity of the movement.

Another endeavor to outline the history of COG has been made by Pritchett (1985, ix-xxix). He begins with the traveling ministry of Berg's parents and concludes with the period in the early 1980's after COG went underground. He detects five formative stages in COG's development, namely: 1) "Search for a Ministry;" 2) "Ministry to the Drug Culture;" 3) "The COG's Radicalism;" 4) "Hostility Towards the System;" 5) "Withdrawal of the COG;" and 6) the "Turning Point," during which period the "deamplification of the group's deviance began" (xxvi).

Pritchett traces COG's evolution in some detail. He specifies the kind of movement that prevailed in each of the last five phases. He examines five main ingredients, namely, 1) authority, 2) doctrine, 3) structure, 4) external relations, and 5) societal control, and tries to demonstrate how these changed over the time span of about 15 years.

The most elaborate outline of COG's history has been formulated by Van Zandt (1991) who, claiming to be following Wallis's scheme (1976), traced the movement's origin and evolution through 12 distinct stages:

1. *The Charismatic Background: David Berg and His Family.* (pre-1968 period.)

2. *Huntington Beach: 1968 through April 1969.*

3. *Road Travel: April 1969 through February 1970.*

4. *Texas Soul Clinic and Skid Row: February 1970 through October 1971.*
5. *Worldwide Expansion: October 1971 through February 1973.*
6. *Litnessing: February 1973 through 1975.*
7. *The New Revolution: February 1975 through May 1976.*
8. *Flirty Fishing: May 1976 through December 1977.*
9. *The Reorganization Nationalization Revolution: January 1978 through January 1979.*
10. *The Nationalize Re-organize Security-wise Revolution: January 1979 through April 1980.*
11. *Consolidation and Migration: May 1980 through April 1981.*
12. *The Fellowship Revolution: April 1981 through April 1982.*

In a postscript to his monograph Van Zandt has attempted to update the history of The Family, not, however, in the same detailed manner as his outline of the first 15 years of its existence. According to him, two major areas in which The Family has changed are its organization and some of its practices, especially the sexual ones. By 1985 Berg used his influence to increase the sales from the distribution of cassette tapes and COG literature. He also adopted a more defined authority structure with the appointment of one area leader whose sole task was to supervise, direct, and intervene in all aspects of communal life. Teen Training Camps were introduced in the mid-1980's, reflecting the Family's need to educate its children.[10] While flirty fishing, whereby the female members (and, in some experimental cases, males) try to attract men (women) to the movement by offering them sexual favors, is now no longer practiced, The Family still maintains that "sex is one of God's gift and that it should not be denied to those who are capable of enjoying it" (Van Zandt 1991, p. 170).

These attempts to write a history of the early phases of The Family, though incomplete, indicate that the movement's belief system, organizational structure, and lifestyle had not been institutionalized. Because The Family has now emerged from its period of seclusion, it has embarked on a new phase during which it might have to rethink its external relations and remodel its internal structures. Judging from the troubles with civil authorities that The Family has had in the last couple of years, the societal response may remain negative and belligerent. And this might, in turn, determine The Family's future developments.

This incomplete history of COG supports the view that it is a viable organization that has adapted to both internal needs and external reactions. While outlining the stages of development that the movement has gone through might contribute to our understanding of its vitality and persistence, one must stress that the four outlines sketched above are academic constructs and therefore, to some degree, artificial. We have only recently begun to obtain accurate information about the way The Family understands its own transitions. Its members distinguish at least three major phases in their development, phases that correspond to the three names by which the organization has been known.[11] The first stage is that of the "Children of God" which lasted till early 1978. The second is that of the "Family of Love." Members point out that COG "was disbanded in 1978 when our founder, Father David, who had retired from administrative functions some years earlier to concentrate on his writing, discovered the mismanagement that was going on within the group. At this time he promptly dismissed the leadership and dissolved the organization. Those who so desired continued to follow the writings of Father David, and established a new group." The third phase, that of "The Family," came into being in 1987. It adopted different methods of operation and abandoned some controversial missionary tactics (especially flirty fishing).

There is little detailed information, however, about the way members of The Family explain the many changes in their movement. It is possible that, because the innovations were initiated by David Berg himself, they are seen as part of a continuous revelatory process. But many questions remain unanswered. Does The Family have a theology of its own history? And how do the members who have experienced the changes interpret them? Does The Family represent the final stage? And can it be said that the movement is becoming an "established" religious sect?

Understanding the Children of God/The Family

A study of the societal reaction to the Children of God reveals, if nothing else, how hard it is to understand their behavior which at times goes counter to the established social and religious mores. Their sexual practices, the prophetic role of their leader, and fluctuating organizational structure require some explanation.

Christian sources have tended to concentrate on the Children of God's belief system and moral practices, all of which are contrasted to, and judged in the light of, what is deemed to be the orthodox Christian position (Martin 1980; Sparks 1977). While some of the moral and theological appraisals of the COG may be correct, they offer us no theories about its emergence, success, and continued presence after a quarter of a century. Moreover they do not provide theoretical tools for understanding the worldview of the movement and seeing its beliefs and practices as a consistent effort to articulate and put into practice a religious lifestyle. It is easy, though academically not justifiable or productive, to dismiss the changing nature of Berg's revelations and his unique reformulation of Christian sexuality as either the results of a psychologically disturbed personality or as an expression of a bizarre and marginal religious and social group that is doomed to extinction.

Ethnographic Research

The first step in understanding The Family must certainly consist in gathering correct information. Much of the data at our disposal is based on interviews with its members, short visits to its communal dwellings, and reports by exmembers. Although such information is not to be disparaged, it must be emphasized that participant observation for a lengthy period of time is needed. There is only one published ethnographic work on The Family (Van Zandt 1991) based on this kind of intensive anthropological method (see Jorgensen 1989).

Van Zandt's research consisted of two brief phases: 1) a short three-week period of covert participation (May 15 to June 5, 1976), during which he actually joined COG and feigned membership, and 2) a two-month spell of overt participation (from late June to late August 1977) when, while living in a communal house, his research intentions were known to the group. Leaving aside the ethical issues involved in covert participation,[12] his work represents a model for gathering accurate information. And even though he spent a relatively short time living with the Children of God, his efforts stand in sharp contrast to earlier researchers who had relied on short visits to COG communes, intensive interviews with members, and content analysis of COG literature. One cannot overemphasize the importance of Van Zandt's anthropological method, even though it can be very taxing, to say the least (Van Zandt 1991, p.178).

Of particular interest is Van Zandt's meticulous descriptions of the witnessing and litnessing (i.e., the distribution of literature) procedures of the members of The Family, descriptions which could not have been made without his active participation in the group. Van Zandt's lengthy narrative of The Family's recruiting tactics helps us understand the evangelization methods of COG, which he sees primarily as a kind of (religious) proclamation. COG members believe that litnessing is efficacious in declaring God's word.[13] It, therefore, cannot be viewed simply as a form of routine proselytization (Van Zandt 1991, p. 28), as Wallis (1976) held. Even more important was Van Zandt's examination of the members' attitude to witnessing and litnessing and eventual discovery that they did not always like the long hours spent approaching strangers, passing out COG literature, and trying to elicit a religious response from their contacts. They even found excuses to procrastinate and hence to spend less time on the road (1991, pp. 156-158). Because he was able to observe members in different activities, Van Zandt was able to conclude that the zombie-like, hypnotized or drugged appearance of COG members was the result of the intense interactive posture adopted by members only while witnessing or litnessing. It was a temporary assumed behavior that was not employed in their other activities (p. 93). The socialization process, though certainly confining, did not "produce COG automatons who are without dissatisfactions or who always 'embrace' their membership in the family" (p. 156). Like members of many religious groups, COG members had their doubts and at times required special reinforcement from their leaders and confreres. It is not surprizing to learn that many members voluntary defected from the movement.

It would be difficult to find descriptions of the COG as thorough and enlightening as those of Van Zandt. Works like those of Ward (1972), Enroth et al (1972), Cohen (1975), McBeth (1977), and Oosterwal (1979) definitely supply us with interesting and accurate accounts of the early phases of the movement, but cannot be compared to the painstaking work of Van Zandt. Some additional material has been provided by Kvideland (1979a, 1979b) who studied the movement in Bergen, Norway. Kvideland (1979b) explores the various kinds of symbols employed by the Children of God and speculates on their religious functions. He carefully explains (Kvideland 1979a, pp. 167 ff.) COG's general view of the Bible and how its members interpret and use Biblical texts.

Sociological Interpretations

If Van Zandt's study stands as a paragon of ethnography, Wallis's research is a paradigm for sociological analysis. Two main areas have been the subject of Wallis's speculations: 1) the charismatic nature of Berg's leadership and 2) COG's sexual practices.

The rise of charismatic leaders, who elicit the undivided devotion and sacrificial dedication of their followers, has been of special interest to sociologists ever since Max Weber (1968). Wallis (1982b) argues that the development of charisma takes place in an interactional context. Berg's charisma grew out of his relationship with his family members and followers and needed constant reinforcement and reaffirmation. Wallis is intrigued by the fact that the Children of God have undergone, over a period of under two decades, frequent and substantial modifications in both their ideology and life style (Wallis 1982a, p. 77). He suggests that the rapidity and extent of these changes, the frequent turnover of leadership, the constant ambiguity regarding what is the correct belief and practice, and the indifference to the failure of so many of Berg's prophesies to materialize, can all be explained by the concept of charisma (Wallis 1982a, p. 106).

David Berg can be seen as an exemplar of the charismatic leader who succeeds in keeping his movement from becoming institutionalized. This is achieved by focusing all attention, not on the organization he founded, but on his authoritative revelations. Thus, for instance, Wallis asserts (1982a, p. 114) that Berg allows democratic decision-making only if it "fully accords with his wishes."

The issue discussed by Wallis is why hasn't Berg's charisma become institutionalized; in other words, why is it that, since charisma is inherently unstable, his movement hasn't become a stable organization that will secure its future even after the death of its founder? Wallis's theory is that Berg has responded to the institutionalization process by resisting it (1982a, p. 120). This he did by such techniques as changing the leadership, refusing to organize his revelations into a fixed ideology and lifestyle, and ousting those members who were not prepared to follow his unpredictable behavior. These tactics helped confirm those who remained convinced that his charisma and prophethood were God-given qualities. Berg's apparently erratic behavior reinforced his hold on the movement and his claim to be God's prophet. In Wallis's opinion (1982a, p. 135), Berg was successful because he "had the foreknowledge of the process [of institutionalization] and the means of forestalling it." And, again according to Wallis, Berg clung consistently to several fundamental elements, particularly the belief that the apocalypse was imminent and the urgency to bear witness to the coming end. The fluidity and mobility of the movement were in harmony with its primary goals and did not demand a fixed organization or institution.

Wallis (1977, 1979, 1986) has also spent some time analyzing the sexual practices of The Family. He observes that some of them are neither new nor alien to the Christian tradition (Wallis 1977, p. 14) and shows how Berg justified these practices, including "flirty fishing," on biblical grounds.[14] In COG's ideology sex and marriage are subordinated to the communal goal of evangelization. Sexual behavior is an expression of love shown to those (insiders and/or outsiders) in need. Sexual liberty, especially flirty fishing, is a kind of sacrifice and "is seen as appropriate only in *special* cases, where God's work can be effectively carried out in no other way" (Wallis 1977, p. 14). Richardson and Davis (1983) corroborate this by pointing out that flirty fishing is based on serious motivations. COG members describe it as a kind of "secret weapon" (p. 409) employed to attract male members to the movement. They think it is a test of their commitment (p. 419). Wright (1987, p. 15) supports the same view since he thinks that sexual pluralism has the function "of securing primary loyalties by diffusing emotional bonds throughout the group." COG's sexual practices create "group cohesiveness by eliminating 'private twosomes' when they compete with commitment to the movement."

In typical sociological fashion Wallis examines COG's practices regarding sex and marriage in the context of the traditional mores in the West. Western customs, he claims (1979, pp. 81-83), are not without economic, social, and psychic costs. COG has developed various structural and motivational factors that diminish the burdens of conventional practices regarding sex and marriage. Their communal nature lessens the economic and household burdens of the monogamous relationship. Wallis (1979, p. 89) sums it up as follows:

> [T]he structure and ideology of the Children of God have facilitated innovation in the sexual and marital life of its members, and in their mode of witnessing to the world beyond. The communal style of life inhibits the development of conjugal economic dependency. The diffuse character of relationships inhibits conjugal emotional dependency. Commitment to a belief in sharing, meeting the needs of all members, and placing God's work above all else, inhibits personal possessiveness and exclusiveness.

One might add that a comparison of COG with monastic institutions in Christianity and Buddhism might throw some light on the way the Children of God understand sex and marriage. Members of traditional monastic institutions have sacrificed sexual relationships for perceived higher goals, namely, the spiritual advancement of the monk and the preaching of the Gospel or the teaching of the dhamma. The monastic lifestyle, even though considered a sacrifice, has its own economic, social, intellectual, and psychological advantages. Its ideology and benefits have contributed to its continued survival. Rather than giving up or limiting sexual relationships, The Family has bestowed upon them a new theological interpretation, which not only justifies their practice but also extends them to areas generally prohibited in Christianity. Both the suppression of sexual desires and the extension of sexual relationships are perceived as sacrifices necessary to achieve higher goals.

The explanation of the sexual mores of the Family does not lie in the supposed pathology of its founder, but rather in the situation in which new religions grow (Wallis 1986, p. 125). In the case of the COG, Wallis sees it as a world-rejecting new religion, led by a charismatic personality who criticizes traditional institutions and resists the institutionalization of his own movement. Change, instigated by David

Berg, becomes a way of life dependent exclusively on himself. It also enables him to eliminate his own constraints and inhibitions, thereby opening the way to more atavistic and antisocial behavior. Hostility to the world creates and/or intensifies anxiety, fear, and paranoia, thus leading to violence[15] or sexual behavior which runs counter to established social and religious mores.

The sexual behavior of the members of the Family raises the much-debated contemporary issue of the role of women in contemporary society. Cohen (1975, p. 38) has no doubt that as a rule "women in COG communities hold extremely inferior roles, and perhaps because of this there seem to be far less women than men." Wangerin's (1984b) evaluation, however, appears to be less negative. She sees the early stages of COG as a form of patriarchal tribalism. Mothers enjoyed social security and, as in the tradition of Pentecostalism, enjoyed leadership roles. Because the movement eliminated the dichotomy between virgin and whore, all women

> were considered both sexy and motherly ('sexy madonnas,' so to speak), sex was a pleasurable gift of God, and virginity was irrelevant. This *was* women's sexual liberation for many converts from Fundamentalist denominations and from Roman Catholicism. And for many women who had already experienced so-called sexual freedom, COG's way of life was liberation from loveless sex (pp. 136-137).

Another area examined by Davis and Richardson (1976) is the way the movement is organized. Admitting that any analysis in this field must be provisional, these two scholars enumerate eight major levels (pp. 328-329) from the local district to the King's Counsellorship. They portray the decision-making process, the rules that govern organizational growth, the types of colonies according to the different tasks they are assigned to fulfill, the way individual colonies are structured, and the management of their finances (pp. 330-335). Davis and Richardson disagree with Wallis because they think that the process of the routinization of charisma had already started by the mid-1970's. In describing the decision-making process, they observe that Berg's power has been limited (p. 329). They seem to think that, by the mid-1970's, the movement was on the way of becoming an established Christian sect:

> It is probably too early to predict the result of these changes, but we expect that conflict areas among the Children of God, the churches and the community will be lessened, perhaps from a clarification of the role of COG (p. 338).

Such a prediction has not materialized. Although, since the early 1990's the members of The Family appear to have settled down into stable communities with a relatively consistent and permanent set of beliefs and practices, it is not certain whether and to what degree will their efforts to improve their relationship with Christian churches and society be successful. None of these above-mentioned writers provide much information about the way the children are educated in the Family. Because of high birth-rate in the movement, it is possible that the growth in its numbers does not reflect great success in their evangelization methods. The socialization process to which young members are subjected was studied by Wangerin (1984a) who maintained that the strict methods employed were taken from the conservative religious tradition. COG educators adopted, with some modifications, the Montessori method with the goal of inculcating obedience and preparing the children to make an economic contribution when they were still young.

Wangerin (1984a) also suggests that the leaders of COG reproduced themselves as a class society in miniature. She explains (p. 5177) that by so doing

> they were able to marry and have large families. Opportunities for leaders came at the expense of the unmarried followers, who contributed cash and labor to support the leaders' families. Marriage for leaders depended on celibacy for disciples, particularly since birth control was taboo. When the Children of God became more democratic and sexually free, the leaders and the parents of large families were forced to find other means of support.

Scholars are especially indebted to Stuart Wright (Wright 1983, 1984, 1986, 1987, 1988; Wright and Piper 1986) for the study of defectors from the Children of God. Wright argues that voluntary defectors have not been psychologically harmed by their membership in the new religion. Rather, most of them have assimilated their experiences constructively. Little evidence was found to support the brainwashing theory of cult formation (Wright 1987, p. 93-98). Wright argues (1984, p. 181) that the highly regulated environment in which the Children of God live did not destroy free will. He further explains in some detail (Wright 1987, pp. 25ff.) how various factors, such as social insulation, dyadic relationships, belief in the imminence of transformation, primary group affectivity, and leadership, influence the defection process. And he identifies (pp. 67 ff.) the concrete steps that are taken by members to disengage themselves from a new religious movement.

The Future of The Family

Recent efforts[16] by the Family to reestablish relationships with the outside world, to publicize its formal statement of belief, to defend itself against the attacks of its detractors, and to achieve the status of a respectable religious entity are all indications that the movement is entering a new phase. It might be too early to predict, however, that the process of its institutionalization has begun in earnest.

Wallis (1987, pp. 84-89) has argued that the conditions of those world-rejecting movements, like The Family, that came into being in the 1960's are precarious because, among other things, their constituency is disappearing. He observes that the Children of God were more radically world-rejecting in their earliest phases of existence. Whether this is a sign that their movement is now in the stage of institutionalization is not easy to determine.   There might be some indications that the routinization of charisma may have already started.   One report by an exmember (Lynch 1990, p. 20, footnote 9) claims that Moses Berg, who "is believed to be living in Brazil," is nearly incapacitated by old age and ill health.   Once their founder is incapacitated or dies, the followers must, if their movement is to survive, redefine themselves and their mission.

The Children of God have been, and still are, one of the more controversial of the new religious movements. Much of the antagonism they have aroused over the years has been largely due to their sexual practices. Recent accusations have also revolved around alleged sexual customs with youngsters. It appears that their views regarding sex remain radical, in spite of the facts that 1) they have formally abolished the custom of flirty fishing and 2) they explicitly discourage sex among children and between adults and children.[17] In a recent (1993) four-page publication entitled "Overview of Our Beliefs and Practices as Expressed in Our 'Statements,'" The Family reasserts its belief in the "Law of Love," which implies "that loving heterosexual relationships between consenting adult members—whether they are married or single—are perfectly acceptable in the eyes of God." In the same "Overview" child abuse is strongly disavowed. "Sexual conduct between an adult and anyone under the age of 21 is strictly forbidden."[18] However, reports by hostile ex-members (a problematic information source) do not confirm this wholesome picture. Whether The Family can now change its negative image is debatable. Melton states (1992, p. 230):

> The sexual manipulation in the Children of God has now been so thoroughly documented that it is doubtful whether the organization can

ever, in spite of whatever future reforms it might initiate, regain any respectable place in the larger religious community.

The Family has indeed already begun the process of painting a more wholesome image of its views on sex, especially among children. Whether these efforts will succeed depends to a large degree on their charismatic leadership and/or on whether the movement can make the transition from a wandering, unstable "cult" to an established sect.

John A. Saliba is a Jesuit priest and professor of sociology at the University of Detroit Mercy. He has published extensively in the field of new religious movements, including several definitive bibliographic surveys of social scientific publications on alternative religions.

Chapter 15

The Children of God, Family of Love, The Family[1]

David Millikan

I. Examining The Family

Unlike many isolated fundamentalist groups, The Family has been active in writing and explaining their beliefs to the world outside. They have an extraordinary quantity of printed literature, videos and audio tapes. There are a number of levels at which one gains access to this material. Like the Mormons and the Masons, there are beliefs held by The Family which have been hidden from the world outside. This teaching is contained in the DO ("Disciples Only") literature. Normally this is kept from people who are not members or who are considered babes in the faith. They believe that some teaching requires a certain level of "faith" to understand or accept, and a person who does not have "the faith for" a particular teaching should not be exposed to it. They see this approach to be biblically justified. The New Testament makes a distinction between teaching that is appropriate for mature believers and those who are "babes." Hebrews 5:13-14 says: "For every one that useth milk is unskilful in the word of righteousness: for he is a babe. But strong meat belongeth to them that are of full age, even those who by reason of use have their senses exercised to discern both good and evil." Again in 1 Corinthians 2:13-15 it reads: "This is what we speak not in words taught us by human wisdom but in words taught by the Spirit, expressing spiritual truths in spiritual words. The man without the Spirit does not accept the things that come from the Spirit of God, for they are foolishness to him and he cannot understand them, because they are spiritually discerned." Those outside The Family and outside of a relationship with Christ are referred to as "Flatlanders." They have the expectation that Flatlanders[2] could not accept or understand many of the things that are contained in the DO literature.

In the past they have maintained a high level of secrecy about their DO literature. Elaborate security measures have been put in place to protect it from outside scrutiny. But in the last three years this has changed. First they have seen much of their DO literature fall into the hands of people who do not have their best interests at heart. Some of this has found its way into the Press and much of it has been quoted and examined in various courts around the world. They have also formed the view that the veil of secrecy which was drawn over this literature has encouraged in the minds of many people an erroneous view of its salacious or deviant character. A policy decision was taken to open the movement as much as is practical to the scrutiny of those who come to them with reasonable intentions. This has been my experience. This is a new atmosphere for many people within The Family but it is one which they all seem to welcome. All of the leaders of The Family that I have met have mentioned to me how much they enjoy the opportunity of being able to communicate their history and beliefs openly.

It is impossible to understand the world of The Family without this level of literature. I requested access to all DO literature and, following a delay of several days during which permission was sought from World Services (the administrative branch of The Family, responsible for publications, communications and statistics, often referrred to as "W.S."), the permission was given and I have had access to everything I have asked for and more.

I have also been in a position where I have been able to record conversations with a broad range of Family members. Some are people who have joined as recently as the last year. Most have been long-term members, including several who where present at the beginnings of the movement in the late sixties. These audio recordings constitute an invaluable and unique opportunity to gain insight into the life and thinking of this group. At the point of writing this report, I have thirty five hours of audio recordings. I also have 140 pages of handwritten notes.

I had the opportunity in November, 1992, to travel to a number of the homes of The Family around the world. ("Home" is the Family term for the communal residence of full-time members. Depending on the facilities, the population of Homes can vary from as few as 12 members, including children, to "Combos" of 100 or more.) I visited a total of 12 homes in Japan, Thailand, India, Russia and England. This occurred during a four-week period. I understand this is the first time a person from the outside such as myself has been given access to the inner life of The Family at this level. It was an access which I requested as the basis for writing this present report. Three of the homes I visited in Britain were in Hampstead, London, the West Country, and Midlands. During these visits I was given unsupervised access to members of The Family at all levels. I was able to have private conversations with teenage children, YA's (Young Adults)[3] and many of the adults. These conversations were either recorded or I was able to take extensive notes.

I have been able to talk with several people within The Family who are known as key thinkers of the movement. This included an exchange of correspondence with David Berg. I have met Peter Amsterdam (who is Berg's executive secretary) on two occasions. These were 2-day sessions devoted almost entirely to the discussion of theology. I have recently begun a fascinating correspondence with Apollos who is regarded (with good reason) as the theologian of the Family (apart from Father David) and I have met Davidito and had the opportunity to talk to him about *The Story of Davidito*.

When reading the literature it is necessary to know its status and what response is expected to it from the people within the group. A number of considerations need to be taken into account when assessing the normative significance of any piece of literature. There are levels of importance depending on when it was written, under what circumstances, and who inspired it. It is not uncommon within the group for literature which was considered normative to be thrown away on the basis of a further revelation from David Berg. This is the situation for example with *The Story of Davidito*. Following the call to remove the book, some 6 years ago, there are only three copies left in Australia (I have one). There appear to be none in the UK. So when examining literature from the group, before one can say that it has authority within the group now, the following questions must be asked:

1. What is the date? Literature which is later may take precedence. That is especially true of matters which are contentious.

2. Who wrote it? There are a number of authors. Berg is the first in authority. But even his writing has different levels of significance. At the lowest level there are recordings made of children's stories and other domestic matters. It then ranges through to the highest level which would be David Berg talking "in tongues." This occurs on occasions when he is under inspiration from Abrahim, or one of the "Spirit helpers." There are also occasions when Berg has dreams which he uses as a means of revelation from God.

There are statements which emerge from the Council headed by his wife, Maria—these tend to deal with practical and ethical matters. They have become more assertive in the last few years, and have authority in setting the manner of the group's behaviour.

There is a central theological reason why it is imperative to remember the date of all literature from The Family before assuming it defines the present character of the group. The Family sees "revelation" as a dynamic thing that changes with time. They are upholders of the concept of "progressive revelation"; i.e. the belief that God did not reveal his mind once and for all, but in part according to the demands of the situation. Some things written in the past can be superseded or "explained" by new insights given in the present. So God has been systematically handing out more and more information about His plans and thoughts throughout history, culminating in His revelations contained in the MO Letters. But even they are subject to the limitations of history.

> God has given His people the basic information that they needed from the very beginning. Then He's given more and more as history went on . . . . He began to tell the Prophets what was going to happen. And then when Jesus came, with His Apostles and the Early Church, He really gave more details. All the time God has been giving more information and more details needed by Man! ("The Word, The Word, The Word!" ML# 2484, *DB8*, p.404.)

David Berg believes he and all Christians have been given the gift of various Spirit Helpers. These are not angels. Rather, they are the departed spirits of people who have been faithful believers in this life. It is a belief not dissimilar to the Roman Catholic attitude to the Saints. He understands that they have a role in Heaven giving them certain powers to become involved in the affairs of this life. The way in which they work is through providing information or insight. Berg has been visited by a number of Spirit Helpers, especially in the early years of the Family. Abrahim became a permanent companion for a number of years, but seems to have appeared less frequently in Family literature since the middle '80s. The following quote from "The Fight Is On!", Letter number 2885, written August 1993, shows that Abrahim is still present:

> So who is going to fight? (Dad bursts out in tongues and weeping:) "How many times do I have to tell you, it's David thy father!" Thank You Lord! God bless Abrahim, he's got some fight! He's been fighting for centuries! He was a martyr. He fought and they wiped him out, along with his whole tribe—men, women, children, babies, everything. The Turks were the Antichrist system of the day.

When he first arrived in 1969, Abrahim could not speak English and it was necessary for Berg to provide translations. Eventually he came to speak directly through Berg. In the midst of a talk Berg will sometimes suddenly break into a message in "tongues," followed by the interpretation. This is the sign that he has been taken over by one of God's messengers.

David Berg uses the term "talking in tongues," but he does so in a way which differs from its use within contemporary Christian churches. The phrase is not unfamiliar to the Pentecostal and Charismatic arms of contemporary Christianity where it refers to the phenomena of Glossolalia. This is an ecstatic utterance in a strange tongue under the influence of the Holy Spirit. It is seen as one of the Charisms or gifts associated with the presence of the Holy Spirit in the life of the Church. David Berg uses the phrase to refer to the state in which he and others are overtaken by one of the Heavenly Helpers to the point that the Spirit Being actually overcomes the person and speaks through them. It is a state which is similar to what is known today as Channelling. "God lets another spirit speak through you in another language, the native tongue of your particular individual guiding spirit who is assigned to you personally." (*DB1*,p.78, 1/74) David Berg talks of a special relationship he has with the figure Abrahim. But he also mentions David (the Old Testament King of the Jews), Ivan (a Russian man), and Moses. It is the presence of the Spirit Helpers and their authority which gives authority to David Berg himself. He points out that his words sometimes have the "sound of God himself" because he is talking in tongues through someone even higher and closer to God than Abrahim and Moses. This is Abrahim's "angelic overseer." "I believe he is the one who speaks like the very Voice of God in some of the revelations I've had . . ." (*DB1*, p.79, 1/74.)

There are numerous occasions in the literature where the individual households are encouraged to judge the truth of the MO Letters on the basis of their own contact with the Bible and their own understanding.

It is their view that they are expected to judge the truth of the things that are sent to them. This is a firmly held belief within the group, although it must be said that there are certain things they cannot challenge. I know of a number of instances in the last three years where Family members have successfully opposed matters of strategy when dealing with local situations. They did this and it was accepted. It is also regarded as a remarkable event. But there is a sense in which the Family is able to engage in an elementary form of discussion within their ranks on matters of doctrine. Their own literature contains the following statement:

> Just because some idea is openly discussed in print within our movement, it does not in any way mean that it becomes, or is even intended to become, standard practice, or indeed is ever practised by any of our membership (Our Replies to Allegations of Child Abuse, June '92).[4]

This is an unusually open attitude to the right of personal judgment. Some people argue that this is a ruse to disguise the true call for total obedience demanded within the life of the group. Indeed, it can be argued that The Family have hidden the true nature of their beliefs from the outside world. So it is not always easy to know what a statement like this means. I am certain it expresses the intention of The Family. My conversations with Family members convinces me that they believe they have freedom to make their own assessments of David Berg's writings. But they also live with a belief that gives them no expectation that David Berg could ever lead them astray. What is unusual is the fact that these calls for personal evaluation even appear in The Family literature. Given the diverse nature of the group and the tenuous contacts between the central point of authority and the individual households, it expresses an unusual openness. Certainly it holds out the right to question, which is rarely present in more restrictive groups.

The most contentious literature emerges from the Family of Love era when the sexual freedoms associated with Flirty Fishing ("FFing," pronounced "eff-eff-ing") and Sharing were introduced. Sharing is practiced widely to this day, but Flirty Fishing is not, and was not universally practiced even during the main years between 1977 and 1984. The literature of this period was full of demands to see FFing as a test of loyalty. There were, nevertheless, acceptable reasons within the group for not participating in FFing. It is also common in all religious groups to perceive a gap between what the leadership or the literature calls for and the way in which lay people respond. For example, the Roman Catholic church has not changed in its teaching that contraception is a sin—in fact, recent words from the Holy Father reinforce the teaching of the church on this matter. But most Catholic couples in Western countries do not refrain from contraception. The fact that they do not practice the Church's teaching on this matter does not diminish their sense that they are still "Good Catholics."

In the same way in The Family, we need to know if the literature on FFing is normative. Was there freedom not to accept it? Was there a pattern of people not obeying it, and did they have a view of David Berg's writings which gave them the freedom to make judgments about what was "essential" and what was the product of his iconoclastic and provocative character?

I spent considerable time talking with members about their experiences during the Family of Love and Flirty Fishing era. Most saw Berg's teaching on FFing to be mandatory. Some women became the key FFers and others proved unsuccessful. Some women were not sufficiently attractive or lacked the right personality and social skills. A significant number of women were almost constantly pregnant during this era, and there were other ways of evangelism which were pioneered during this time. There was a considerable geographical difference in the way it was applied. It was not particularly successful in many parts of Asia, whereas Hong Kong was regarded as a successful FFing scene. In some areas and for a limited period, FFing fell into ESing. This was the use of Escort Agencies. It was a logical extension of many of the principles of FFing, but it did not last long. There were some in leadership in some homes who insisted on FFing with greater enthusiasm than others. There were a large number of members who went into bars and other places and allowed a style of contact which was open and flirting, but they refused to advance to the point of sexual intercourse. I have talked with others who did "go all the way." There is no question that most of the contacts which occurred with outsiders as a result of FFing did not result in sexual contact. There were a number of conditions which had to be in place before it was deemed appropriate to proceed to sexual intercourse. So it is reasonable to say that FFing was most characteristically a shared glass of beer or orange juice in an "up market" bar or hotel and did not normally end in sexual relationships. Many in The Family talk about the exaggerated and shocking style of David Berg's letters and say that he is a man who is iconoclastic by inclination and his letters should not be read as literal statements of what must be.

A. Ex-members:

Conversation with ex-members is essential to forming a comprehensive view of The Family. But when talking with ex-members, one needs to understand the pressures and expectations with which they live. It is characteristic of people who remove themselves from the rigours of life in a group like The Family that they leave with a complex mix of emotions. It is my experience that most people do not leave such groups because they have come to the realisation that the world they are in is aberrant or their beliefs a sort of madness. They usually leave because of disillusionment with their own capacity to maintain the purity of commitment and belief required by group membership. Even with those who become fierce opponents of the group after leaving, there remains a sense of nostalgia and acceptance of the group's basic tenets. They may now be consumed by anger and frustration and try to bring the leadership of the group down, but they tend to still hold the beliefs of the group to be admirable.

Many ex-members find life in the world outside the group difficult. They have lived for many years in a highly structured, communal life style. There is a certain security and protection from many of the frustrations of life. Outside The Family they are thrown into an uncertain world in which the entire responsibility for their employment, the care and education of their children, their housing and continuing spiritual life are now their own. This often occurs at a time when they are struggling with self doubts and uncertainties about matters which have to do with their fundamental belief system. If this situation is complicated by a sense of grievance following frustrated leadership aspirations or personal conflicts within the group, then they can become prey to certain groups which have a vested interest in seeing the group to which they belonged brought down.

Discussion of membership of strongly authoritarian religious groups, be they a monastic order or a group such as The Family, takes us to the difference between the way of freedom and the way of law in religious belief. It is part of the universal debate in all belief systems. Family Membership is a way of order and precision in all things having to do with faith. The life of the believer is ordered and circumscribed. This is a way which offers the security of rule and law where the choices have the promise of precision and clarity. The price of this security is the loss of a certain personal freedom. But it is a choice that many people are prepared, even anxious, to make, not only in religious faith but in politics, education and many other areas of life. On the other hand, there is the way of freedom which is a decision for individuality and personal choice. But this is a way which requires that we live with ambiguity and uncertainty. For those stepping from one system to another, it can be a profoundly disturbing experience.

There is no question that all groups that demand the degree of loyalty The Family does will be surrounded by individuals, families, and anti-cult groups which believe the very existence of the group is an evil. This is true of strongly authoritarian Charismatic churches and groups like Sahaja Yoga and Scientology, The Moonies, or the Exclusive Brethren and so on. It is my view that many of the advocates of the "Brainwashing" or "Mind Control" theory of sect membership find their most enthusiastic supporters in ex-members who may not be in a position to judge truly the situation they are in.

It is inevitable that people stepping away from a group like The Family will experience periods of disorientation and frustration, and, at times, even deep psychological unease. For many of the people who leave The Family there exists a structure which allows them to maintain contact with the group while still operating in the world. This level of affiliation is called TRF (pronounced "turf") Supporters or TSers. ("TRF" is an acronym for Tither's Report Form, which is a monthly activities' log and statistical report filled out by all D.O. and T.S. Homes.) This is a recent development within The Family. Most highly authoritative groups view ex-members with disdain and suspicion. This was the case 8 years ago in the Family, but the situation has changed. There is a realisation that ex-members are an important half-way house for some of the young adults and others in The Family who want to look at the world outside at closer quarters. The TSers have also proved to be an important source of financial support, especially in situations where legal expenses have been excessive. But there are some who leave and remain distressed for many years. They find their greatest difficulty is in coming to terms with the sense of disorientation. This is often accommodated in a simplistic statement from "exit counsellors" and others who introduce them to the concept of Brainwashing. It can become for some an uncomplicated explanation of why they feel the way they do. It accounts for their difficulties but it does not necessarily adequately describe what actually happened. I raise this issue because I approach the view of ex-members that say they were brainwashed with a certain caution.

B. Is sect membership the refuge of the weak and easily led?

One popular response of outsiders to the rigours and eccentricities of life in a group like The Family is that the people who join are by nature weak and easily lead. This has not been my experience. It is also tempting to look to psychology for a set of definable characteristics that describe the susceptible "sect" person. This has been attempted in the past, where it has been assumed there is some defective aspect to a person's character which makes them prey to the control of people like David Berg and others. Such an assumption does not survive the test of experience. The discussion of this matter in the psychological and sociological literature has been silent in the last ten years. There is too much diversity in the backgrounds of the people who join and remain happily within groups such as The Family.

The early attempts of the social sciences to account for the phenomenon of "sect" membership has floundered on a lack of precision. I do not believe it possible to say that there is a "typical sect type of person." Nor can we say that members of these groups are weaker or more damaged than the norm. Indeed, it is my experience that they tend to be people who are strong and who have a higher than normal expectation of what the life of faith is meant to be about. They are people who are prepared to sacrifice their comfort and security in the pursuit of an ideal. They are prepared to step away from the norm. It is my experience in dealing with families that have one of a number of children who have joined a group like The Family that the one who joined was usually the strongest and most serious minded of the children. Eileen Barker observes: "Those who join New Religious Movements are by no means always, or even usually, the pathetic, weak or susceptible characters that is sometimes assumed they must be."[5] Indeed, it takes a certain strength and conviction to join The Family. It is a heady experience to become part of the group. The disciples and their children are encouraged in the belief that they are at the very forefront of the battle for the life of this world. It is their conviction that their membership in The Family gives them a place of extraordinary privilege once Christ returns. These are people who have been willing to give their money and talents to a cause they believe to be an expression of the very mind of God. Membership in the group has given them a sense of identity and meaning which they would recover only with the greatest difficulty if they left. It is for this reason that leaving such a group can be so difficult, and why it is not uncommon for people to be filled with bitterness and anger for reasons which have more to do with their own sense of loss and dislocation.

C. Cult and Sect:

There is considerable discussion about the use of words like "cult" and "sect" in relation to groups like The Family. It is important to state clearly what these terms mean and how they should be used. The term "cult" has become overloaded by sensationalist reports in the media to the point that it is a difficult word to use. Most academics interested in this field prefer to use the term "New Religious Movement." It is my opinion that there are some groups whose life is so aberrant and destructive that they move beyond the realms of what is acceptable in human society. Such a group I would call a "cult." I do not, however, believe The Family fits this description. I have had close contact with several cults, including one which led to the publication of my study *Imperfect Company: Power and Control in an Australian Christian Cult,* William Heinemann, 1991.

D. Is The Family Christian?

In matters of doctrine, The Family's theology is a mix of apocalypticism, evangelical southern American Protestantism, and universalism. They see themselves as Christian and hold the basic doctrines of Christianity without question. They believe in the Triune nature of God—God the Father, God the Son, God the Holy Spirit. Although in the expression of that teaching they suffer the difficulties of all Christian exposition which tend between Tri-theism (i.e. the idea that there are in fact three Gods) and Modalism (which sees God as one person in three modes). Their tendency is towards the later.

Much of the attention of the world outside the Family is directed to their teachings on Sexuality. But the theological concepts which do most to influence their life are those associated with eschatology. At the heart of Berg's vision, and indeed his greatest theological passion, are his revelations concerning the end of the world. This more than any other aspect of Berg's theology, including his current views about sexuality, defines the character of The Family. They believe the world is about to end. Most of the Family members I have spoken with about the subject believe it will take place within the next six or seven years, although there is the beginnings of a difference of opinion in the last eighteen months. I have encountered a number of people, especially in upper leadership, who prefer to talk about the "possibility" of the end occurring within seven years.

The Family believe this end will occur over a series of stages including a terrible time of persecution on earth known in the Bible as the "Great Tribulation" (Matthew 24:21), the Second Coming of Jesus Christ and the Rapture of the saved (Matthew 24:29-31), the awesome Wrath of God which culminates in the Battle of Armageddon (Revelation chapters 15-16), followed by the 1,000-year rule and reign of Christ on Earth, known as the "Millennium" (Revelation 20:1-6), which ends with the cataclysmic Battle of Gog and Magog (Revelation 20:6-10), and eventually the end of all punishment in Hell and the restoration of all—or nearly all—souls into a heavenly existence either inside the Heavenly City or on the recreated New Earth.

They believe that the heart of the Christian message has to do with the need for salvation in Jesus Christ. Outside of this relationship, they do not allow that there is any salvation. And yet, unlike many fundamentalists, Berg is a universalist. He believes that people who never heard the Gospel in this life are not condemned, but are given a chance to receive it in the next life. He believes that even many of those condemned to Hell will finally be released in time, to live outside the Heavenly City on the paradisiacal New Earth described in Revelation, chapters 21 and 22. But Berg is not a strict universalist. There are some who will never know salvation.

> I think I'm getting more and more to where I don't know whether you could ever rehabilitate or convert some of those guys, like the Devil and the Antichrist, the False Prophet, Hitler and some of the worst characters in history and the cruellest tyrants and whatnot. I'm beginning to be a little doubtful as to whether there's any hope for some of those guys, they've just gone too far! They can be thankful they're just going to be annihilated and they don't have to be tormented forever. They're going to have been tormented for quite awhile, the Thousand Years of the Millennium and some things like that, so after the Great White Throne Judgement it looks to me like the best thing to do is get rid of the whole bunch that can't be rehabilitated! ("Judah on Pearly Gate & the Doctrine of Annihilation!" D.O. 2142, 02/85, *Vol. 17*, p. 71.)

The Family has a literal view of the Devil or Satan. They see him as a formidable and frightening figure utterly devoted to the destruction of God's Plan and all who follow Him. The Devil is a fallen angel who is in an unrelenting struggle against God, and is assisted in his activities by a force of lesser spirits like demons and souls of people who have died in a state of rebellion against Christ. The Family is conscious that the time is short and they are shortly to enter into the Tribulation. This is a 3-1/2 year period when the constraints against the Devil and his Antichrist are removed and evil will expand in ways that are unimaginable to us now, followed by the Rapture and Second Coming of Christ.

There is a paradox in The Family's view about the role of Satan in this world. It has to do with the freedom which Satan has to harass and disturb the faithful. One of the dilemmas which all Christians face is reconciling the omnipotence of God with the power of Satan. It is one of the most difficult theological questions. Why is evil and Satan in the world if God is loving and all powerful? It is a problem which theology has been unable to solve without falling into intolerable paradox. The two extremes which are considered unacceptable to Christian theology are the way of Dualism and the way of Theodicy. Both attempt to preserve the righteousness of God. Dualism possesses the solution that there are in fact two entities in the universe, separate from each other and locked in a deadly battle for supremacy. Theodicy argues that this assigns to evil a status which rivals God and necessarily suggests that there was a principle for evil in eternity prior to the creation of the world. Theodicy's solution is to state that evil is an invention of God— that Satan is God's creation. This is the option that Berg has taken.

> Don't forget, the Devil's working for the Lord too! Didn't you ever think about that? He's God's little devil and demon and imp and chore boy to whack us around with God's permission when we get out of line! But otherwise he doesn't have a right to put a finger on us. ("God's in Control!—Nothing can happen without His permission!" DO 2084, 12/85, *DB3*, p. 158.)

This position does of course raise some tortuous dilemmas. On the one hand this position has the advantage of protecting the sovereignty of God. But it ultimately makes God responsible for all the evil we see in the world. The barbarism of this century, including such events as the Holocaust are caught up in the larger plan that God has to teach the world about sin and bring all people to salvation. Berg does not shrink from this conclusion. They make much of the verse in Isaiah "I form the light, and create darkness: I make peace, and create evil: I the Lord do all these things." (Isaiah 45:7) It means that Satan is an instrument of God. The evil things that happen on the earth are not random acts of venom from Satan, they are often God allowing Satan to bring disaster or misery on people so that they will understand what is at stake in this world. "God allows these things to happen!"[6] Berg is saying that evil means one thing in the hands of Satan but is transformed when used by God. The acts may be the same but they take on a different meaning when you see who is behind them. Even the death of someone in a terrible famine may be an act of mercy, for God would know that they were better off in the next life. God does not actually have anything to do with the evil—but he has control of the one who is the source of evil. So although Satan fights to free himself from God's authority, he is being used. God will allow him to bring suffering on people who deserve punishment. So Satan becomes an instrument of justice. On many occasions God will allow people to be killed. "When they get to the point where they're possibly suffering *beyond* endurance, He releases them and takes them into a better world where they're relieved of all this pain and agony and poverty and suffering and starvation and sickness . . . all of it caused by sin of *some* kind."[7] And again: "Therefore great disasters that sweep thousands of lives into the next are undoubtedly in some way good for the people involved. Those who die go right into a life where they'll certainly be taught what's right and wrong."[8] So death is not the end of the line for salvation. Many possibilities lie beyond the grave.

God lets Satan loose in the world for another reason. The havoc which Satan inevitably brings into the lives of those who are prepared to entertain him is a warning to others. It shows the world that God is not to be treated lightly. There is a feeling abroad which is even entertained by some Christians that God is a gentle character who will accept everybody no matter what they have done. This is definitely not the case and it needs the occasional demonstration of God's power to let people know who God is and the way he deals with the World. The riots, fires, and earthquakes in Los Angeles over the last four years is such a warning. God is clearly angry with the city. This provides a way for explaining disasters in one's life. If you are in the midst of a divorce, you become sick, your daughter is killed in a car accident, and within a matter of months you are broke, the first question The Family will want to ask is, "Why?" They would want to know where the problems were coming from. It is entirely possible that they are from God, who has been trying to say something to you for some time but you have not been listening. He has been "spanking" you with minor upsets to your life. But now this is what it has come to. He has had to do all this to bring you to a relationship of obedience and yieldedness in Him. This has been part of Berg's theology from the beginning: "God loves to chastise you! He loves to chasten you! He enjoys spanking you, in a way. Why? Because He watches it bring out the *best* in you!"[9] Spankings always appear in your life as moments of disturbance or suffering. It is what Berg calls God's "intolerable compliment." He quotes the verse, "Whom the Lord loveth, He chasteneth, and scourgeth every son whom He receiveth" (Hebrews 12:6).

It means that this life is lived in the midst of a very dangerous situation: "This is more or less his [the Devil's] territory, his domain. He said; 'it's all given to me and I can give it to whoever I want to.' (Luke 4:6)"[10] Berg often talks about the earth as "dangerous territory," and there is little to comfort in the midst of this. And it must be said that he is among good company when he takes this position. It was the view, perhaps not stated with quite the same bluntness, of the great Church father, Augustine. But it could not be said to be a position that has many advocates in contemporary theology.

On the question of the person of Jesus Christ, they are essentially orthodox. They believe Him to be the Son of God, and Saviour of the world. "Jesus is God, in a way, part of God, part of the Trinity or a part of the oneness of God, the same way we're one Family, where husband and wife are one but they're different personalities" (*MOP* 65. p.540). And what Berg says about salvation through Christ has the ring of orthodoxy about it:

Question: What makes Jesus' teachings different than any of the other great teachers like Mohammed and Buddha? — Mary.

Answer: The difference was that though they all *talk* about love, He *was* Love and He was *God*, so He really knew what He was talking about! Not only that, He was the only One that died for the sins of the World and rose from the dead! So you can't even class Him along with other teachers. He's in a class all by Himself. They may have taught similar doctrines, similar teachings, but nobody taught like Jesus. He taught with authority, He really knew what He was talking about. Because He's the only *Saviour:* "I am the Way, the Truth and the Life! No man cometh unto the Father but by *Me!*" (John 14:6.)"[11]

They understand the atonement in orthodox terms, in that they emphasise the vicarious character of Christ's death as a propitiation for the sins of all mankind. But there is also a strong theme within their writings which elevates the exemplary aspect of Christ's death. As "Love" is the ethical reference point within the life of the group, they look to Christ as the model in this respect. As one of the thinkers of The Family put it to me: "The highest expression of love is the sacrifice of Jesus on the Cross for the sins of all mankind." They believe salvation is achieved when a person invites Christ to come into their lives. This is done through the simple act of praying to Jesus and asking Him to come in. It is one of the distinctive aspects of the their belief that they place great significance on this act of prayer. Even if there is little outward sign of repentance or change in life style, or even if a person cannot say that they experienced anything of any significance following the moment of asking Jesus to come into their hearts, they regard that act as the dividing line between those who "know the Lord" and those who do not. This is what separates a person from being saved and not being saved. It is this act which takes a person from the reign of darkness to the reign of light. When The Family records in their statistics the number of "souls" they have won, this is what they are talking about. They further emphasise the decisive nature of this act by saying that it is eternal in its effects. They follow the school of thought which says, "once saved always saved." They do not follow the equivocal position that one can be saved and later lose that salvation. They believe that there are many "worldly" Christians in the world.

The distinction between different degrees of Christians is taken into the next life. The Family believe that God will divide Heaven into many classes and hierarchies. The level at which one will live in the after life is determined by the sort of reward God gives when you die. The Christians alive now are likely to see the return of Christ, and they will be raptured to the Marriage Feast of the Lamb. This feast will last for

70 days while God lets his anger loose on the unsaved and the followers of Satan who remain on Earth. At the Feast, God hands out the gifts and rewards He has in store for all who come to heaven. There will be a great ceremony, during which each person present will go before the judgment seat of Jesus. They will not be asked if they are saved—that has already been established. They will be asked to account for the quality of their lives after they have been saved. The nature of the reward will depend on the way in which the person has worked: "We can *earn* special *praise* and special *commendation* from the Lord . . . He says some He will make rulers over one city, some over a few cities, and some over many cities . . . so your works have a great deal to do with your *reward,* a great deal to do with the way you *shine* and a great deal to do with your *position* once you're there."[12] This is a powerful inducement to good behaviour in the Family, for no one wants to be down the ranks when it comes to ruling in the Millennium. It is also a way of providing The Family with a promise of justice. The Family has sacrificed much in their pursuit of the right life with Jesus. They are well aware of the sacrifices they have made in the cause of the Gospel. There have been many occasions when they have been under enormous pressure to concede to the demands of the world outside. They have given up any of the career aspirations which are the normal lot of people outside. The women particularly have borne a heavy burden within the family—they have had large numbers of children—been subject to their husbands—been called on to meet the sexual needs of brothers (and, in the early days, women) within The Family, and many of them gave themselves to the sexual desires of men outside the movement. They need to know that there is a reward for this commitment. It would seem a cruel injustice if they were to arrive at the Marriage Feast of the Lamb and discover that the lukewarm Christians they have often despised from the mainline churches are treated on equal terms. Berg will have none of that. He repeatedly reassures his people that in heaven they should be at the top of the pile. As for the rest of the Christians, especially those who have not really tried to do the right thing on earth, some of them will be in trouble: "Some are going to have to bear everlasting shame and contempt because they didn't do their job and they weren't faithful and they lived selfishly."[13] The distinctions based on the quality of one's life in this world are severe. And the levels of reward offered in Heaven operates as a powerful inducement to obedience in this life. Berg offers a number of Biblical passages as the basis for this belief, a key one being Daniel 12:2,3:

And many of them that sleep in the dust of the earth shall awake, some to everlasting life, and some to shame and everlasting contempt. And they that be wise shall shine as the brightness of the firmament; and they that turn many to righteousness as the stars for ever and ever.

To encourage his followers to be faithful witnesses, Mark 8:38 is quoted, where Jesus said, "Whosoever therefore shall be ashamed of Me and of My Words in this adulterous and sinful generation; of him also shall the Son of Man be ashamed, when He cometh in the glory of His Father with the holy angels."

Berg seems quite unconcerned that he is introducing an element into heaven that compromises its perfection. He talks about some people scraping in with such sorry records from this life that they will have to hide away from God. They could be stuck in the basements of heaven shining shoes like the poor of this earth because they will be unable to bear God's sorrow and anger at them. In the absence of an eternal hell it appears to me that Berg has created a division of heaven which amounts to the same thing. To live in Heaven, "yet be *ashamed* of yourself forever . . . that's almost as bad as having to go to *Hell*."[14] Of course for The Family, the warning in these words is palpable. It is the murmurers, those who are disobedient and unyielded who will be put away in the basements.

The Rich Young Ruler in the Gospel stories is a good example of the sort of person who is not going to do well in Heaven. He came to Jesus full of expectation that he would find from Jesus an easy way of salving his troubled spirit. But when Jesus told him to make the sacrifice and sell all that he had and follow him, he went away sorrowful. He respected Jesus, he came to him as a teacher and even called him Lord, but in the end he was not prepared to pay the price. That is what Berg wrote to me. He told me I was like the rich young ruler: I was not prepared to go all the way and put aside my attachments to this world. He challenged me to throw caution to the winds and join him—if I did not, I was choosing the easy way and I must assume that what awaits me in Heaven is a lowly place, perhaps not too far from the basement.

If asking Jesus into one's life is the beginning of salvation, they emphasise another act, which is the receiving of the Holy Spirit. They say that the Holy Spirit is "part of our salvation," but they allow that there may be many Christians who are saved but have not achieved the full benefits of that salvation. That begins only at the point one receives the Holy Spirit. This may occur at the same time as receiving Jesus into one's heart, but it normally occurs later. There are many people who are saved but do not know the "Baptism of the Spirit." This is a term well known to Charismatic Christians, and there is a considerable body of theological literature on the matter.

Berg uses the term "Baptism of the Holy Spirit" to describe the moment when the dynamic or power of salvation comes to reality in a person's life. The Spirit is not entirely absent from the original act of salvation. On that occasion there is a "measure" of the Spirit. That is necessary to awaken the person to their need for salvation in Christ, and gives a sense of assurance that it has been achieved. But the subsequent "Baptism of the Spirit" is the arrival of the Spirit in full measure into the life of the Christian. This is what provides the active force and the psychological dimensions of salvation, and renders the work of Christ effective in the life of the believer. Berg talks about the Gifts of the Spirit as a set of capacities or powers which are delivered as a sort of package by the Holy Spirit or one of his helpers after a person gives their life to Jesus. Some people receive some of the gifts of the spirit. Some get none. (See 1 Corinthians 12:4-11.) It is extremely rare for anyone to receive all the gifts of the Spirit. Berg talks about his own introduction to the gifts. It occurred when he was still working full time with his mother on the evangelistic circuit, when he was 19. He says he was fundamentally changed at this point. Up till then he had the habit of reading anything he could lay his hands on. After this he read only the Bible and devoted himself only to the study of God and His plan for this world and the next. At this time Berg says he only received *some* of the gifts. The others came later.

The first evidence of the Spirit's presence was his loss of shyness. He immediately became bold in telling others about Jesus Christ. But he claims a lot more happened at this moment. "I had the gifts of discernment, wisdom, knowledge and faith ever since I got the baptism of the Holy Spirit when I was 19."[15] It was not until he grew older that he received the remaining gifts of the spirit. He goes through the list: *Wisdom*: "I know that God gave me that gift a long time ago." *Miracles*: "I have seen **some** miracles that the Lord has wrought through me." *Prophecy*: "I did not have prophecy until after I received the special anointing of the Lord when the Jesus Revolution began." *Tongues*: Some years later with the coming of Abrahim. Then came "unusual *Faith* and *Knowledge*" which he defines as knowing certain things "supernaturally"; he claims to have this. *Discerning of Spirits*: "That I think I've had almost since I was a little boy."[16]

It is a formidable collection of gifts which, not surprisingly, has given him a firm view of his status. He has made many allusions to the implications of his receiving such attention from God. One of the famous MO Letters written about the Holy Spirit and gifts is *Holy Ghosts*.

During the recording of this letter, he talked about the way in which the spirit of tongues operates within him. While he was delivering the letter he suddenly stopped his talk and broke into a series of unintelligible sounds directed to Maria. She naturally asked him what he had just said. Berg become coy and said he was unable to say. He said he was unable to speak because of the enormity of what he had just been told in tongues. She pressed until he finally answered: "Forgive me for my pride, Lord, the gift of pride sure isn't from You! I don't like to tell some of these things, because then it gives me too much responsibility and then I'm afraid I'm going to have to live up to it! The Lord just said: 'Behold, who has greater wisdom than the wisdom of the ages that I have given unto thee through My gifts of the Spirit? (Maria: Praise the Lord, that's right)."[17] For further reinforcement, he adds another scripture the Lord gave him several nights earlier, "Behold a greater than Solomon, is here!" (Luke 11:31.)

Along with a number of Feminist theologians today, David Berg argues that the Holy Spirit is the female aspect of God. "We talk about the Holy Spirit *wooing* us, so that means the Holy Spirit makes *love* to us. Let's face it!—She stoops to make love to *all* of us just like *Jesus* did and like God does!" (*DB1*. p.414. DFO 1304. 10/82.) The drawings and cartoons of the Holy Spirit present in The Family literature all portray the Third Person of the Trinity as a young, beautiful, and sexually rich woman.

The point at which Berg tends towards Modalism in his theology is where he talks of the Holy Spirit as an "expression" of God or as the effulgence of God's personality. He also sees the "Baptism of the Spirit" as something that is not exclusive to the Holy Spirit. He does not allow that the Baptism can occur without the Holy Spirit, rather he sees it as the occasion that other Godly spirits as well can be involved.

> *The so-called baptism of the Spirit* is therefore not only the baptism of *the* Holy Spirit, but a sudden yielding and surrender to *one* of these holy spirits of God. So along with *the* Spirit of God, we receive specific spirits who have these specific gifts. How about that? ("Holy Ghosts—More Holy Ghosts!—The Spirit World!" *DB1*, p.78, GP 620-622, 27/1/74.)

The Family has a distinctive understanding of the purpose of the Baptism of the Holy Spirit. It is first of all a power to witness. It is the task of the Holy Spirit to produce within a person an attitude of boldness, and dynamism in the area of witnessing. The literature of The Family abounds with stories of people who talk about their lives before and after the Baptism of the Spirit. The most important difference is

always the capacity to witness. The singular example of this is David
Berg himself:

> *I was very shy when I was young extremely shy.* I was one of those little
> children that when a stranger comes to the door he runs and hides behind
> mother and holds onto her skirt . . . . *It wasn't till I was 19, when I was
> filled with the Spirit, that I lost the fear and the shyness* and all just overnight
> like that, just the Lord! I was anointed with such power of the Spirit, I
> really didn't care what *anybody* thought then. I just socked it to them!
> (*DB1*, p.23 1, DFO 1032, 9/8/76.)

II. Early History

The late sixties saw the emergence of an extraordinary range of
religious groups in America and England. Many of these groups
flourished for a season within what was known as the "Jesus Revolution."
These groups saw themselves as radical Christians whose goal was to
break free from the jaded conservatism of the Western Churches. In this
they saw themselves as being in the tradition of the Anabaptists,
Moravians, the early Methodists, and other reform movements present
within Christianity from the beginning. Most took as their model the
New Testament accounts of the early Christian Church. The features
which most attracted the Jesus Revolution were:

— The fact that the early church held a common purse and distributed the
wealth of the community evenly amongst all members.
— There was a sense of focus and total commitment to the cause of faith in
Christ.
— They lived in the imminent expectation of the return of Christ.
— There was a sense of urgency in the way in which they aggressively
evangelised the world around them.

Other groups grew around the teachings of charismatic figures from
the East, like Bhaktivedanta Swami Prabhupada whose devotees became
established as the Hare Krishnas. They offered a decisive break from
what they believed to be the discredited traditions of Christianity and
strove for religious meaning through renunciation of the world and the
flesh and a single-minded devotion to Lord Krishna. Other groups grew
from a belief that the way to truth lay in a union of the two visions; in,
for example, the teachings of the Unification Church (Moonies). Others
believed the way forward lay in putting religion on a quasi-"scientific"
base, such as in the visions of L. Ron Hubbard. The Children of God
was formed in the same time of ferment, and, like the Moonies, had a
continuous, powerful leadership which has enabled them to survive. Like
the others, they too are undergoing a significant metamorphosis.

The Family began to be given shape in the late sixties by David Berg. Berg is a child of fundamentalist, evangelical, millennialist, southern American Protestantism. He was born in February 1919. His parents were both active as preachers and pastors in the small denomination, The Christian and Missionary Alliance. This same denomination has a number of churches in Australia, and some 10 years ago established a theological college in Canberra. Although this is a somewhat isolationist denomination, in recent years they have worked hard to become part of, and have been accepted into, the theological debate in Australia. Berg and The Family have no links with the denomination now, although he was ordained by the denomination around 1947-8.

In 1944, Berg married Jane Miller, who is known within the group as "Mother Eve." She remains in good standing with the group. He had four children: Linda, known as Deborah, and Paul, known as Aaron, Jonathan, known as Hosea, and Faith. Linda left The Family following a major controversy, and has since written a scathing book published by Zondervan in the USA.[18]

From 1948 until 1951 Berg pastored a poor Christian and Missionary Alliance church in Valley Farms, Arizona. From 1951-1953 he taught at a Christian secondary school in Los Angeles. During the next 12 years he worked closely with Fred Jordan in the "Church in the Home" television programme and Jordan's American Soul Clinic school of evangelism. By 1967, he had left Jordan, and along with his wife and four teens, travelled over 10,000 miles evangelising, and took the name "Teens for Christ." They moved to Southern California and took over the activities of a Teen Challenge drop-in Christian coffee shop at Huntington Beach where their numbers quickly expanded to over 50. He had taken on the style and many of the attitudes of the hippies and street people amongst whom he moved. They lived with little financial support and began to develop the skills of "provisioning" which is still a feature of the group's life.

Between 1969 and 1972, the group began a period of wandering. They saw this in religious terms as an experience similar to the wanderings of the Children of Israel in the wilderness described in the early books of the Old Testament. Berg and a flock which had grown to over 100 followers moved around the United States and Canada in a caravan of camper vans. The move was made in circumstances which became a common feature of the group. They had begun to attract unfavourable press, following a series of public demonstrations in which they condemned the evils of American society and stated a prophecy that an earthquake was about to devastate Los Angeles. During 1972, large numbers of the Children of God began to move out of America set up homes in other countries. They moved into Europe, England, and Asia. Some forty moved into Australia and set up homes in Sydney, Melbourne, Hobart, Adelaide, and Brisbane. They were driven by a firm conviction that the end was near for America. The average age of those coming to England was 21 years. Some of them sought citizenship in the countries to which they had travelled. By 1975, the movement had shifted its centre from America to England, where the headquarters was based in London.

III. Some Distinctive Aspects of The Family Theology

The theology of The Family is practical rather than philosophical or speculative in the classical sense, so one does not encounter extended discussions of the theological issues raised by what David Berg is saying. His writings tend to be extended, even rambling and imprecise expositions of matters which have to do with the activities and organization of The Family's colonies and homes. They do not see themselves as being in dialogue with the contemporary theological scene, and make no attempt to participate in any of the scholarly journals or forums. In fact, it would be true to say that like many fundamentalist groups before him, Berg regards the theological community as populated by arrogant, self-opinionated people who are more concerned about ideas than they are about the practical business of spreading the Word of God to people outside. He shares the views of many fundamentalist Christians this century that the academic theological world has been wooed by "modernist" theories and attitudes which are sceptical of the simple truths of the Gospel. This was certainly the view of his mother, Virginia, who I believe has been influential in forming many of the views that Berg holds. The result has been that Berg has a dismissive and sceptical view of most branches of academia, especially those which impinge in his area of knowledge.

The movement which David Berg formed in 1968 has undergone some convulsive changes. The Reorganisation, Nationalisation Revolution (RNR) of January, 1978, dissolved the entire management structure of the movement in the midst of the early years of FFing. Since then, there have been other moves which have seen dramatic (if less convulsive) changes, but the principles of Berg's theological vision have remained constant. The central ideas of his vision are these:

A. Eschatology:

David Berg took the millennialist beliefs popular in American fundamentalist Christianity with radical seriousness. There is little, if anything, that is original in his vision. He has done little to advance the descriptions of the Antichrist put foreword by Lactantius in the fourth century and the best selling Brother Adso's *Letter on the Origin and Time of the Antichrist*, written in about 915 A.D. David Berg and the members of the group believe that they will witness the great events which will see the end of the world. What they believe in this matter is of great significance to the way in which they behave in the present.

Berg believes that the Bible can be read as a virtual text book of the events leading up to the end of the world. He has arrived at a way of interpreting the strange prophecies and visions of Daniel and Revelations which he sees as spelling out in detail the rise of Russia, the birth place of the Antichrist, the location of the battle of Armageddon, and the date at which these events will occur. These same verses which Berg interprets as prophecies directed at this present age have been the source of similar speculations in the life of the Church from the very beginning. But Berg believes that he has been called as the last in the line of God's prophets. What he is saying is this: "Everything's going just like the Bible predicted and we've explained to you: It'll all eventually erupt into the Atomic War, from the chaos of which will arise the A.C. [Antichrist] who will temporarily sign a *compromise* with the Jews, Arabs, and Christians to neutralise Jerusalem and let the Jews rebuild their Temple. (Daniel 9:27a) When he has everything under control 3 1/2 years later, he'll break the Covenant, declare himself god, set up his *image* in the Temple area, try to force everyone to worship him, and try to kill all who won't, thereby bringing on the *Great Tribulation,* ended 3 1/2 years later by the *Second Coming of Christ* and Rapture of the Saved, Wrath of God on Earth, and *Marriage Feast* of Christians with Jesus in the Heavenly City above! (Daniel 9:27b; 11:30-31; Matthew 24:15-31; Revelation 15-19.) Then we return with him to conquer and rule the earth for 1000 years of Heaven on Earth like the Garden of Eden, with worldwide peace, no more wars for 1000 years, Satan and his forces bound, the curse removed and *Paradise Regained!* (Revelation 20.)"[19]

The major events of the end times will center on the Middle East. The Antichrist is said to be a man who was born in the middle east and is presently making his way towards his goal of world domination. Most of The Family members I talked to believe the Antichrist will come from among the Jews. At first he will appear to be an attractive person who is able to bring some order into international affairs. This will occur at a time when people will have become so disillusioned with the degeneration in world affairs that they will gratefully look to him as an antidote to the chaos. He will set up his headquarters in Jerusalem where he will work relentlessly to create reconciliation between the warring factions of the world, including the world religions. For the first time in history, all the major world religions will recognise his authority and unite under him in one form of worship, based on the Temple in Jerusalem. "For a while it will seem to be absolutely heaven on earth . . ." (*The Book of the Future*, 01/84, p. 55.) There will be a large number of Christians who will be fooled by his early appearance. They will think that he is a man of God. Because the Antichrist will encourage the Jews to begin again the sacrifice of animals in the Temple, there will be many who will see him as the Messiah. In fact, it will be the Jews who make the first move to proclaim him as divine.

The Antichrist, along with his right-hand man, the False Prophet, will have the power to do miraculous things. He will cause disturbances in the natural order and he will be able to heal people of sickness. (Revelation 13:3, 13, 14.) But after 3 1/2 years, he will suddenly change. God will pull off the restraints which have kept him in check and evil will be let loose: "like a dam being opened or removed a *flood* of *iniquity* is going to circle the World under the reign of the Devil himself in the person of the Antichrist."[20] At this stage the relationship between the Antichrist and the devil will undergo a decisive change. The distance between them will collapse and Satan will come to possess the Antichrist until he will be the Devil himself. In effect the Devil will incarnate within the person of the Antichrist. (Revelation 13:2.)

Once the true colours of the Antichrist are revealed he will set about the task of bringing the world under his control. To achieve this end he will use the most sophisticated applications of modern technology. In particular, Berg has described a central super computer that will differ from other computers in one fundamental respect—it will have a soul, given to it by the Devil: "I'm convinced that the super computer will actually be *demonically inspired* to where it actually *does* have *demon intelligence*, . . . it will be a real *wonder,* and will really be *worshipped!*"[21] With this computer and other sophisticated devices the Antichrist will take charge of people's lives. He will enforce a financial system which uses an identification number that everyone will have branded on or implanted under their skin. Family members are convinced that the world is rapidly being prepared to receive the "mark of the beast" foretold in Revelation chapter 13, verses 14-18:

> And he [the Antichrist's false prophet] deceiveth them that dwell on the earth by the means of those miracles which he had power to do in the sight of the beast; saying to them that dwell on the earth, that they should make an image to the beast. . . . And he had power to give *life* unto the image of the beast, that the image of the beast should both speak, and cause that as many as would not worship the image of the beast should be killed. And

he causeth all, both small and great, rich and poor, free and bond, to receive a *mark* in their right hand, or in their foreheads: And *that no man might buy or sell, save he that had the mark,* or the *name* of the beast, or the *number* of his name. Here is wisdom. Let him that hath understanding count the number of the beast: for it is the number of a man; and his number is *Six hundred threescore and six* [666].

The mark of the beast is one of the most feared dimensions of the end time. The Family believe this will be achieved through the implementation of a computer chip either in the hand or forehead.

Following the trends of the moment, it will become a cashless society: "Men will no longer buy or sell with money as a means of exchange, but with a number, a number which will be given to them *permanently,* without any possibility of counterfeit, change, manipulation or forgery, because it will be branded on each person."[22] This will occur either on the right hand or the forehead. This will be the instrument of his control, and with this in place no one will escape his scrutiny. The Family are very concerned at the use of bar codes and the growth of a cashless financial order. They are alert to the recent moves in agriculture to inject animals with miniature plastic tags with identification numbers placed permanently under the skin. They oppose these moves not only for the civil liberties implications, but because they see it as part of the inexorable progress of the Antichrist. They are alarmed that our societies seem so unaware that they are actually aiding and abetting the progress of the Antichrist by delivering the most powerful tools into his hands.

The control that Satan will exercise over the world through the Antichrist will almost be total. There is a verse in Revelations which Berg reads to indicate that this control will extend to war and victories over the saints: "and it was given unto him to make war with the saints, and *overcome* them . . ." (Revelation 13:5). But these victories will not be decisive: "[He] . . . will be allowed to overcome us *physically,* obviously destroying the organised *temporal* power of the Church, he will not and cannot overcome us *spiritually* . . ."[23] There will, of course, be a great difference between the way in which the Family survives the Tribulation and the mass of Christians in the Churches. The mainline churches will be ill prepared for these events. They will not understand what is happening. They have no stomach for a fight, and in most cases they will simply lie down and refuse to fight back. But the Family will be equipped with the Power of God. They will be given a special measure of the power of the Spirit which will not only protect them, but give them the power to win some victories themselves. "I believe we're going to have a time of greater power even than the early church, greater manifestations, mightier works, mightier witnessing than has *ever* been done before!"[24]

The Tribulation is a time of terrible persecution for Christians. Despite the protection which God will give through the special powers He gives, many of them will succumb to the persecution. "For then shall be great tribulation, such as was not since the beginning of the world to this time, no, nor ever shall be" (Matthew 24:21). "And some of them of understanding shall fall, to try them, and to purge, and to make them white, even to the time of the end" (Daniel 11:35).

It is a sober picture for The Family, and the fortune of The Family is a little ambiguous. Berg is not sure if most of The Family will survive or most of them killed. He is certain that some of them will succumb and be martyred, but in his more pessimistic moments he suspects that a large number of them will be taken. The weight, though, is on the side of optimism: Berg is certain that God will make a special point of protecting them. After all, there must be some reward for the present years of sacrifice, obedience, and discipline. They will, for example, have learnt Scripture by heart in readiness for the day their Bibles and Mo Letters will be taken. They will have leaders who have the spiritual power to draw on the resources of heaven and protect the Family: "Certain very powerful men and women of God, like the ancient prophets and prophetesses of old, are going to be the leaders and have these supernatural miraculous powers to protect and defend their flocks and followers and help them to survive to the very end . . ."[25] Such powers are vividly portrayed in Revelation chapter 11, where some of God's final witnesses against the Antichrist world call down fire from Heaven, smite the earth with plagues, etc. Towards the end when things are at their worst, God will enter the struggle directly by initiating a number of attacks to divert the attention of the Antichrist away from the Christians. God will let loose a range of monsters and plagues that will target the forces of Satan: "They'll have so much on their hands defending themselves from these monsters and these plagues that they won't have much time to persecute you and me!"[26] (See Revelation chapters 8 and 9 for a description of the trumpets of tribulation that sound at this time, summoning plagues, judgements and strange monsters to torment the ungodly followers of the Antichrist.) But in the last few days, the protection of God will be withdrawn even from the Saints. In a period of 3 1/2 days before the return of Christ, "[Satan] will finally be allowed to kill them, that the cup of iniquity of the wicked may be filled!"[27]

During this time the Antichrist will align himself with "10 Kings", with whom he will attack and destroy the mysterious Whore of Babylon, described in Revelation chapters 17 and 18. From the first century until now those interested in apocalypticism have identified the Whore as a wide range of figures. It was seen by some of the early Christians as the Roman Empire; during the Islamic expansion into Europe the Moslem religion was the Whore; in the 16th century the Whore was said by the Protestant churches to be the Roman Catholic church; in our century it has variously been identified with Hitler, Stalin; and the Jehovah's Witnesses again see it as the traditional churches, in particular the Roman Catholics. Berg believes the Whore is epitomized by the international commercial system, centred on the United States: "I am convinced that today's capitalistic commercial system, led of course by America, is the epitome of the Great Whore of Revelation, and is in fact its ultimate fulfilment!"[28] Berg insists that Bible passages such as Revelation 18:3 are fulfilled in the U.S.: "For all nations have drunk of the wine of the wrath of her fornication, and the kings of the earth have committed fornication with her, and the merchants of the earth are waxed rich through the abundance of her delicacies."

During the time after the Rapture, when there will be rewards and feasting in Heaven for the saved, the 15th and 16th chapters of Revelation portray an earth that will feel the full fury of God's anger. Only the unsaved will remain and God's wrath will have no reason for restraint. The Seven Vials of Wrath described in these chapters of Revelation will be let loose. God will send plagues and disasters into the world in the same way He did with the recalcitrant Pharaoh. The first of these vials of wrath will see a sudden spread of terrible suppurating sores on the bodies of those who have accepted the mark of the beast. It will be like skin cancer. Then the sea will turn to blood and the creatures left after the earlier attentions of God, will all be killed. The sea will be left stinking and dead. The third vial will see the rivers and lakes and streams of the world suffer the same fate as the sea. They too will fill with blood so that all life within them will suffocate. There will be no fresh water left to drink, to survive they will have to drink blood. Fourth, God will intensify the heat from the sun seven times. The searing heat will shrivel life so that nothing will be able to move in the open and survive. Fifth will come permanent darkness: "[they will be] . . . left to their sufferings and torments, their tortures and their plagues, licking their sores, drinking blood, scorched with fire and now finally in darkness!—Groping around in such thick darkness they can't even find their way!—How horrible!"[29] The sixth vial of wrath will see the Euphrates river dried up to make way for the kings of the world to gather for the final battle. One has to wonder how anything at all would be possible in a situation where everything was in darkness, there was no water no electricity, no food, and no communications. It is the end of all forms of civilisation: "[It means the] . . . destruction of so-called modern civilization and return to savagery and return to native type living in the wilderness or on the farm."[30] But somehow the forces of the world will respond to the call of Satan and come together in the valley of Jezreel in Israel. This is the site of the Battle of Armageddon.

The seventh vial sees the arrival of Jesus and the warrior saints. They will stream out of Heaven mounted on white horses and dressed in beautiful sparkling white robes. But before they arrive a hail of fire will be poured out of heaven accompanied by thunder and lightening. The final act before the battle will be a devastating global earthquake of such magnitude that all the world cities will be reduced to rubble: "One great final earthquake is going to destroy all the hell-houses of Satanic power called cities, those horrible cancers on the body politic of man, those cesspools of iniquity in which man prides himself—his cities. God's gonna throw them all to the ground!"[31]

The carnage of this event is impossible to imagine. It is a vision of such unrelenting destruction that one has to wonder at the mind that brought it to be. Berg sees these passages from Revelation in literal terms. A Christ-rejecting world is reduced to a hideous inferno of total darkness, populated by people without food or water who are suffering from painful cancerous sores and who are ultimately defenceless against the weapons of war God brings against them. The surface of the earth will pile high with the rotting corpses of the Antichrist's hordes, so God will bring in his "garbage men." Drawing on the images of Ezekiel and John, Berg talks of scavenger birds like vultures and buzzards invited by God to feast off the flesh of the millions of dead. (Ezekiel 39:17-20; Revelation 19:17-18.)

There is a powerful and unmistakable note of apocalyptic retribution in Berg's interpretation of these Biblical visions and prophecies. He looks for vindication and even revenge in the next life, because of the indignities and lack of respect that Christians have suffered in this life. The battle of Armageddon is the moment the Family will be able finally to settle some old scores: ". . . all the enemies we've had, we're going to get our *revenge* in that day. We're going to get vengeance in that day against our enemies! It's going to be a *righteous* vengeance!—They're going to get what they *deserve* and *we're* going to give it to 'm!"[32] Berg defends himself against the charge that he is being uncharitable or unchristian by pointing to the Book of Revelation which tells us that the souls of the Christian martyrs in Heaven cry out for vengeance in a similar manner:

And when He had opened the fifth seal, I saw under the altar the souls of them that were slain for the Word of God, and for the testimony which they held: And they cried with a loud voice, saying, How long, O Lord, holy and true, dost Thou not *judge and avenge our blood* on them that dwell on the earth? (Revelation 6:9-11).

The Battle of Armageddon will be the final and greatest act of carnage before the Millennium. There will be blood flowing from the slaughter over a distance of 200 miles. In some places the blood will rise to a height of a horse's bridle (Revelation 14:20), and the millions of rotting corpses will fill the air with a suffocating putrid stench. Berg quotes from Ezekiel chapter 39, indicating it will take 7 years to dispose of the destroyed weaponry (vs. 9), and that grave diggers will take 7 months to dispose of the corpses (vs. 11-13). By the end they will be putting "little signs or markers" over what remains of the bodies exposed to the hot sun and the vultures. "And the passengers that pass through the land, when any seeth a man's bone, then shall he set up a sign by it, till the buriers have buried it in the valley of Hamongog" (Ezekiel 39:15).

Clearly Satan will be exposed as the instigator of the entire episode. He and his minion the Antichrist will be decisively defeated. A group of them who are the real recalcitrants and haters of God will be thrown into hell and chained to "a bottomless pit" located within the bowels of the earth for 1000 years. (Revelation 20:1-3) During this time he will remain there without influence on the earth. But he is not finished, for in the last years of the Millennium God will once again pull off his constraints and let him loose to stir up the final confrontation at the battle of Gog and Magog. (Revelation 20:7-9) In the meantime, out of the devastation of the Battle of Armageddon, some people will survive. With considerable understatement Berg says of them: "they must be pretty tough or they must live a pretty charmed life . . ." These are the people who Jesus and his helpers are going to rule for the next 1000 years. And this is the time for which The Family waits. It is the reward and the vindication. It happens in the same cities and before the same people who were their detractors and persecutors in the past. Their real spiritual powers will be obvious, and they will rule with authority: "We are going to rule and reign and teach and train, to show how the World *should* have been run and to be an example to the Universe of what kind of government man *could* have had it he had only obeyed the Lord."[33] Again, the Bible is quoted:

And he that overcometh, and keepeth My works unto the end, to him will I give power over the nations: And he shall rule them with a rod of iron;

as the vessels of a potter shall they be broken to shivers: even as I received
of My Father. (Revelation 2:25-26.)

The Millennium is about giving people another chance at salvation.
It is also about justifying God's anger and the annihilation of the
unsaved. If God acts with such fury, there has got to be a
counterbalancing display of his mercy and grace. After the horrors of the
battle of Armageddon, God steps back to show that He still has the best
interests of the world at heart. He draws together the shattered remains
of the earth and gives it a possibility for peace: "The Lord will set up His
kingdom here on Earth for a thousand years to try to salvage what He
can and who He can and give them another chance or perhaps their first
chance . . ."[34] Once again the note of vindication emerges. Berg is angry
at the way he and his people have been treated by the world. He has had
to hide and creep around like a criminal. He has seen The Family
vilified and attacked and abused. And he has been given no respect or
honour in this life. He has been mocked and treated by the world as a
fool and a criminal. The Millennium will finally put that right, and his
tormentors will be forced to respect The Family's authority: "We will no
longer be the poor, persecuted, hounded few of the poor bedevilled sects
or cults or whatever they want to call us . . . we are going to rule the
Earth with Jesus Christ over our God-damned enemies who have
tormented us and persecuted us and hounded us from country to country
throughout the Earth . . . so don't worry, we're going to have a country
to call our own one of these days, thank the Lord!"[35]

The character of life in the Millennium will in many ways be like the
best of what we know now. But there will, of course, be some
fundamental differences. The first will be the change in the bodies of the
saved. They will be given spiritual bodies that will not age or become
sick. (Philippians 3:21.) So The Family and all of the rest who have
been savedthrough the ages will not die. Those who are not saved will
go on as usual, but because the Curse will be lifted from the Earth, like
the Old Testament characters before the flood, they will live for more
than 900 years. But they will still be subject to many of the limitations
which we know in this present life.

The first task in the Millennium is cleaning up the carnage and
wreckage of Armageddon. As mentioned earlier, the prophet Ezekiel
says it will take seven months to bury the dead and seven years to
destroy the instruments of war. It will be a formidable task, but with the
organisational directions from the Lord and the added powers given to
the saints in their supernatural bodies, it will be done and the earth will
be restored to the state of paradise. The eighth chapter of the New

Testament letter to the Romans talks about the expectation with which the Earth waits for the moment of liberation from the effects of sin. It is like a woman in the pains of childbirth, it groans as it waits to be released from the bonds of mortality. The Millennium is when it happens. Berg draws a utopian picture of the whole of nature blossoming in the joy of paradise. The birds will stop singing in a minor key, the animals will all turn to herbivores and people will become vegetarian. This Berg believes was the state of people before the Flood. The removal of sin will mean that the earth will be able to flourish without the evil things like weeds and thistles and thorns and flies. There will be no cars, it is going back to ox and horse power and on the seas there will only be sailing boats. There will be much less disease and for the people who are not saved, life will go on but in more pleasant circumstances. They will marry, have children and go about their business.

The resurrected saved of all ages are going to rule the world with a "rod of iron." There is still some sin left in the world, so they are going to force people to be good. They will have to teach them about the ways of the Lord, and they will be forced to listen and obey. They will initiate sessions in which people will be required to confess their sins and put things right with the world around them. The style of government will be strictly authoritarian: "They will all be *compelled* and *forced* to obey whether they like it or not—Absolutely no democracy, absolutely no freedom of man, or wicked man!—No more wicked democracies with wicked majorities voting for wicked governments and wicked rulers in a wicked world—but a complete totalitarian *dictatorship* of the *righteous* with Jesus Christ as Dictator."[36] Berg clearly relishes the prospect of these years in control for he emphasises over and over the role The Family as the ones who run the show. He has given a description of the sort of powers they will have to allow them to assert their authority. He speculates that it may involve a capacity to immobilise people, or perhaps cause them to go blind: "We'll just *look* at them or *think* or point our finger at them or whatever we want to do! And they won't be able to touch us or do a thing!—*We* will be the power and the government in control!" He also sees some parallels with what he has seen in *Star Trek*: ". . . where they freeze when they point their finger at 'm or they disappear or they wind up in a different place or something— that's actually going to happen, we'll have such powers! That's one reason I enjoy 'Star Trek,' I think that guy was almost inspired!"[37]

It must be emphasised that this is a widely held belief within large sections of Christianity. A number of large theological seminaries, such as Dallas Seminary and Bob Jones University in the United States teach this view of the End Times as standard theology. It is, for example, the generally held view of the largest denomination in the U.S., the Southern Baptists. The Jehovah's Witnesses hold a similar eschatology. There are numerous other groups who would be in complete sympathy with this vision of the End Times. They would differ only in detail.

This matter raises an interesting issue concerning the nature of reward and the doctrine of "works." The literature of The Family is keen to make a distinction between salvation by "grace" and salvation by "works." They make it clear that salvation is not earned, or in anyway contributed to by the actions of mankind. They see it as an act of divine grace, unmerited and undeserved. But they go to some lengths to indicate that there are various levels at which one can enjoy the benefits of salvation. So salvation itself is not at stake, but the level at which it may be enjoyed is. They see support for this in various places in the Bible. The most pointed is Matthew 5:19, which reads, "Anyone who breaks one of the least of these commandments and teaches others to do the same will be called least in the Kingdom of Heaven, but whoever practices and teaches these commands will be called great in the Kingdom of Heaven." The way this is interpreted in The Family is as a series of rewards for righteousness: "The Lord is keeping books on everyone, but it's hard in this life to know who is going to get what."[38] It is hard to avoid the feeling that this view of reward has a salutary effect on the behaviour of Family members.

It must be understood that The Family have a palpable sense of the Millennium and Heaven. These are physical realities in which they will be present in the resurrected body. In fact, in Japan at one of the major training facilities for The Family in the world, Tateyama, there is an elaborate model of the Heavenly City held in a pyramid building on a hill above the training centre. The Family have a self-conscious commitment to the Christian teaching concerning "resurrection of the body." They see Heaven to be a physical "place," indeed a city, somewhere above the earth. Their descriptions of the New Jerusalem, based on St. John's vision in Revelation chapters 21 and 22, have allowed The Family to produce detailed maps, including descriptions of various structures, the layout of streets and the nature of the materials used. It is in the shape of a pyramid 1500 miles high, 1500 miles wide, and covering an area of 2-1/4 million square miles.

B. The Role of Women in The Family:

There is a complex and interesting relationship between men and women in The Family. At one level, the teaching of David Berg is unequivocal in assigning to women a subservient role in relation to men. This is certainly true when it comes to the relationship between husband

and wife. But he also gives to women a high status within the organisation of The Family, and he does not exclude women from any of the spiritual dimensions of The Family's life. In the last few years, his earlier hard stand against women has been modified. This is an example of Berg's earlier views:

> It's part of the Devil's corruption, trying to throw a monkey wrench in God's machinery! God's law was that woman's desire shall be unto her husband (Gen.3:16), and the Devil's been trying to overthrow that ever since, of which Woman's Lib is a classic example. They don't desire to *please* their husbands, they desire to *rule* over them. They don't want equality, they want to *enslave* their husbands and to be the boss! It's rebellion against the plan and order of God. The Devil inspires women to rise up against it and rebel against it and hate it and fight it.[39]

This is a view of the role of women which would be greatly applauded in many fundamentalist churches. It is an attitude not unknown in certain places in the mainline denominations. Certainly many of the opponents of women's ordination would hold the view that women are circumscribed in the way in which they can exercise authority. Although this is a different argument to the role of women within marriage, it is not uncommon to find the opponents of women's ordination holding a view concerning the "headship" of the man in marriage which is similar to that put forward by David Berg. But within The Family the role of women is very much more complex.

The role of women has changed in the life of the Family. In the early years, Berg stated a typically hardline fundamentalist view of women and their relationship with men. In the last few years this has changed, and changed dramatically. The rise in status of Maria, the place of women and their achievements during the FFing period, and the relative success of men within The Family has led to a change in policy. In the early days the position was strongly conservative and unrelenting in it's view that the role of women was circumscribed. "You women are unfathomable! We're not supposed to *understand* you, we're just supposed to *love* you, that's all! *You're* supposed to *understand* us! You were made for us, to understand us, we're not supposed to understand you. Well the Lord helps us though."[40]

The role of women in The Family is complex—within the world of personal relationships with their mates, the woman must recognise that the Bible sets a hierarchy. The man is the head of the household, for that is the way the Bible states it and that is the natural order of things and that is the way Berg treated his first wife and that is the way it operates in The Family. But in all other areas of The Family's life, women have equality and women are represented well through all levels of authority. The Family recognises this, and is proud of their record.

So women step between two worlds when they go from their mates to the larger responsibilities of The Family. The following illustrates what I mean. A woman within the Family had written asking for advice about her relationship with her partner. She was clearly the dominant figure within the life of The Family, but within the relationship with her partner she was being asked to submit to him. This was Berg's summary of her situation: "*Don't either hinder the other! Obey God! Work Together!* Know your limitations! Use all your talents! In the operation of spiritual gifts there is true equality for women! He promised to pour out His Spirit upon His sons and daughters! But when it comes to the operation of sex and the home and the husband/wife relationship, God has made it very clear who's the boss! Only in the physical, material hard labour of some tasks do we recognise the superiority of the man as the stronger one, as well as in the home relationship of husband and wife, although there is equality here also in the Lord."[41]

He repeatedly warns the men not to limit the exercise of spiritual gifts should they appear in the life of their mates. He makes it clear that in the role of wife, the women are required to be submissive. But in the area of spiritual gifts there is no hierarchy. "In the operation of spiritual gifts there is true equality for women . . . But when it comes to the operation of sex and the home and the husband wife relationship, God has made it very clear who is the boss!"[42] This was the way things had worked out for the best in Berg's life before his life in The Family. He recalls the best times of his life with his wife Jane were when things were running according to this order of things. It was in the early days of his marriage, when he was still on the circuit with his mother. He had a job to do, leading the singing, giving his testimony, and occasionally preaching. Jane was supporting him, playing the piano, and at home she knew her place: "That was a very happy time, to be married and have a wife to fuck whenever I wanted to and I loved the babies and the children . . ."[43]

There is a signal example of Berg's teaching on the relationship of women and men in an exchange of letters between him and his son Ho. It occurred in 1980, when various letters were published which dealt with a series of problems that Ho was having. He had been given the job of publishing certain volumes of MO Letters, and he had not done it well. He had also shown signs of a spiritual laxity, which had led to him becoming wooed by the System. Berg chose to blame much of the problem on Esther, Ho's wife, who was spending most of her time away from home and her children, out FFing and socialising excessively. In a stern rebuke, Berg called her "an insipid snob who was a society climber and always wanted to be a star . . . I think she's actually feeble-minded. And anybody that's as weak-minded as she is a channel for the Devil."[44] So as far as Berg is concerned, the problem with Ho is that he has not asserted his role as the authority in the home: "You need to start being a man in your family, Son, and wear the pants and tell her off to either toe the mark or get out! (Ho: Amen, yes Sir!) . . . Now you either get her under your control and get her home there and make her get down on her knees and wash and scrub floors and do the washing and the laundry and the dishes and the cooking and take care of the kids, or GET OUT! (Ho: Amen, yes Sir!) That's the way I feel about it. Do you hear me? (Ho: Yes Sir, yes Sir.) All right. Now you either do that or you're going to be out and I warn you! (Ho: Amen)."[45] It is the sort of talk that will drive feminists into paroxysms of anger: "Now be a man, son and get your pants on and give that woman hell! I mean it! I'm sick and fed up with her . . ."[46]

As it happens, Esther did see the light and returned for a season to take up her proper role within the household: "I've been a real backsliding hypocrite, even worse for pretending to be someone I wasn't and have something I didn't . . . I resented and despised the simple and greatest calling the Lord gave me as a mother and housekeeper and have been reaping the havoc of it in myself and worse Ho and the Children."[47]

Within the Royal Household, the division of labour occurs along traditional lines. Although Maria is increasingly assuming the role of leader and prophet within the movement, in the years of Berg's vigour the women were the ones brought in to look after them. And it was seen as an example of their ideal role: "[Sue] does everything you can possibly imagine hand and foot! She waits on us hand and foot, so she's not only a hand maiden but a foot maiden! Praise God! She's a sex maiden too! She really supplies all our needs. Sue feeds us and makes the bed and vacuums the floor and fills the bottles and empties the bottles and does many of the things that need to be done for us personally."[48]

C. Women as Heroes

It was the FFing period that changed the role of women. This was the most demanding thing Berg has asked of his followers, and it was the women who bore much of the weight of FFing. They put themselves at risk in ways that is nothing short of heroic. It suddenly liberated women from a subservient role with their men within the Family and gave them a place of prominence. They were the front line troops in the battle against Satan, and many of the women did things that they never thought possible. Witnessing stories are the tales which stir the hearts of The

Family most, and, despite the current reluctance of some of the women to tell their children about those days, the sense of pride they have in what they did is significant. As Berg said at the time, is was a form of martyrdom.

As early as November 1976, as the FFing movement was gathering momentum, there was a growing recognition of the cost of FFing to the women of the Family. It was not only the reality of sexually transmitted diseases which the women were contracting, nor the "beasts" that they occasionally encountered, it was the dangers and the traumas which resulted in the homes and their relationships with their mates. Berg said of it: "That is as close to martyrdom as you can come without dying or being tortured or something. That is really laying down your life, that is real crucifixion!"[49]

Since then there has been a change. In the last 7 years there has been a growing sense that women should be on equal terms in *all* aspects of The Family. An unpublished letter by Maria illustrates the way in which The Family has shifted on this matter. She avoids the unpalatable option of saying that Berg was wrong but says that the situation has changed. The most important change is the proximity of the End. They believe that the Lord is giving progressively more freedom, and the release of women in a broader sense is an expression of a greater freedom. She is also saying that the nuclear family to which women were subject is becoming less important. The nuclear family is giving way to the larger Family and in the larger context there are no restrictions on women. It must also be remembered that Maria is assuming a greater authority and she has always had a sense of the practical situation within The Family.

> *In some of the earlier Letters Dad gave marriage counsel which indicated that the wife should be very submitted to the husband* in personal little family unit matters, but that in the Lord's Work the husband shouldn't interfere with the wife's ministry, especially if she was a leader & he wasn't. But the Family has changed since those early days, we've become more 'One Wife' & there is virtually no distinction between our work for the Lord & our 'little private family units.' We're no longer little family units, we're one big Family, & we're getting more & more that way as we progress.
>
> *I think right now, things are getting so late & we're getting so close to the End,* that all of us, & especially our *Teens.* are going to have to be more *dedicated.* Maybe we're going to have to forget all this 'women be in submission to the men' kind of thing. It doesn't seem to jive with the need of the Church & the Ministry, & because of that, *something's* gotta *go!*
>
> *You can't have both, it doesn't work.* It puts the poor women under too much pressure & takes their ministry away from them.[50]

The other teaching of The Family which greatly effects the life of women concerns the matter of contraception and child birth. While a woman is in a position to have children, then her child bearing takes precedence over all other activities within the group. If, for example, a woman is the National Shepherd (as is the case in Australia), then she will be given whatever assistance is necessary with child care to allow her to continue in the job. Even though she may be performing that job with great distinction and enthusiastically elected to the position, she cannot claim this as a reason for practicing contraception. Child birth takes precedence. But if she does become pregnant, she will be given every assistance to continue in the job. She will work up to the last moment before the birth. She will be given 6 weeks off. During this time, she will still maintain the authority of the position, but one of the teachers or someone appropriate will be assigned to help. She will then return full time to the job and normally take the child with her, but with the assistance of a full time child care helper, who would normally be an older teen. I have seen instances in several Family homes where teen boys have shown an aptitude for child care and have taken the task on full time.

One of the factors which changed the role of women within the Family was the FFing era. As that period in the life of the group developed, it was the women who were involved in the front-line encounter with people outside the group. Even though FFing was not originally seen as an exclusively female activity, it emerged for a number of reasons that it was the women who were going out and putting themselves in the situation where they were having sex with "Fish." (Family term for a receptive person being FFed during the FFing era.) This proved extremely difficult for many of the men. Jealousy was not tolerated, and for many of the men the prospect of seeing their women out in these situations proved almost impossible. It was in these situations that Sharing was encouraged, and some of the women asked others to "look after" their husbands while they were out FFing. The status of women who were active through the FFing period is high within The Family. In many ways they are seen as spiritual heroes. I believe it has done much to elevate the status of women within the group. For they are the ones with the stories and the experiences which have become part of the folklore of The Family.

D. The World and the System:

As might be expected, The Family have a highly dualistic view of the world. Given their understanding of the role that Satan has in these later days, it is to be expected that they look on the world outside as hostile to the Gospel and all who are its representatives. It is this which has encouraged their isolation and rejection of much that the world offers. The suspicion is deep because they believe there are hidden forces within the world which are moving inevitably to a historically predictable end. But it is important to say that the experiences of the last two years have produced a modification in this view. They have found themselves in an increasingly complex relationship with the world outside. Particularly following the incidents in Japan and Australia and London, they have found themselves obliged to enter into relationships with people who have proved to be trustworthy and supportive of them. They have been required to develop a degree of sophistication in their handling of the media which is a new experience. This I believe has led to a softening of their language and attitudes to the world outside.

While God may be the creator and eventual victor in the struggle for the souls of mankind, there is a session during which the forces of Satan have effective control. The temptations of Christ portray the Devil showing Jesus all the kingdoms of the world and saying, "To You I will give all this authority and their glory; for it has been delivered to me, and I give it to whom I will, if You will worship me." (Luke 4:5-7) This they see as evidence that Satan in fact has control of the world. Scriptures such as 2 Corinthians 4:3-4 are cited to justify this view, where Satan is referred to as "the god of this world." This is a widely held view within orthodox Christianity. But there is a distinctive aspect to Berg's theology at this point. He takes the view that the outcome of the spiritual battle is in part dependent on the role which human beings play. So he is limiting the power of God to determine the result.

> The warfare in the Spirit World is very important, but it all hinges on us and has to do with us . . . because the hands of the powers of Heaven are tied according to our decisions! If we make the right decisions and operate by faith, then the forces of good are loosed and empowered to help us and to overcome the forces of evil! But if Man makes the wrong decision and goes the wrong direction, then in a sense their hands are tied, and the hands of the devils and demons and of Satan are liberated to bring about devastation amongst humanity.[51]

What I understand Berg is saying is that God chooses to limit Himself in this matter. This has the effect of increasing the responsibility and the weight which is on human beings. In a sense it is part of the spirit of Berg's theology that emphasises the freedom people have in this world. He goes to great lengths to give substance to this freedom, by assigning to people a certain autonomous ethical function. But this cannot be done without also withdrawing God from the process to some measure. There is also an extent to which Berg assigns to people a role in determining the outcome of their salvation. One can earn merit or preferment in the Next Life by the quality and consistency of our life in this.

He is also assigning to human beings a role in determining the outcome of the end of the world. Berg believes that God has given to The Family the task of speeding the Second Coming by bringing to an end the obligation on all people to spread the Gospel to the furthest ends of the world. When this task is finished, then the great events of the End Times can begin. A Scripture which is quoted to lend credence to this view is Matthew 24:14, which says, "And this Gospel of the kingdom shall be preached in all the world for a witness unto all nations; and *then* shall the *end* come." Berg says,

> "He's waiting on us to finish the job, to get out the Word, get out the lit, get out the Posters, get out the witness, to get in the souls and the disciples, before He's going to let it crash and the night comes when no man can work." (Jn.9:4)[52]

They do not have a "high" view of original sin. They do not locate the full responsibility for sin on individual people. This is because they draw a distinction between the presence of evil within the individual and the evil which comes as a force from outside. So the struggle of individuals is on two fronts. First, one is required to overcome the residual influence of sin within one's own self, which they believe is independent of Satan. And one also faces the wiles of the evil one in the world outside. Their view of this situation is influenced by their reading of Ephesians 6:12: "For our struggle is not against human foes, but against cosmic powers, against the authorities and potentates of this dark age, against the superhuman forces of evil in the heavenly realms." They see evil manifest most significantly in the structures of the contemporary world—in business, the media and politics and so on. In this they are influenced by the Anabaptist strain in David Berg's thought which sees the Christian position as one which puts a person in a critical attitude to the political structures of the day. The Family have a modified fundamentalist theology in relation to the world. They see the world as evil in its structures, but they draw a distinction between people who are captured by the system and those who are not. The "Systemites," (although they do not use this term in recent literature) are those people who have been taken in and use the evils inherent within The System.

They see a clear distinction between those who are in the faith and those who are not. They are part of the "born again" view which sees conversion to faith in Jesus Christ as Saviour and Lord to be the essential and only point of entry into salvation. They have a liberal attitude to the possibility of salvation outside of membership in the group. They draw a distinction between those who are saved but not living godly lives and those who live in total obedience to the principles set down in the New Testament and God's revelation in MO Letters. The inner circle are the disciples who have renounced the world, joined a Family household, and given themselves to the disciplines of witnessing and the other duties of the group. They have a circle of friends who work in the world, maintain ordinary lives, but are devoted to the teachings and beliefs of The Family. These people form a support base. There is, for example, a taxi driver in Sydney who pays the telephone and electricity bills for one of the households. This is not uncommon.

They allow people to move out of the inner circle of total commitment to take up life in the world. I know more than 10 people who have been full time disciples in The Family, but have moved outside the homes and still maintain friendly relationships with ex-disciples. Their literature has a number of discussions about the way to treat people who have left on good terms. This is one of the characteristics of the group which makes them more liberal and open than some others. It is most unusual for a group like The Family to allow their members to move away from total commitment and still maintain a relationship with them. It is a characteristics of many intensive religious groups that they find even the possibility of a person moving away anathema. Some such groups maintain that there is no life outside of their walls. They will go to great lengths to hold onto someone who indicates a desire to leave. Movement away is threatening to the integrity of the whole membership. It is a challenge to the very existence of their ideal. It is normal that once the break comes, all contact with that person is severed. Even people with family ties with the person leaving are obliged to desist from all communication in the life of many isolated, fundamentalist groups.

Deviation or diminution of commitment is regarded as a serious life-threatening apostasy. So it must be seen as significant that The Family accommodates the possibility of people leaving, and even provides a number of facilities for ex-members to maintain relationships with them. The Family does reserve scathing treatment for "backsliders." These are people who have left the group but have done so harbouring grievances or who have turned their back on the teachings and directions of God through the Word and the MO Letters. They are people who have been given a vision of the Gospel but have not been prepared to make the sacrifice necessary to reach for its true holiness. In the minds of The Family, they are people who once knew the truth but have turned away and become infected by attitudes and thoughts that put them in conflict with the group. Such people are viewed as backsliders, as described in 2 Peter 2:22: "It is happened unto them according to the true proverb. The dog is turned to his own vomit, & the sow that was washed to her wallowing in the mire."

The group is not as isolated or closed as many other groups that operate in the name of Christianity. The categories are not as limited as that of many other fundamentalist groups. Several factors put them in a more liberal posture than many others. These factors are, that:

— they can accept that people are capable of salvation outside of their walls.
— they can allow that there are people in the world and in the church with whom they feel a close and genuine sense of fellowship
— they allow a remarkably open and free range of contacts with people outside of the Family
— they recognise that there are people who preach the gospel and win others to Christ outside of The Family
— they allow that people within The Family can have reasons for leaving full time involvement without jeopardising their salvation or poisoning the life of the group through continued contact with them.

E. Attitude to the Mainline Churches:

Until recently, Berg despised the Churches with a fierce passion, but according to Apollos: "He has mellowed out in this regard considerably, citing advantages of the churches, even encouraging Family members to direct converts to acceptable churches. We see that the Lord is directing us to work more closely with other Christians as we come closer to the days of Great Tribulation when all Christians will need each other like never before." This is a considerable change in Family attitudes. But certain things have not changed. Berg still holds the churches responsible for much of the dark attitudes to the flesh which Christians hold: "The churches have made illegitimate almost everything that's pleasurable, the Lord's God-given blessings." (*MOP.* p. 82)

Berg has expressed distress that most churches show no understanding of the proximity of the End and do not share his urgency for the conversion of others: "I hate the System from which I came with a perfect hatred, because it is a lie and a delusion and a deceit and is damning souls to Hell when it ought to be saving them!" (*Ibid.*) At the same time he recognises that the Church has many within it who are good and strong Christians. As far as he is concerned, they exist within the Church despite the structures. He has recently developed a more conciliatory attitude to the churches, and has even suggested the possibility of The Family establishing a co-operative relationship with certain churches, with a view to them working together in following up some of their converts. Given the hostility of The Family in the past, this is a remarkable development.

Like many alternative Christian groups before them, they see themselves as recovering the original essence of Christianity. They have little respect for the history of the churches since the first century:

> "I sometimes think there is a greater gap between us and Churchianity than there was between the Christians and the Jews!—I mean we agree with the whole Bible, every bit of it that is up to date. We probably agree more with the Bible than the church people do, because we bring out all the parts that they don't obey and they don't agree with regarding the present and the Future, as witnessing and winning souls and evangelising the world and getting ready for the Tribulation." (*DB2*, p. 107, 8/83.)

These beliefs remain, but the Family has become more accommodating in its relationships with the mainline denominations. I was involved in a series of negotiations in Melbourne, Australia, following an approach from two Uniting Church ministers alarmed that The Family had turned up. The minister and elders of the Church came to the following arrangement. The Family were welcomed, but they were not to take any leadership positions in the church. They were not to attempt to evangelise any members of the church, and they were to keep clear of any discussion about their open sexual beliefs.

F. Persecution:

They believe there is an inevitability that they will suffer persecution. They regularly quote 2 Timothy 3:12, "All that live Godly in Christ Jesus shall suffer persecution." They see their own values and beliefs to be so repugnant to the world that they will be misunderstood and attacked. "If we continue as we're now going, we stand to be the greatest threat on this earth to the Devil's kingdoms. The Devil's got to rule our generation, because they're going to be his kingdom on Earth and he's going to be their Antichrist." ("Judas!" DO 71, 3/71, *DB4*, p.258.) "We are one of the few religious outfits in the whole world that is really on the attack for Jesus! We are invading the Devil's territory! We are attacking the gates of Hell and we are winning! (Mat. 6:18.) Winning souls and winning citizens from his kingdom! Satan hates us for it, therefore he attacks us on every hand, every way he possibly can to stop us—But he can't stop us! Hallelujah." ("With Persecutions!—Mark 10: 29, 30," DO 1967, *DB8*, 1967, p.567.) He sees persecution as a mark of the true Christian life. In fact, he argues that a lack of persecution is an indication that something must be wrong. He quotes the Biblical verse.

"Woe unto you when all men shall speak well of you, for so did their
fathers to the false prophets." (*DB8*. p. 577.)

G. Security and Fleeing:

Berg's writings have a strong emphasis on the need for vigilance and
self protection. He makes a number of references to the risks to his own
safety, and talks of occasions when he has narrowly escaped death. The
instructions about security are detailed, and driven by a highly developed
fear that they are in a hostile situation in imminent danger of attack, or
at least a Police raid. The first principle David Berg advocates is the
protection of all identifying material, such as mailing lists, addresses,
maps, phone numbers. They are required to keep all records either in
memory or to the barest minimum. Next in importance is the protection
of the leadership:

> I've always advised leadership to live separately, totally anonymously and
> totally selah from the rest of the Family. If possible, *top* leadership should
> live completely alone and isolated and privately, so that they are unknown
> and unrecognised and cannot be connected with the Family in any way.
> (*Security under Persecution*, DO 953-2, 13/12/80.)

Many Family homes around the world keep contact with each other
through modem, fax and telephone. And in my contacts I have
discovered a high degree of computer literacy. There are a number of
homes where this is not true, but the opportunity is present within the
Family to develop these skills. They use standard software. In Australia,
when all their records where taken during the raids in May 1992, a
number of floppy disks were removed which contained (amongst other
things) lists of those who supply them with clothing and food. These
disks were in code and the police took some time before they were able
to break the code and gain access to the lists.

Recently an elaborate attempt was made in the Philippines to take
over one of the Family homes. A person masquerading as David Berg on
the telephone set up a situation where the leadership of the Home was
flown to California and two people from outside moved in and took over
the Home. They were supplied with counterfeit MO letters, and they
were obviously well supplied with information about the inner workings
of the Family. It was an elaborately planned exercise. It resulted in a
number of sensitive files falling into the hands of outsiders and a
significant amount of the home's money was spent. A significant amount
of the home's money was stolen and misappropriated and over a dozen
trunks of irreplaceable master audio tapes of Family music recordings
were stolen. The Philippines National Bureau of Investigation arrested

the two detractors, but they managed to flee the country. An outstanding warrant for their arrest has been issued, as well as an extradition request against Priebe from the Philippines government to the Canadian government. Incidents such as this have encouraged Berg to remain aloof and even reclusive within the movement. Very few people I have met within The Family have met David Berg, even though there are a number who have been in the movement and in positions of leadership for 15 and 20 years. On occasions when I have met Peter Amsterdam it has occurred in a secret location of which even other members of the Family in the country were not aware. Strict security measures were implemented regarding transportation and communication to and from these meetings.

The Family have had a history of responding to situations of difficulty with local authorities by fleeing, citing Jesus' advise that "when they persecute you in one city, flee ye to another." (Matthew 10:23) This has changed in the last 3 years. They have taken to heart Berg's words in *Stand Up & Fight* (ML# 2476). They now believe that they will be a more effective witness if they resist the urge to flee and stand and answer their critics. As Apollos put it: "we believe the Lord has led us to in order to be a better & more far-reaching *witness* than ever before, which has been the case—Persecution has proven to be a great blessing in disguise, enabling us to meet many wonderful new friends."

H. Witnessing:

The primary way in which they believe they resolve their responsibilities to the world outside the group is through "witnessing." They have a remarkable preoccupation with the task of convincing others of the need to find salvation through Jesus Christ. As one of the leaders of the group in Australia said to me: "That's why I joined, that's what I am called to, and that's what I do." The imminent return of Christ, and their view of Satan's domination of the world creates great urgency in telling others about Jesus. There is a sense of mission within the group which creates a certain pressure to achieve results. There has been a habit of keeping records on their rate of witnessing. They report on the number of pages of literature they have distributed, the number of people they talk to, and the number of people who have actually been converted. In the Australian situation, one household in Sydney had been achieving conversions at an average above 70 per month. This was regarded as normal. A conversion is a situation where a person has been explained the basic beliefs necessary to understand the gospel. They are asked if they wish to "accept Jesus Christ as their Saviour from sin." If they say yes and pray a standard prayer, then they are considered to be a convert.

It could be said that the entire activity of The Family is devoted to the end that people outside may be won to Christ. The only activity which may compromise that view is their relationship to their children. But even this is seen as a form of preparation for their future activity as witnesses for Jesus. They are taught that all activity, whether it be directly involved in bringing the Gospel to others or activity around the homes working in the garden or caring for the children, is directed to this one end:

> "Lord, we're trying to help the whole *world* to get saved and everything we do, Lord has a part in it, whatever we do, Lord, whether its maintenance work or washing dishes or scrubbing the table or whatever, Lord, we're having a part in our worldwide ministry of saving souls for Heaven! TYJ! (Thank You, Jesus!)."[53]

They have not been able to adequately follow up on all their converts. This has become a concern within the group and there is discussion of setting up structures which will allow them to nurture the new converts in the faith. It is this which is leading to some discussion with certain mainstream church figures with a view of establishing a relationship where the facilities within the church to care for their converts are used. In the Anabaptist tradition, Berg maintains a persistent criticism of the evils of the political and economic excess of Capitalism. He believes a modified form of Socialism to be a closer approximation of Christian principles than Capitalism.

I. Changing styles of witnessing, and recruitment of disciples:

There have been dramatic changes in content and style of their witnessing. In the early years their witnessing sometimes took the form of prophetic gestures, including dramatic "sackcloth vigils." The first of these demonstrations occurred in 1969, in Washington, D.C., at the U.S. Capitol Building where Senator Everett Dirksen was lying in state in the rotunda. Seventy of The Family disciples marched in perfect unison to the site of the demonstration. Each carried a seven-foot wooden staff which they struck on the ground simultaneously making a loud and frightening sound. They walked in silence. They assumed fierce looks, wore large wooden yokes around their necks, ashes smeared on their heads and wore long red hessian robes as a sign of mourning for the imminent destruction of American society. Their message was one of warning and doom. They engaged in no discussion nor did they try to persuade or convince. It was what they saw to be an act of "prophetic declaration." They stood for a period of time, then unfolded large handwritten scrolls of Bible verses. Some of the most common verses were: "The wicked shall be turned into Hell, and all the nations that forget God" (Psalm 9:17), and "But if they will not obey, I will utterly pluck up and destroy that nation, saith the Lord" (Jeremiah 12:17).

This early stage was one of attack and condemnation. In the coming years David Berg was to change his attitude on this matter. He became more and more concerned at the need to bring people into a relationship with Christ and membership in the group. So the group demonstrations turned into personal one-to-one contacts. The object became the statement of the gospel and the particular vision of The Family. This personal contact began also to change with the introduction of literature, then FFing, and more recently the emphasis on personal witnessing has begun to shift more to the consolidation of the home environment. David Berg is now allowing that there are aspects of the education and nurture of the children which come before witnessing. In 1993, The Family in the U.S. revived sackcloth demonstrations to warn what they perceive to be a decadent and backslidden America of God's impending judgements which will come upon her for her sins. However, one-on-one witnessing and literature distribution remain the most common modes of witnessing, in the U.S. and elsewhere.

There has been a diminishing commitment to gathering disciples into The Family. In the early years, quotas were not uncommon, and it was expected that each colony bring in at least one new disciple each month. That was changed to one disciple each 3 months, but, since April, 1978, all quotas were abolished. In fact, as the sense of the approaching End gathers momentum, within the life of The Family there has been a diminishing emphasis on gathering new disciples. The emphasis is more on winning souls. In 1987, Berg was saying, "I am absolutely against this business of grabbing somebody out of the park or off the street and taking them straight home as a 'new disciple.' They're not a disciple yet, you're not even sure of them at all!—And you are not at all sure what their relatives will be like!" ("Honour the King—1 Peter 2:17" DO 2383, 11/87, *DB9*, p. 82.)

There have been only 4 new members join full-time in Australia in the last 2 years. This would have been intolerable some years ago. There are a number of reasons for this shift in emphasis. First, Berg seems to have a distaste for complexity and largeness in The Family. He has maintained his image of The Family as a lean organization which is broken into small and unencumbered home groups. He is dominated by his belief that the End Times and the persecution which will occur will put enormous pressures on any concentration of activity with The

Family. He believes The Family homes will be broken up, and they will lose the capacity to sustain themselves in the way they do now. For this reason, he believes The Family should prepare themselves for a time when they will be split up and each of them will be required to take secular employment simply to sustain themselves. He has the view that they are being well prepared for this situation now, through the life they are leading in The Family. It is a problem which occupies him at some length: "When the Antichrist System takes over completely, almost everybody's going to have to get a job, more or less. How are our people going to survive outside . . . ?" ("The Crash Continues!" *DB9*, paragraph 36.) He makes various suggestions. For example, he believes the girls will be in a good position following their life in the Family:

> I've looked at these dance videos recently and I've thought, well thank God, if we didn't do anything else, we've taught these girls a trade, a skill, a talent! They're beautiful, and that's something the World will always want and they'll always have no matter what! They'll always need beautiful women—and if they like beautiful women, they will have need of beautiful dancers. I believe they've got a trade that they can earn their living if they had to. ("The Crash Continues." DO 2381.27/10/87. *DB9*. p.63.)

It must be noted that Berg wrote this at a time when the production of such videos had already ceased, and since then Berg has suggested a number of other more "acceptable" occupations which members could pursue if and when necessary. There has also been a shift in emphasis from a total concentration on activities outside of the homes in the way of witnessing to a recognition of the role of the children and the demands of their care and nurture in the faith. This again has shifted some of the urgency away from recruiting new disciples. In 1980, he was saying, "We have a tremendous number of children of our own, children now to educate, and while we're busy having these children and you women are really bearing them and caring for them and teaching and training them, that's just about all some of you women can do!" (*New Year's Eve Praise.* No.957:183. 1980.) In the past the group was sustained by a influx of new members bringing new resources. Today, the large number of children has changed the emphasis; 50% of the group is under 15 years of age. The literature from Berg and World Services has in the last four years increasingly developed an emphasis on children, their nurture and education. It is clear that Berg sees the future of the group to be in the development of the children.

The process of joining The Family as a disciple has changed greatly. In the early years it was a simple matter of the young people moving in, and, within a matter of weeks, making a formal commitment to forsake all and submit themselves to the discipline and leadership of the group. Today it is very much more difficult. There are a wide range of people whom The Family would regard as unlikely possibilities for membership. For example, it is almost impossible for The Family to think of a whole family joining. They are so conscious of the demands of Family membership that they would have to be certain that all members of the family seeking membership were united in their commitment to join. Again, they are wary of any person over thirty who has a history of commitments which may complicate their life within The Family. They are particularly wary of people who come into the movement with considerable resources. They have had experience of people who came to The Family and brought with them large amounts of money, only to discover a year or so later that they wished to leave. This can create problems should they leave asking for some of the money back. This is not Family policy, but they have regularly helped people who have stepped away from the movement in order that they may re-establish themselves in the world. For example, they provided $5,000 to assist Rick Dupuy aka "Watchman" when he made the decision to leave the group.

It is for this reason they have generally slowed the process of joining, even for those who are their best prospects. Single, young, unencumbered people whose families are not hostile to what they are doing; these are the most likely candidates for joining. Even then it will take at least 3 months, and often 6 months. Normally this would involve a growing level of involvement in the life of the group. This would progress to the point that the person may well be coming to one of the Family homes every day. They would be expected to participate in worship and witnessing, and they would be expected to participate in extended teaching sessions concerning the teachings of the Bible and the literature of The Family. It would also be necessary for the prospective disciple to indicate clearly that they have considered all that is involved in joining. This is what is called "counting the cost," which is a concept taken from Luke 14:28. When this process has run its course, only then will membership be considered. The final decision to accept a new disciple will usually involve not only the Home Shepherds, but leadership at the District and National level.

J. Discipline and Leadership within The Family:

The Family is one of the few communal groups to survive from the days of the Jesus Revolution. They have been through a number of significant changes in leadership structure, and seemed to have settled on an interesting mix of centralism and democracy. Part of their success must lie in the commitment they make to maintaining discipline within the life of the group. The Family homes are run on strict, even military lines. All people within the home have tasks assigned, and these are required to be carried out in an attitude of acceptance and cheerfulness. Demerit points are used as a mechanism for maintaining discipline for the young people and a series of punishments are meted out. A certain number of demerit points will lead to the loss of video viewing rights, for example. In the last couple of years there has been a modification of this scheme. It became a matter of concern that some areas went overboard on the issuing of "demerits" to young people. This has been sculled down recently and a number of homes have discontinued this method altogether. There are certain situations where children are punished through smacking, but I have talked with children who have been smacked. They tend to look back on the incident in a way which does not create any alarm.

I have observed a group of young children, 4 to 6 years, being disciplined. They disobeyed a request to stop running noisily in a corridor. When this continued, one of the Home Shepherds went outside. With a stern voice he called the children to him. He explained that he was unhappy at what they were doing. He told them clearly what they had done was wrong, and said as punishment they were to stand in a line with their backs to a wall for a period of 5 minutes without making a sound. They were silent and subdued, but not frightened during his talk. They took their place along the wall, and stood silently. Two minutes later, he turned to them and sent them on their way. What they had done was regarded as a breach of discipline within the Home. There was a note of humour in the way in which he metered out the punishment, and softened once he sensed that the point had been made.

The problems of discipline within The Family of young people, led to the establishment of "Victor Camps." In a limited number of locations in Macau, the Philippines, Norway and elsewhere, problem adolescents were separated from regular Family activities. They were submitted to a strict discipline of hard work, long hours of "Word" study, and for the recalcitrant, extended periods of isolation. The last of the "Victor" camps was closed in England in 1992. They have been the attention of close examinations, in particular, of a wardship court case in London. Some of the accusations of excessive discipline and physical beatings have been admitted to be true. These accusations have been brought by ex-members, including Berg's granddaughter Mene Berg, who described a regime of discipline which went beyond the bounds of what could be regarded as acceptable. In April, 1991, Maria wrote a series of Letters which became know as the Discipleship Training Revolution (DTR) in which she called for the diversification of the positive lessons learned in the Victor Camps throughout The Family. It signalled a softening of the approach to discipline.

Open Heart Reports (OHRs) are required to be completed at least once a week. Some Homes enforce the discipline of OHRs more strictly than others. These amount to confidential accounts of a member's life within The Family. It gives a description of the state of that person's journey, and gives the member an opportunity to share whatever is on his or her heart. They are expected to give an account of the way in which they have been witnessing, any major "victories" or blessings and any difficulties with life within the Home situation and so on. This is often the point at which potential problems are discovered. If a person is going through a period of doubt or is finding themselves in an untenable situation within the group, this will become obvious. Usually this will be resolved in the normal course of Family life. They will talk the matter through with someone close on a one-to-one basis. If the problem persists and the person concerned is judged to be wilful, certain decisions will be taken. The leadership in the Home may decide to give the person a day off where they can consider the situation and spend the time in reflection and reading the Word. If the problem persists, then a "Walkie Talkie" may be organised, in which a Shepherd takes a leisurely walk with the person, discussing their problem and hopefully offering solutions. Or they may be given a reading list by the Home Shepherds. In both cases a "reaction" is asked of the person spoken to. They will be asked to write down their response to the talk and their encounter with the Word.

Should the problem persist further, then the Home Shepherds will arrange to meet with the person. Two of the Shepherds will be present. Often, one of the Shepherd's will do the talking and put the case that the person is "out of fellowship" with the Home. The problem will be aired, but the object of the occasion is for the Shepherds to hear the person state their grievance, but also to state what the Home Council considers to be the situation and what is required. The function of the silent Shepherd is to act as an objective observer of the situation and give feedback to the other Shepherd and comment on how the counselling proceeded and assess whether the real problem was being isolated, etc. If the problem persists and the person wishes to continue as a member of The Family, then they could be asked to attend a Retraining Centre (RTC).   This is a situation where the person is isolated from the normal affairs of The Family. They will be put in company with some chosen Shepherds and asked to submit to a regime of considerable discipline. Their lives will be highly ordered and a hard program of Scripture memorization, study and reflection on The Word will be required. Their every move will be watched and they will be asked to submit willingly to the authority of their Shepherds. This can last from between 6 weeks to 2 months. If a person remains rebellious following this, then no further measures exist within The Family of full-time disciples, and that person will be asked to consider becoming a TSer, or part-time live-out member.

K. Renunciation of the World:

An early and persistent theme of Berg's, was his call for total commitment and renunciation of the world. It is a long-standing aspect of Christian monastic life that a person turn from all worldly ties, take no secular job, and recognise no allegiance either to family, friends, lovers or financial security which will threaten the primacy of one's total commitment to Christ.

David Berg is asking the same degree of commitment from The Family. All Family members are required to turn from all worldly supports and live entirely by faith. There are exceptions when someone is in debt, or it is deemed that they can be a better witness and by retaining their secular job. For example, there is a live-in Family member in California who is a doctor, who continues her practice, giving free medical care to Family members, and using her income to repay government grants which enabled her to go through medical school. Remaining income is a great help to her Home. So there are rare exceptions to the "forsake your job" standard. When a person has been through this, a period of some 6 months elapses. At the end of this, if all else is acceptable, the person is expected to leave their job, join a household, sell all that they have, put the proceeds into the hands of the group and give themselves to the discipline of the leadership and share in witnessing and the other duties of the group. There are cases where they will allow that a person can join without bringing their money with them. For example, it was put to me that a person may come to the group with certain assets, although they believe the best place to put those assets is in the service of God in the group, if there was serious trouble from that person's family over the transfer of the funds, they would allow the money to remain outside. But this is the rare exception.

IV. Ethics:

For a fundamentalist Christian group, The Family have an unusually liberal ethical system. They believe that the break between the Gospel and the Law or the religion of Jesus and the religion of the Old Testament is the difference between night and day. Berg believes that the progress of Christianity is a movement towards greater and greater freedom:

> Each age or generation of the Church has taken another step or some new step toward total freedom in the last generation . . . from harsh restrictions of the law to the total freedom of love through the grace of God. (*DB1*, p. 8).

This is at the heart of David Berg's vision. He believes that he was given the task of ushering the final statement of the Gospel before the end of the world. In the context of this belief, Berg makes judgments about behaviour, not by law, but by love. So selfless, unconditional love become: the principle which now guides all behaviour. To restrict the freedom of people for Berg is tantamount to denying the message of Christ for them—Or to return to the Law is a denial of the Gospel. They regard the teaching of Jesus to be crucial in establishing the supremacy of Love. In Matthew 22, verse 36, the question is put to Jesus: "Teacher. which is the greatest commandment in the Law?" The answer is, "Love the Lord your God with all your heart and with all your soul and with all your mind." This is the first and greatest commandment. And the second is like it: "Love your neighbour as yourself. All the law and the Prophets hang on these two commandments."

So in all ethical judgments, it is love which guides their decisions, not law, or regulation, or tradition. They do not believe it is possible to make ethical judgments about certain acts by an examination of the acts themselves. They depend on a verse in I Cor 6:12, "All things are lawful for me, but not all things are helpful. All things are lawful for me, but I will not be enslaved by anything." They believe that the principle of "Love" is the primary moral arbiter and one judges the moral virtue of an act by examining the quality of one's attitude of love.

A. Sharing:

Sharing is an expression of their ethical vision. It is an essential aspect of The Family's view of itself. It symbolises and embodies their freedom and adventurousness, and their over-arching view that love and commitment to their own brothers and sisters is what keeps the life of The Family whole and alive. In an exchange of letters during December, '92 and January, '93 I put it to David Berg that Sharing was now the only barrier to acceptance between them and the mainline Christian denominations. He replied:

> I'm sure you can see that we *cannot* recant on our stand on *sexual freedom* as a beautiful and wonderful *creation of God* for our *good, enjoyment and*

complete unity of both flesh and spirit, as well as *excellent children!* 'By their fruits ye shall know them!'—Mat. 7:20—and you've certainly seen that! They are proven glorious fruits of our true, tender, loving care and good training—And have shown no evil effects of genuine loving honesty and freedom about sex as God's own gift for our good!—and not bad and evil as Satan proclaims—even by the churches and some Christians!

Sharing not only embodies the ethical vision of the group, but it is also a way they have developed of dealing with the sexual life of the disciples within the confined environment of The Family homes. It must be remembered that no sexual relationships are allowed between Family members and the world outside. It is also a principle of The Family that the individual homes are required to be as autonomous as possible. This means that no relationships which involve a sexual dimension are allowed between homes. So the prospects for sexual intimacy for a single person within a home are extremely limited. This has been seen as a problem early in the history of The Family. I believe it was present in some situations prior to FFing, but it was FFing which established it as a general practice within the life of The Family.

Two factors precipitated Sharing during FFing. First, as mentioned above, many of the wives who were FFing found that the best way of dealing with their husband's jealousy was to ask one of the other women in the home to "baby sit" their husbands while they were FFing. It also occurred to The Family that there was an inconsistency in having their single women have sex outside of the family and not allow the same freedom within. If there was a single male within a home who had no sexual opportunity, then it seemed foolish to them that the women within the home should not accommodate him when they are having sex with outsiders.

Sharing is based on three principles. First, it proceeds from the ethical standpoint that there is no evil in any sexual act (except sodomy), provided it is done as an expression of love. But even within this freedom there are still constraints. The expressions of love are kept within the confines of the behavioural code developed by the group. Second, the primary responsibility of all members is to the larger life of The Family. The relationship between a husband and wife is secondary to the love which all members should have to all others in The Family. So, the needs of another brother or sister cannot be avoided because of a prior relationship to a spouse or mate. In other words, the moral obligation of The Family is larger and prior to the obligations of a one-to-one relationship between two mates. Third, the needs created by sexuality are given a certain moral weight. Within the life of The Family, the sexual need in one person creates an obligation in others. By elevating sex to make it a moral good, they have created the obverse, namely that the denial of sex to another in need is a moral evil.

One of the most characteristic statements made by Family women describing their first sexual encounter in FFing was the fact that they saw in the man "a real need." In fact, they saw FFing as a loving response to a person who had a need. The best prospect for FFing was a single, older man, with some prominence in business or government service, away from home or separated from his wife, or divorced, or with a history of sad relationships behind him. They believed that FFing put on them an obligation to show love and affection to that person because of his need.

So, Sharing is a manifestation of the Law of Love. It operates within all homes where there are singles or there are mates who are separated for reasons of Family business. The simplest form of Sharing is if two single people within a home decide to join together in a sexual relationship. That can be done without much discussion or counselling. If one or both of the parties are married or with mates, then the Home Teamwork would be involved. The final arrangement may be negotiated through the third party of the Home Mother. Whatever emerges as the Sharing arrangement will involve discussion and prayer with all the parties involved. If the husband of a woman being asked to Share is not happy, then it will not proceed. But, it is also true that the obligation is on all adults within the Family to share unless there is good reason not to. I put this last proposition to Apollos, who made the following comment: "Sharing is something that is supposed to be purely voluntary, without any pressure or undue persuasion from others. Sharing takes place because people *want* to help each other out. However, it is true that adults within the Family feel that they are their 'brothers keeper,' and that they should do what they can to meet the needs of single members who are desirous of sex, unless there is good reason not to." Such reasons are, recent child birth, the pressures of important work within The Family. It was also put to me, that Sharing tends to keep within levels of authority in The Family. So, a person in a high leadership position would not normally share with someone lower down the ranks.

Four principles are applied by the Home Teamwork when considering a Sharing situation. If the following questions can be answered satisfactorily, then Sharing will proceed:

— Is it something that is motivated by love?
— Do all parties involved approve and recognise the love in this act?
— Is anyone being hurt?
— Has it been talked through and submitted to counselling?

— Does this have the Lord's blessing?

Normally it will occur no more than once a week and no less than once a month, but it may not always result in a sexual relationship. It may be that what is asked is simply that the other person makes themselves available once a week to have a meal together. They may decide to go for a walk and talk, hold hands, and perhaps kiss and cuddle. But it is most likely that it will result in sexual intercourse.

Sharing has changed in its character over the years. It was not uncommon in The Family of Love era for Sharing to involve single members of The Family participating in sexual activity with married couples. This was on occasions extended to include a sort of unfettered situation of free love. This is not the case now. The present situation is highly ordered and couched around with counselling and guidance.

Within The Family there is a concerted attempt to maintain Sharing, but at the same time preserve the integrity of married relationships. In fact, it is my impression that the emphasis is shifting towards the latter. Although Sharing is central to their vision of themselves, we may be seeing a shift in emphasis. Sharing will be seen more as a safety valve for unmet needs, rather than an occasion to extend the sexual possibilities of individuals and couples. It is not the occasion for free love.

The people I have talked with deal seriously with the complexities of relationships Sharing raises. I have talked at length about the way they make a division in their emotional life between the one with whom they have a primary sexual relationship and the one with whom they are Sharing. Some find it easier than others. Most seem to go into the Sharing relationship with the view that certain areas of emotional expression and intimacy are not allowed. More recently, they have been allowing a greater focus on the married life of people within The Family. For example, each week one day is set aside for married couples and their children to spend time together. During this day they are given time off from the normal demands of Family life. It is specifically a time for nurturing the married relationship. At the time of writing this report. The Australian families, following the rigours of the Sydney case, have been given money from "the folks" to hire an apartment on the Queensland Gold Coast, so that each of the couples within the Family in Sydney can spend several days together alone.

One of the complicating factors which Sharing raises is the matter of pregnancy. Sharing occurs without contraception, so it is not uncommon for a woman to become pregnant and give birth to a child not fathered by her mate. In this case, the obligation is on the married mate to accept the child within his own family. In other words, the married relationship forms the primary point of identification in the life of a child. He/she will not be excluded or kept from his biological father. But she/he will be virtually adopted by her/his mother's mate and relate to him as father.

B. Authority and Revelation Within The Family:

All religious groups have clear understandings of the way in which they arrive at truth. The central task of all religions which recognise their allegiance to a transcendental power, is getting to know the mind of this God in the midst of an ambiguous and compromised world. The normal "sources" for this knowledge or "revelation" in orthodox Christianity are:

— Through the Bible as the infallible source of all truth in matters of faith and behaviour, as tends to be the emphasis within Protestantism, especially in fundamentalist denominations. The Bible becomes the exclusive source of revelation and truth in these churches, who see it as divinely inspired and literally true in all that it says, even in English translations.

— Through personal and direct experience with God. This is the case with the Quakers, who have no clergy, and allow nothing to compromise the right of the individual to access God directly.

— Through the assigning of authority and ultimately, infallibility to the Church hierarchy, who act as the guardians and dispensers of God's revelation. This was to a large extent the attitude of the Roman Catholic church prior to Vatican II.

— Some assign authority to an independent vision which is regarded as an "extension" or "fulfilment" or "further revelation" beyond the Bible and the history of the church. The writings of Mary Baker Eddy performs this function in the Christian Scientists, Joseph Smith and the Book of Mormon has this role amongst the Mormons.

David Berg sees himself as a person called by God in a manner similar to, but nevertheless different than, the Old Testament prophets. It is similar in that he can claim authority as a revealer of God's Word to this generation. He is greater in a number of ways. First, he has the status of being the last in a great line and also he is the one who will actually see the final events happen. He will gather together the holy remnant who will see the great events of the End Times.

"We, being the *last* generation of Christians, are extremely important to the Lord, just like Jesus was with the *first* generation of Christians! In a sense I am the final Prophet of this Church of Jesus Christ, Jesus is the Saviour, the King of Kings, the Lord of Lords, the Prophet of all Prophets, but God has sent you a Prophet in these Last Days to feed you & to love you & to tell you the Truth,"[54] and again: "We are God's last Church, the last step in God's progress towards total freedom for His Church and the last chance to prove that the ultimate Church can be trusted with total freedom in this last generation!"[55]

David Berg's claim to authority stems in large measure from several references in the Old Testament which they believe refer to him specifically. For example, Ezekiel 34:23,24 reads, "And I will set up over them one shepherd, my Servant David, and he shall feed them: he shall feed them and be their shepherd. And I, the Lord will be their God, and my servant David shall be prince among them; I the Lord have spoken." Encouragement is also taken from Hoses 3:5, which says, "Afterward, shall the children of Israel return, and seek the Lord their God, and David their king; and shall fear the Lord and His goodness in the latter days."

Berg sees himself as speaking God's mind to this generation and asks that this be recognised within the life of the group. He does not claim to be infallible. In fact, he goes to some length to state that he is capable of making mistakes. But, he also makes it clear when he is speaking in a manner which requires the attention and obedience of the group. It is similar to the utterances of the Pope on those occasions when he speaks en cathedra. It is only then that infallibility is ascribed to what he says. Berg describes MO Letters as "extensions" or "enlargements" of the Bible. So he sees the Bible as limited by its history and its preoccupation with theological matters which have ceased to be relevant in the urgency of "these present evil times." In some cases, the MO letters actually supersede the Bible in authority. Referring to David Berg's MO Letters, Maria says,

> We don't even need to read the Book of Acts, because you have told us how to live it! We don't even have to look back at that because you've told us exactly how it should be today! ("We're Still the Jesus Revolution—Our foundation is *Jesus* and the *MO Letters!*" DFO 1592. *DB2*. p. 105.8/83.)

In his own words, he appropriates the words of the Old Testament to himself and assigns a similar authority to the MO Letters.

> And I will set up one Shepherd over them and he shall feed them, even My servant David; he shall feed them and he shall be their Shepherd—Eze. 34:23—And he shall give them the MO Letters. ("Training and Shepherding Babes!" DO 734, *DB8*, p.56, 2/77.)

V. Later History

In 1978, Berg initiated the Reorganisation, Nationalisation Revolution (RNR). He believed the leadership had become distant and cold in their relationships with the members. Information about the life of the colonies and homes, he believed, was not being directed through to him. Certain tensions had developed between him and his daughter Deborah and others who were taking on lifestyles more appropriate to the easy life of the world rather than the constraints appropriate to a missionary group. For example, the story is told of Rachel (who later left the movement) who was spending more and more time with her "fish" and was becoming bolder and more dismissive in her comments about Berg and the Family. In the minds of the Family, she became arrogant and disrespectful and flaunted the lavishness of her lifestyle in the face of Family members who were living in near penury elsewhere. Peter Amsterdam told me of one occasion she was entertaining some Family members newly arrived from the Middle East. They had come from extremely difficult circumstances and she served them rice cooked in the finest French Champagne. She was given to making cruel and mocking remarks about the sexual prowess of a number of the men she had been with. Berg responded by sacking some 300 leaders throughout the group, and called for a new regime and called on the homes to begin again and elect new leaders.

The RNR occurred at the same time that FFing was under way. Berg virtually destroyed the entire management structure of the group overnight. Contacts between the homes began to break up. It was a time when many in the movement were grappling with Flirty Fishing. Many found it too difficult to accept and walked out of The Family. Others who stayed were attempting to put it into practice, but were unsure how. In some places the standards of the movement began to drop. A number of homes became absorbed with FFing, to the exclusion of other activities.

This was the most fluid period in the history of the Family. As large numbers of people left full-time involvement, membership in the group began to lose some of its significance. The finances of the movement were devastated. It was also a time when the uniformity of the movement began to break down. Today there is a remarkable continuity between the homes from country to country. The level of communication is very high. During 1978, this was not the case. There was a marked difference in the behaviour of various homes. It is for this reason that FFing proceeded more effectively in some areas than others.

A. "Flirty Fishing":

In 1976, a series of MO Letters called "King Arthur's Nights" began to talk about a new form of witnessing that Berg and his partner Maria and other members of the leadership had been engaged in. He described incidents in London dance clubs and Teneriffe where Maria and other women had used their sexuality to establish contact with outsiders. This developed through the series of Letters to an argument about the sacrificial nature of FFing and the need to see sexuality as a tool in the next stage of witnessing in the life of the group. The fact that sexual intercourse was the natural outcome of what was being said was allowed and even encouraged. The theological influences which produced this were these:

— The urgency and insistence on witnessing.
— Their ethical beliefs did not necessarily regard sexual intercourse outside of marriage as adultery,
— Berg described FFing as an outpouring of sacrificial love. He believed it was possible to participate in FFing with a form of love which was not driven by prurient or lustful motives.

Berg insisted he was calling for an outpouring of pure love in response to what he saw as the hunger for love present in the people they met. In "The Family of Love!—Sin or Salvation?" June '77, he said: "We soon found there was no stopping place, no limit to which God would go to save a poor lost soul with His infinite love and unlimited mercy!"[56] This took shape in Berg's theology as a view of love which The Family would take to the world as a higher and more Godly way.

Berg saw a similarity between the act of the women giving themselves to the sexual needs of their "Fish" and the act of Christ dying on the cross for the sins of mankind It was an act of love and sacrifice. Its motive was love and the desire to see the salvation of others. Their ethical theory had prepared the way, in removing from sex with others apart from one's spouse, the sense that it was wrong.

I have spoken with 20 women within The Family who were involved in FFing. All of them began early and continued until the early '80s. There was a marked drop off by 1985. Many of them were FFing on an average of 2 nights a week. The vast majority of their FFing contacts did not result in sex. FFing often started and finished with a conversation with someone in a bar or hotel. There were normally a series of meetings, during which she would be witnessing to the man about faith in Jesus. If this proved to be a warm and open conversation, then the woman would allow the sexual aspects of the relationship to open up. It was also normal for the Family member to include other Family members in the situation to assist in witnessing and also to provide some support in making the decision as to whether this may be a person with whom they would "go all the way." On average, the women who were active in FFing had sexual intercourse with between 20 and 30 different men during the 9 years that FFing occurred.

There were certain reasons which allowed a woman to participate in the life of The Family without FFing. In some limited places it was seen as a test of loyalty. In most, there were a number of acceptable reasons for not participating, such as pregnancy or nursing small children. This was particularly true of the women in Australia. They have large families, whose children would have been babies during the later years of this era. Some did not believe they had sufficiently "good looks" to do it effectively. Some did not have the personal confidence to initiate contacts of this nature. Some were active in other forms of ministry which put them apart from FFing. There was much else that was happening within the life of The Family. The literature and music ministry was developing and the growing number of children was placing an increasing demand on the home life.

FFing was open to all group members. There was no distinction between women and men, married or single. Women were able to FF men, and, in a few rare instances, other women. Men were allowed only to FF women. The group believes male homosexuality is a sin; they are more accommodating to lesbianism, but do not see it as a normal form of sexual expression. As FFing developed, it became almost exclusively a ministry conducted by the women. The men found it more difficult than the women to disengage from the FFing relationship. Because they did not use contraception, the possibility of pregnancy proved to be a larger problem for the men than the women. If Family women became pregnant as a result of FFing, they were happy to bring the child into the life of The Family. If it was appropriate to tell the biological father that he had a child, they would. But they did this only in situations where this would not disturb the father's marriage, or where there was not likely to be any legal or emotional difficulties. I have discussed some of the ethical issues surrounding this matter in the appended conversation with Ammi and Joan (Appendix A).

For The Family men, the prospect of having a pregnant woman on the outside created much greater difficulties. In fact, this led to several men finding it impossible to continue in the life of The Family. They talk about some of the men "being FFed out of the Family." It is a prevailing view of women within The Family that they tend to be more grasping and tenacious in holding onto relationships. This is one of the main reasons they give for explaining the difficulties which the men experienced. As Ezra, a senior member in Japan, put it to me: "If a woman takes the bait of FFing, they do not just want the worm. They want the line, the fishing rod, the boat, the man, the house, the whole thing."

The years following this were ones of considerable sexual freedom within the group. All forms of sexual interchange outside of male homosexuality were allowed. It was around this time that the *Story of Davidito* was written in which instances of sexual contact, including oral sex between Maria's three-year old son and his young nanny Sara, were related. This was described enthusiastically as an ecstatic and important experience. "So guess what happened? For a bouncing climax (ha!), he spoke out in excited foreign tongues! He sounded very gypsy similar to Abrahim!" This is significant, because Abrahim is the spirit guide who communicates through David Berg.

It is clear from the literature and history of the Family that there were occasions when the sexual divisions between adults and children were blurred. I am aware of a number of instances where the literature led some Family members to explore the fullest dimensions of sexual freedom, even with children. But the literature in the last 7 years has unequivocally stated that any such involvement of children in adult sexual activity is banned. Since 1987, there has been a much narrower view of the role of children in the sexual life of the Family. All acts of sexual activity between adults and children are punishable with excommunication, and there are at least two cases I know of where this has occurred.

In the last two years, there have been raids against Family homes in Japan, Spain, Australia, France and Argentina. In all cases the claim has been made that the children seized have been abused. Despite extensive examination and probing by police and others, no charge has been sustained. No one has been found guilty. The pattern established in Australia is now being repeated. More than 600 children around the world have been taken from their parents. Dozens of court appointed psychologists, child abuse specialists and social workers have examined them at times for periods of up to seven days, and no one has produced any evidence to support the allegations that they have been sexually abused. It is significant that none of the children asked to be protected from The Family or confessed to any incidents of sexual abuse. In many of these raids The Family has been treated shamefully and with scant justice. I believe the ardour of those who accuse The Family of abusing their children is misplaced. In the absence of any evidence to support these charges along with my extensive contacts with the Family, I believe the children are not being abused.

B. The Present Sexual Activity of The Family:

There is no question that all sexual activity with people outside of The Family has now ceased. The only possible exception may be a person with whom contact was established during the FFing era (meaning before the practice was discontinued in 1987), who has been a very close and active long-standing friend of The Family, someone who is virtually a live-out member. If closing all sexual contact with this person would possibly be harmful to his spiritual well being and against the best interests of The Family, then, in a few extremely rare and exceptional cases worldwide, sexual intercourse has continued, providing condoms are used. I know of only two such relationships persisting, though I am sure there are others, but they are very much the exception. So there is effectively no sexual contact between The Family and the world outside. If a married couple come to the point that one finds it impossible to continue in full-time membership of The Family, even if that person remains on friendly terms and lives close by, all sexual contact with that person will cease.

In 1987, the policy toward FFing dramatically changed. In "Summary of AIDS Rules and Policies" (*DB7*, p.500, 9/87), it was stated, "All sex with outsiders is now banned!—Which means ESing and FFing with sex is now out!" There were three main reasons. First there was a genuine fear of AIDS and other sexually transmitted diseases. In the years before the pronouncement against sex with outsiders, Berg had been struggling with the issue of sexually transmitted diseases. He had been convinced that the Lord would protect the women if they had the faith for it. But he could also see the work of the Devil in the problem. In Novermber 1976, a Letter was published entitled "Afflictions!—A Powerful Revelation!" (D.O. 569, *Vol. 4*, p. 4188) in which he conceded that the FFers were putting themselves at great risk. In the terms of The Family, he described this as a demonstration of the verse, "Greater love hath no man than this, that a man lay down his life for his friends." (John 15:13) It was the argument that FFing is an analogy of the crucifixion. Jesus submitted himself willingly to his executioners because he was driven by love for them. The girls of The Family were doing the same, but the problem remained. What were they to do about the sexual diseases? They had never used contraceptives. They had gladly accepted all the consequences of their actions. They kept the babies and nurtured them within the bosom of The Family. They kept their secrets and for the most part, allowed their fish to retire in peace and ponder the extraordinary nature of the experience.

They were also discovering that FFing was not the only way of spreading the Gospel. Some of the husbands, like Andy in Hong Kong, discovered a style of witnessing that was proving to be more effective. His wife, Sue, was not one of the most attractive women in The Family, and she was returning night after night with no effective contacts from the bars she attended. Andy began to move around the offices of the business district talking to people and showing them photos and giving them tapes of their music. He found that the contacts he made were more effective and he discovered that he was bringing more money into the Home than his wife.[57] This became the experience of many people in the Family and led to the development of "tapenessing." Later, a further development gave rise to DFing (distributing *Daily Food* devotional booklets) and a new form of witnessing that was to take over where FFing stopped.

FFing created a stratification between some of the top FFing girls and the rest. No matter how spiritually significant FFing was, it depended on a number of very worldly qualities. The good-looking and vivacious girls were the ones who achieved the greatest success, and they became an elite group within the Family. Some of the "shiner" FFing girls found themselves in positions which were alien to the rest of The Family. They were propelled into a world of videos, money, clothes and expensive gifts. These girls were soon in demand, and a number of the homes vied for them to join them. A number of appeals for FFers with references appeared in the literature. The homes which were able to attract these girls would be the homes with the best FFing statistics, and the most secure sources of income. They arrived with wardrobes of beautiful clothes, and they filled their rooms with TVs, video cameras, stereos, and so on. They kept private funds and spent much of their time outside the homes, hob-nobbing with the world. It was not long before others were beginning to feel like second class citizens. One Family member recalls that situation:

> There were the "really haves" & the "haves" & the "have nots" & the "absolutely have nots," in a sense. There were the girls that could really FF & were very gorgeous & were almost to the point of being virtual prostitutes or hookers in some respects, & they were the "really haves." These were often a married couple with their children who travelled with their TV & video machine & SLR camera, the latest video camera for filming, a library of movies, & they would usually be able to rent a nice place & furnish it well & live quite well, dressed very well, & had gold necklaces & gold in their flee funds, & Swiss Francs, & were well to do in a lot of ways. Some of these people looked down on those who were the "have nots," as though they were lacking in faith. This was starting to creep into the Family & destroy our living communally & common potting of living Acts 2:44-45, "And all that believed were together & had all things common," but things were not so common—we were slowly regressing.
>
> Sometimes it was difficult during these days because the ones that were doing very well made you feel that your faith was not so good, but then you wondered really how their ministry was for the Lord & how lasting their fruit really was & how much fruit they were really bearing. This has really proven true after we moved from FFing. A lot of these so called fish have drifted away where a lot of them weren't there so much for the message but more for the girls & the relationships that they were having. In other cases some of the girls left the Family because it meant

sharing a more deeper message with their fish & getting more of a commitment out of them & knowing that they could possibly drift away, & some of these girls were attracted to the materialism side of things & left The Family not wanting to make that sacrifice.

This, in fact, created a tense debate within The Family which was addressed in the MO Letter, "*Rewards!*" Some of the homes were finding that they were being disadvantaged because they did not have women who were effective Esers or FFers. This was the case in London where Jed and Esther complained in 1983, "some homes or couples are making great sums of money mainly through ES-work on the one hand, where as on the other extreme there are families who are just as dedicated and working and trying hard but financially don't make enough headway for the shortage of time involved. A problem is that money is such a sensitive area to most, especially at this present time."[58]

At this time in The Family it was not necessary for these women to "forsake all" to The Family. They were certainly expected to tithe, but for the first time it created a division at the grassroots level of The Family which was disruptive to the spirit of community and togetherness that they sought to foster. Some of the women were spending most of their life outside the Family Homes. Their lives were lived out in the night spots and hotels of the major cities of the world. Some of those who were left behind, looking after the children and doing the chores of the Home, began to feel that they were lesser beings in the scheme of things. For some there was a "worldly" spirit which FFing brought into the Homes, which at first was exciting, but soon began to pall. Some of the women who were doing a lot of FFing were finding it difficult to stay within the confines of The Family. There was a growing concern that FFing was not only bringing people into The Family, it was also FFing some out of The Family.

The most recent documents to emerge from World Services have been remarkably candid in their repudiation of FFing. They have written frankly about the period during which it was happening, indicating the initiative of Berg in setting it in motion.

C. Children and Sex:

In the matter of Sex Berg's concern for children is that they are given the greatest degree of freedom possible. Berg believes that sex is a natural need and expression which is given by God and must therefore be good. In a sense, the defense of freedom in all forms of human pleasure is a statement of the Gospel. It is the forces of darkness and the apostasy of the churches which have produced the guilt and restraints that destroy the true purity of sexual expression. He is also convinced, by the popular Freudian view, that the repression of sexual needs produces physical and emotional harm. It is also his view that cancer and other sicknesses can be caused by people living with the mistaken idea that sexual expression is wrong or bad.

> It's a physical need! It's a God-created. God-implanted physical need! It is a necessity! It is an urge which needs to be satisfied, and if you don't get it satisfied somehow, you can develop all kinds of complexes and neuroses and all kinds of things! (*DB2*. p.568.)

It is for this reason he insists that the children be brought up in the group with no inhibitions with sex. This was one of the messages of *The Story of Davidito*. This is the most contentious publication to emerge from the group. It is a book of 750 pages which covers the birth and rearing of Davidito, the son of Maria and adopted son of David Berg. It has the appearance of a large and indulgent family album with numerous photos. It shows Davidito in the indulgent environment of The Family immediately around David Berg. Most of the book is given to stories of Davidito. But there are some 20 pages which deal with The Family's attitudes to Davidito's sexual development. It gives examples of the sort of sexual freedom which were sanctioned as acceptable in the life of the group. It describes him as being involved in a wide range of sexual behaviour with the adults. He watches couples having sexual intercourse in various situations. He is allowed sexual contact with the women around him.

> When playing on the floor he'll oftentimes spread his legs open for me to kiss his penis (what we call his 'penie'). He got to where he liked it so much he'd pull people by the hand down onto the floor and would spread his legs apart for 'the treatment.' So we had to explain to him that there are a lot more important things in life than just sex, and a time and a place for everything! (*The Story of Davidito*. p.335.)

Material of this nature in *The Story of Davidito* is at the heart of the problem which The Family face in courts around the world. But the following arguments can be put in their defence. First, it is clear that this was an experiment which was tried by Berg and his household and briefly in several other Homes. One I know of was in the *Music With Meaning* group in Greece. But there is no doubt that most of The Family did not consider this to be appropriate for them. The purpose was not to provide an opportunity in which adults could find sexual gratification for themselves. Second: the book was removed from circulation in 1987 and prior to this was not read by a majority of the group. I had the impression on showing various sections of the book to group members in Sydney that they were seeing it for the first time. Third, it was not a book which carried the same authority as MO Letters and other direct communication from David Berg. It is written by Sara, one of the women close to Berg, who had primary responsibility for Davidito's mothering. It was first published as a series of individual chapters in 1977 and 1978, and these chapters were compiled and re-published as a book in 1982. David Berg's direct comments are infrequent. At the conclusion of the particular section dealing with Davidito's sexual activity, Berg makes a generalised statement about the goodness of sex, with a mild call for restraint:

> God made children *able* to enjoy sex, so he must've *expected* them to!—I did!—*All* my life!—Thank God! I love it!—And it didn't hurt me any! Nearly all kids do anyhow, despite prohibitions!—And the only reason the System frowns on it is that the churches have taught sex is evil!—Which is contrary to the Bible!—How could God-created sexual enjoyment be a sin? The System really screwed up! God help us! They're the ones not normal— But 'let not your good be evil-spoken of'—So take it easy! (*The Story of Davidito* by Sara Davidito, 01/82, from chapter 45, written 05/77, p. 393).

Peter Amsterdam claims that this was a particularly experimental time which quickly passed, and what happened with Davidito never occurred with Techi, the second of Maria's children.

> I've lived with the Folks for 15 years. The time those Letters were written was at Teneriffe at the FFing period. At that time that Home was pretty sexual. It was a new thing & it was being pioneered at that time. You have to discuss it a lot. Once those Letters were addressed you'll see that it doesn't continue in the Letters. Dad taught us what to do & we did it. By the same token, that sexualized atmosphere of Teneriffe changed considerably when the Folks were no longer FFing in their personal Home. Maria had stopped regularly FFing by 1979 because when I was there she didn't do it, except once in South Africa. By the time they got kicked out of Tenerife they were pretty selective after that. She may have been doing a bit more when they were in Spain or Portugal. By the time they moved to Switzerland in March or April of 1978, she didn't do any except for the one time in South Africa. My point is, from the time I was there the Folks' Home was never highly sexualized. Like it shows the picture in there of Timothy & Maria & the description of having a love demo. I was never in any kind of situation like that with the Folks.[59]

I spent two days with Davidito in January 1994, and managed to question him at length about his sexual life. The resemblance to the photographs when he was 6 are unmistakable. He is 18 years old, and shows the Spanish influence of his Father, whose identity I have never discovered. He is a relaxed and easygoing young man, and has the American habit of showing respect to his elders. He was unafraid of my questions and answered them reflectively and on occasional with moments of thought. There was no sense of tension or uncertainty. He enjoys the tussle of conversation and, on a number of occasions over the cause of my conversations with Peter Amsterdam, he joined in with views that were not always according to Family orthodoxy. He is obviously used to being in a situation where he has been encouraged to question and argue, which he does in a way that indicates he has had practice.

He said that the incidents recorded in the Story of Davidito were done for his benefit—he said: "I was a test tube," and ". . . people feel that the sexual activities I had occurred so much more than it really did. They believe it had a bigger emphasis & played a greater part than it did. If they think my early life revolved around sex it's going to seem very weird, but I know that wasn't the case, so it was not such a big deal to me." It must be remembered that he lives in a somewhat isolated situation within The Family, the security demands surrounding Berg exclude him from many of the normal interchanges that a young man would expect. But he has a girl friend and enjoys relationships with young women. He shows no signs of being reluctant to talk about his early sexual experiences. He does so with in an unthreatened manner. In the end he said: "I really don't think it hurt me in any way. I never felt uncomfortable with it."

This is not conclusive evidence that the sexual freedom of his childhood has caused him great damage, but it is important to bare in mind that it was a situation where he was not preyed on. It was an attempt to live out a utopian vision. I pointed out to him that under most legal definitions of sexual abuse, Sara and the others who participated in sex with him would be found guilty. But the point they are making is that it was done not as a means to indulge adult lust, but as an attempt to save him from the disadvantages of a repressed sexual life which so distressed Berg. It must be remembered that during this time the organisation of The Family was looser and more diverse than was the case before, or since. There was a more fluid membership and less sense of cohesion in the relationship between the households. This meant that some households embraced the new freedom with greater enthusiasm than others. I have searched for an accurate picture of what the situation was in the rest of The Family. I believe the following statements are representative of the parents:

> We wanted them [the children] to have no inhibitions. It was the style of that period and we were like Hippies. We never either encouraged or

discouraged sexual contact between the children. And sexual contact was never encouraged between adults and children. But it was looked upon as 'cute' during the Davidito time, whether it was kids expressing themselves or whatever. But now we have changed and my own kids are grown up. They were only small then. Since that time I still want the kids to have a natural outlook towards sex, and I am sure we are a lot freer than most people, but now it is more discouraged.[60]

it was permissible for kids to fool around before the onset of periods or semen. But in most cases we didn't pay much attention to it. My kids were all young then. In fact this appears to be the case with most of the children in The Family.[61]

D. Changing Policy Towards Children:

David Berg has maintained a somewhat ambiguous attitude to the education of the children. In 1971, he wrote:

> We are not entirely against all education, in fact, we have quite a bit of our own, and actually, do educate people in the things of the Lord, even in our witnessing, which is our major task. (*DB4*. p. 160. 3/71)

In 1981, he wrote:

> I wouldn't at all advise any of our children to look forward to trying to get any kind of education above the high school level, even junior high school level, as long as they can read & write & figure—the 3 R's: Reading, 'Riting & 'Rithmetic—and the 3 G's: General Biology, General Social Studies, General Science, etc. (*DB1*, p.237, 1/81.)

There is also a concern to educate the children in practical matters:

> . . . how a pump works and how a motor works and all the little practical things that most everybody has to deal with.

As to the humanities, they are less interested, but do not exclude children from their personal interests.

> We don't need to get into literature except as each individual person is particularly interested. We've got enough literature in the Bible and MO Letters to keep them busy with all the literature they'd ever need to read! If they're interested in poetry or various other kinds of literature, you could let them read it if they want to, the writings of various famous Godly poets and authors, like Shakespeare, Sir Walter Scott, etc. (*DB6*, 11/75.)

The reasons given for the restriction of the children's education are not unfamiliar to those of a large number of fundamentalist Christians who have the same concern about the "secular" tendencies in the educational system. David Berg sees the fundamental task to be that of preparing the children for witnessing and leadership in the Millennium.

I'm not worried about our children's education.—They're getting the best education they could possibly get—In the Word and the nurture and admonition of the Lord and growing in faith and living by faith fulltime and witnessing and litnessing and learning to be mobile and to live *selah* and to survive. (*DB1*. p.238.)

I am not without some reservations concerning the education of the children above the primary school level. Up to that point what I have seen of the education of the children around the world is excellent. They are taught in a loving and open atmosphere, and they appear to enjoy the experience. The level of educational skills the children enjoy is above average. This is also the opinion of the NSW Department of Community Services. In the opening remarks in the case brought against The Family in Cobham Children's Court on July 28th 1992, Counsel for the Department. Ms. Robyn Tupman made the following remark:

. . . The children who they tested in fact were in many cases well above average and on the whole above average in the areas of reading, writing and comprehension. But that in the other area for which they were tested in the limited time available, that is the area of mathematics, the similar above average results were not seen.

I understand Ms. Tupman was saying the children were above average in the basic aids of reading and writing and comprehension, and average in the area of mathematics. This is the opinion shared not just by me, but other people who have had opportunity to test the children formally. One such person is Dr. Tim Watson-Munro. He was employed by the Police Department in Victoria, Australia, to prepare a report on the Buckley children from The Family. Watson-Munro formed the opinion that the children were well adjusted and well-educated. His only reservation (which was not a serious one) was similar to my own, that the educational environment was less than full. For the teens, the educational materials available are limited to a narrow band of publications emerging from fundamentalist, Creationist frameworks, although it must be said that there is a concerted attempt within The Family to address this situation. They are at an early stage in developing educational materials for this age range. They are in a sense growing up as a movement with their children, and what I observe is a change to greater diversity in the education.

What disadvantage the teenage children do suffer is not as bad as what I see operating in a number of the Christian educational schemes that are used widely in fundamentalist churches which have set up their own schools, in particular those using the Accelerated Christian Education scheme. Whatever disadvantage there is is certainly not, in my view, sufficient to warrant the action that is being advocated by the various government services, which have made it clear that they wish to remove the children from the influence of The Family. One must remember the obvious benefit which exists for the children in being nurtured in an atmosphere of love and constant care. If what is being suggested as an alternative is that these children must be educated within State schools, then I believe this cannot be argued as being in the children's best interests. I believe the limitations present in their education must be balanced against the obvious sense of security and self assurance which the children display. The argument has been put that these children are being educated in a way that puts them apart from the "values of the dominant society"; that this disadvantages then in that they are ill prepared to operate effectively in the world outside. I do not accept this argument. What is primary in my mind is the emotional and spiritual health of the children. That I believe is not at risk.

Above the teenage level, life within The Family for young adults can be an exciting affair. Travelling through their homes in Japan, Thailand, India, Russia and London, I encountered a number of young adults who were actively involved in the business of The Family. It was normal to find these young people fluent in at least two, often three languages. They take their language training seriously. Many of them were extremely competent in computing to the point that they were modifying software packages, operating at an advanced level in Desk Top publishing, and communicating in a sophisticated manner through modems throughout the world. In Russia, for example, The Family has a massive literature distribution under way. In the last 4 years this has involved the printing and publishing of over 6,000,000 posters, most of which are coloured. This is a complex and demanding situation, especially in contemporary Moscow. The young adults in Russia were heavily involved in organising this operation; it is a rich world of experience for these young people. In Britain, the young people in The Family were part of the purchasing and preparation of vehicles for the European sector. They were learning a high degree of mechanical skills involving major engine overhauls and modifications to the interior of vans.

I believe we must retain within society the right of groups such as this, when driven by powerful religious or philosophical beliefs, to put themselves at a distance from the dominant values of our culture. The rights of children in this situation is complex, and under certain conditions should be allowed to compromise the right of a group to stand against our culture. But it is not a sufficient argument to say that a group is aberrant and dangerous to its children when the only reasons advanced are that "the group is isolated, or holds eccentric beliefs, or restricts access to the state educational system for its children, or advocates an openness in sexual expression."

VI. Evaluation

The Family are a fundamentalist Christian group who hold a series of theological views which are not unfamiliar to the history of sects who have surrounded the mainline churches. Their isolation is similar, and in some ways less severe, than groups like the Exclusive Brethren, the Church of the Brethren, the Amish, and a wide range of small sects and cults which group around the teachings of particular individuals.

The first thing that needs to be said is that this group has had a history of change. They have undergone quite radical shifts in policy and behaviour since their beginnings. In fact, it is part of the theology of the group to expect change.

The changes in behaviour and theological emphasis have been signalled in the literature emerging from World Services and David Berg. The most recent moves, which shifted the group away from the liberality of The Family of Love era, have been as significant as those which occurred at other times in the group's life. One cannot judge the present behaviour of The Family on the basis of literature which was written before 1986/7.

The underlying principles which have driven Berg from the beginning have not changed, but the elaboration of them and the way in which the group is called on to act has changed dramatically. There has been a genuine consistency in their commitment to the underlying beliefs which relate to the end of the world, the coming Millennium, their attitude to sexuality, and their view of the world outside. But as is the case with all religious groups, the way in which those principles are lived out in the life of the group has accommodated to changing circumstances.

The influences which are bringing about the present retreat from earlier patterns have to do with the advancing age of the older members, the arrival of many children, and a general sense of conservatism which has developed with the passing of time. In the early days of the movement the membership was mainly young single people from the hippie era. Throughout the life of The Family, David Berg has shown himself capable of significant change when the environment around him changed. In many ways The Family, like the Moonies, are becoming more conservative in their attitudes.

As to the beliefs of The Family and the manner in which those beliefs influence the education and attitudes of the children. I do not believe we can say that they are beyond the bounds of what should be tolerated in a liberal pluralist Western culture. There were certain forms of behaviour prior to 1986 in relation to child sexuality which I believe are alarming. I believe David Berg sought to live out an ideal of freedom which is impossible in the compromised circumstances of this world. In that sense, Berg's theological system is flawed in that he does not adequately account for the nature of evil and its manifestation in this world. He has fallen prey to one of the seductions surrounding Christianity, namely the belief that it is possible to create the Kingdom of God within the world of the believing community. He sought to produce a model of Paradise within the life of The Family. In the process, he opened the world of human sexuality to the point that the distinction between Adult and Child sexual experience was lost.

I believe it is essential that children are recognised within the world of sexuality as being in a different category than adults. Indeed, I believe children must be protected from the world of adult sexuality. To do otherwise is to open children to situations which are abusive. There were a limited number of cases in the literature of The Family which encouraged the view that adult/child sexual encounters were available. This was a limited part of The Families literary output and did not lead to the widespread practice of adult/child sex within the group. I am of the opinion that all sexual encounters between adults and children have ceased. The present literature is unequivocal in its rejection of this behaviour and the people within the group are clear about their own changes.

The way in which The Family conduct their lives is the product of a coherent and elaborate theological system. They are responsible and sincere people who have gone to great lengths to arrive at an expression of faith which is consistent with what they understand to be the intention of God. They base their beliefs on a literal interpretation of the Bible and a firm view of David Berg as prophet and sage. In the context of religious history, there is nothing arbitrary or astonishing about their views. The Family as they present themselves now have a right to be respected within the diversity which makes up the contemporary pluralist nature of our society.

Dr. Millikan is an ordained minister with the Uniting Church of Australia, former Head of Religious Broadcasting of the Australian Broadcasting Corporation (ABC) and winner of the United Nation's Peace Award, Human Rights Award and New York Radio Awards. He is a former editor of *National Outlook*, and currently serves on the Commission for Doctrine in the Uniting Church. Dr. Millikan is the author of a number of articles and books on New Religious Movements, has produced several television documentaries and is an acknowledged expert on the theology of New Religious Movements.

Afterword

The Family: Where Does It Fit?

J. Gordon Melton
Institute for the Study of American Religion

In the midst of the controversy over The Family, which has been largely focused on its sexual teachings and practices, little is often said about the larger context within which the group functions. This brief article was originally written in response to several specific inquiries into ISAR concerning the place of The Family in the larger Christian community and the world of communal groups.

Q: Within the spectrum of Christian churches, where does The Family fit?

The Family is representative of American Protestant Evangelicalism, and in the majority of its beliefs and practices is indistinguishable from literally thousands of independent evangelical denominations and organizations. Evangelicalism, as it developed in both England and North America in the nineteenth century called for a return to the Bible as the only authority of faith and practice. To some extent it called for a de-emphasis upon church history and a testing of all beliefs by direct reference to Scripture. This appeal to Scriptural authority has led to a variety of interpretations of the Bible and the emergence of different theological ideas by the different Evangelical groups which otherwise share a common allegiance to the central teachings of the Christian New Testament. The Family assumes a minority position within the larger Evangelical community in its acceptance of several beliefs and practices which it finds mandated in the Bible, such as communalism and its sexual teachings.

The Family, as a separate religious group, emerged at the end of the 1960s as part of a larger movement generally referred to as the Jesus People Movement. This was one of a host of new religious movements which attempted to relate to the hippie street people subculture of the period. The Jesus People first appeared in California, but quickly spread along the West Coast of the United States and Canada, and then across the continent and into Great Britain and continental Europe. The Jesus People had their origin in the broader movement which had come to be known as Evangelicalism. Evangelicalism emerged in the 1940s as a second generation stage of American Protestant Fundamentalism. Fundamentalism arose as American Evangelicals perceived a crisis of faith within the development of American Protestant denominations.

In the early twentieth century all of American Protestantism, but especially the Presbyterian and Baptist denominations, participated in a great debate. It concerned the historic doctrines of Christianity which some, in the light of modern natural and social science, felt a need to discard or restate in different terms. These people were called Modernists, from their desire to "modernize" the faith. Fundamentalists felt that there was a need to affirm certain fundamental beliefs which were essential to the faith and defined the very nature of Christianity. Among the beliefs affirmed were the authority of the Bible as the Word of God, the Trinity, the divinity of Christ, the virgin birth and physical bodily resurrection of Jesus, and the Second Coming.

Fundamentalism was set firmly in place by the production and distribution of *The Fundamentals*, a set of eight booklets, the first of which appeared in 1910. It was a broad interdenominational movement which tried to emphasize those beliefs which all Protestant groups traditionally held in common. The controversy split some churches, especially the Northern Baptist Convention, the Congregational-Christian Churches, and the Presbyterian Church. Other more conservative denominations such as the Christian and Missionary Alliance generally aligned itself with the movement over against the Modernists. Among those who left the larger denominations were some who rejected the idea of denominations and advocated the idea of establishing independent Bible-believing ministries. They and their heirs have perpetuated an anti-denominational perspective among conservative Protestants.

As a second generation of leaders emerged in Fundamentalism in the 1940s, those leaders who still found themselves within the larger denominations controlled by Modernists suggested that conservative Protestant leaders needed to examine their separatist position and begin a new engagement with modern culture from the standpoint of their strong affirmation of Christian fundamentals. The great majority of Fundamentalists accepted that position and took the name Evangelicalism both to describe their emphasis upon evangelism of the world and to distinguish themselves from the image of the Fundamentalists of the 1920s and 1930s. Denominations and local churches who wished to identify with the movement could become members of the National Association of Evangelicals, the evangelical equivalent of the National Council of Churches.

Evangelicals emphasized the traditional doctrines of Protestant Christianity and the need to call the world's attention to the good news of salvation in Jesus Christ. Evangelicalism emerged in strength with two fairly separate wings. The Baptist/Presbyterian wing grew directly out of the Fundamentalist Movement of the 1920s. It emphasized doctrinal purity, Bible study, and the proclamation of the gospel.

The second wing was called Pentecostalism. It grew out of the Methodist Church and was distinguished among Evangelical denominations by its belief in the baptism of the Holy Spirit. The baptism of the Holy Spirit is a particular religious experience in which Christian believers feel that God's Holy Spirit comes into their life and empowers them for service. The baptism experience is usually manifested by the individual's speaking in tongues, i.e., the person begins to verbalize what appears to be a new language which the person did not previously know. The experience of the Holy Spirit also generally led to the person demonstrating one or more of the gifts of the spirit in their life. These gifts, enumerated by the Apostle Paul in the biblical book of I Corinthians include healing, prophecy, discernment of spirits, and the working of miracles. The Baptist/ Presbyterian wing of the movement generally believed that the gifts of the spirit operated during the first century but had ceased to operate once the church was well established.

Once the hippie street people culture emerged on the West Coast, Evangelical ministers from both wings of the movement began work trying to evangelize what they saw as a lost generation of young people. Prominent leaders of what became known as the Jesus People movement came from the Southern Baptist Convention, the Presbyterian Church, various Pentecostal denominations, and independent evangelical ministries. Through the 1970s, independent Jesus People ministries were soon established across America, primarily in the urban areas where a community of hippies could be found.

The Jesus People movement developed several distinctives. First, it emerged around a set of communes. Communal living had emerged spontaneously among the hippies, many of whom had adopted a lifestyle that included poverty. Communes, at first an economic necessity, then became a preferred way of life. Jesus People soon discovered their Christian communal roots. Protestantism, in reaction to the communal religious orders of Roman Catholicism, had generally eschewed communal structures in favor of middle class values. The Jesus People began a new era of appreciation of communal living among Protestants. Secondly, the hippie converts to the Jesus People retained their hippie subculture distinctives. They had long hair, enjoyed psychedelic art (while rejecting psychedelics), wrote their own rock music, and generally challenged the average middle class Christians with whom they came in contact to accept them as Christian brothers and sisters. Most were finally accepted. Most Jesus People ministries were eventually absorbed into more established denominational structures. As they aged, most hippies also shaved, cut their hair and gave up the more visible aspects of hippieness.

The Children of God

David Berg, the founder of the Children of God, was primarily associated with a conservative Protestant evangelical group, the Christian and Missionary Alliance. The Christian and Missionary Alliance, founded in 1897, was an association of evangelists and missionaries who placed a primary importance on converting the world to Christ. Its founder, Albert Benjamin Simpson, propounded what he termed the four-fold faith proclaiming Christ as Savior, Sanctifier, Healer, and Coming King. Simpson was one of the founders of the modern divine healing movement, having experienced a personal healing while a pastor in the Presbyterian Church. His teaching strongly affected the Pentecostal movement, which absorbed much of its emphasis on healing from him.

Berg also associated with Teen Challenge, the organization he was working with at the time he began his work in Huntington Beach, California, where he converted the first people who would later constitute the Children of God. Teen challenge had been founded as an independent ministry by David Wilkerson, a minister with the Assemblies of God. The Assemblies of God is one of the largest Pentecostal denominations in America. Wilkerson had caught the attention of the nation in the 1960s by his ministry among New York street gangs. It was only natural that he would develop a ministry to the street people. Berg was also associated for many years with Fred Jordan's Soul Clinic. The Soul Clinic was an independent evangelical ministry which had conducted rescue mission work in the inner city of Los Angeles for many years as well as other ministries at several locations around the country. When Berg founded the Children of God, he brought with him the consensus beliefs of American Evangelicalism as represented by the Christian and Missionary Alliance, Teen Challenge (and the Assemblies of God), and the Soul Clinic. These beliefs were shared by the Jesus People movement. The Children of God affirm the Bible as the Word of God, the Triune God, the Fall of Humanity, and the deity of Jesus Christ. It teaches the way of salvation that comes by the grace of Jesus Christ through repentance of sin and faith in Him. As Christians they accept as their basic mission the duty to evangelize the world. Every member of the Family is dedicated to this mission and spends the largest block of their time each week in that activity. They also believe in the imminent second coming of Jesus Christ and the added urgency given to their missionary work because of the near end of the world. The imminent second coming was a common belief of the Jesus People Movement and is shared with relative degrees of emphasis by the evangelical movement. From the pentecostalism of the Assemblies of God the Family also believes in the baptism of the Holy Spirit, and its members occasionally speak in tongues. It also believes in the gifts of the Spirit and its members claim the gifts of healing and the discernment of spirits.

In terms of its history the Family is representative of the Evangelical Movement, and in its primary beliefs and practices follows the Pentecostal wing of that movement. As with every other group, it has developed some peculiar beliefs and practices. In the case of the Family, in spite of sharing the overwhelming number of its beliefs and practices in common with all evangelical groups, several of its peculiarities have tended to push it to the edge and even separate it from fellowship with other evangelical churches.

Its peculiar beliefs include its reception of messages from the spirits of the departed, the prophetic role of Father David, and the living out of what is termed the Law of Love. The Family's initial break with the rest of the Jesus People came in the early 1970s. Few within the Family today remember the cause of that break concerned their belief in communicating with disembodied spirits. This belief was first spelled out in several letters concerning Abrahim, a Gypsy spirit guide, who spoke to Father David at various times.[1] Father David's relationship to Abrahim smacked of spiritism to many Evangelical leaders.

Second, the Jesus People rejected the Children of God because of the assumption by Father David of the position of a prophet and reception of revelations which they considered above and beyond the text of the Bible. Typical of such offending document is MO letter #93, "Heavenly Conversation," in which he asserts his special place as a prophet of God and calls upon the Children of God to believe his words. Father David's role in the Family's thought is still a matter of concern to Evangelicals.

Not at issue in the early 1970s, but by far the most important issue which today separates the Family from main body of Evangelicals, is their allegiance to the Law of Love and the sexual behavior which flows from it. While almost never a matter of doctrine, Evangelicals have placed great emphasis upon a sexual code which limits sexual activity to a single partner with whom one shares a monogamous marriage. Thus Evangelicals part company on the Family's allowance of heterosexual relationships between consenting adults which otherwise conform to the Law of Love. In may ways, of course, Evangelicals and the Family are very much alike and would agree on a variety of sexual issues. Both condemn abortion and homosexuality. Evangelicals disagree on birth control, but most have no problem with it. Evangelicals would welcome the emphasis upon family values so emphasized in recent Family policies and the "no sex" policy concerning minors.

The Family practice a form of spiritual or Divine healing. They believe that the Lord will heal people in answer to prayer. While this is no substitute for medical attention, it is a regular practice. They inherited this practice both from their reading of the Bible and from the growing healing movement which was initiated in Great Britain and the United States in the nineteenth century. That healing movement had its early major exponents in the Church of England and the Episcopal Church in the United States.

Albert Benjamin Simpson, a Presbyterian minister, was healed through the ministration of Episcopalian Charles Cullis. Simpson went on to become the major voice in spreading the healing ministry in Holiness and Pentecostal churches in both America and England. Through the these several churches the prayer healing ministry has spread through all of Protestantism and into Roman Catholicism.The practices of the Family in this regard (including the deliverance ministry of exorcism) is identical with that practiced in these other churches, though, of course, it takes on a slightly different flavor in each group.[2]

Q: Is The Family like other communal groups?

Along with the rest of the Jesus People movement, the Family adopted a communal life style quite early in its existence. For some, communal life was briefly abandoned in the period from 1978 to 1981, but today it has matured into a stable structure. As with all Christian communal groups, the Family looks back to the New Testament church as its model. It believes that the church described in the New Testament, which held all things in common, is a pristine model which God intended each generation to follow. The communal life style has both practical and personal spiritual benefits.

As a communal group, the Family fits into a history of communalism which has been an integral part of the Christian church in every era, but especially since the formation of the religious orders in the Roman Catholic Church in the early middle ages. Today the Roman Catholic Church, the largest of all Christian bodies, nurtures literally hundreds of communal groups consisting of people who have adopted an ordered life in order to dedicate themselves to God and their mission for Him in the world. At the time of the Reformation, most of the Protestant groups rejected communalism, but groups of free churches, part of what is popularly called the Radical Reformation (Mennonites, Brethren, etc.) adopted and have perpetuated a communal lifestyle. After three hundred years the Hutterites, an international Mennonite group, now has over 150 colonies located in several different countries (though most are in Western Canada and the American Northwest).

America became the home to a number of Christian communal groups in the nineteenth century, the United Society of Believers in Christ's Second Coming (popularly known as the Shakers) being the most successful. Protestant Christian communal groups have existed more-or-less to the present, however, in the last thirty years a marked increase in what are termed "covenant communities" has been noticed. Many were spawned by the Pentecostal Charismatic movement of the 1960s and others by the Jesus People Movement.

Communal groups can be classified by their means of production and consumption. All communal groups have to have a means of gaining the resources by which to live and all groups have to dictate rules by which those resources are allocated to the members. Communal groups are usually defined by their adoption of a community of consumption, i.e., the community allocates resources more-or-less equally to the members according to need, and excess resources are placed at the service of the group as a whole. Communal groups most frequently strive for a community of production, i.e., a system of economics by which all the members work within the group to gain the resources upon which the group lives. This community of production contrasts with communes in which each member is employed outside the community and brings their salary checks to the community treasury. Religious communes which have a community of production receive their income primarily from (1) from gifts of non-community members who support the goals of the group and (2) from income derived from businesses operated by the group. Some Roman Catholic and Anglican orders operate businesses from wineries to publishing houses and colleges, but the majority of the support of most comes from friends (members of the Roman Catholic Church, Episcopal Church, or Church of England) who support their religious work.

The Family is analogous to most Catholic and Anglican orders in that it has both a communalism of consumption and production. Members share the resources of the group relatively equally and according to need (as appropriate to their age). Surplus resources go into the distribution of religious literature. The group has also adopted a communalism of production. With few exceptions, no member of the group is employed outside of the community. It lives completely off of the gifts of friends who support its religious work, including businesses in their community who include them in their corporate giving. The Family also operates a publishing concern which produces items that are "sold" for a donation.

It is important to note that successful communal groups always assume some authority in reordering the sexual relationships of the members from that commonly practiced in society. Such assumption of authority is most easily seen in the chastity required in most Roman Catholic order communities. In groups where monogamous marriage patterns are held, the groups will often assume authority to approve marriages before they occur, dictate methods of birth control, and control sexual contact by its scheduling of group activities. On the other end of the spectrum, groups will offer patterns of sexual activity which are considerably more liberal that outside society. In such groups it is noted that multiple sexual contacts build the group and prevent special relationships between individuals from competing with their relationship to the group as a whole.

Two fairly famous groups, both of which are analogous to the Family, are the Oneida Perfectionists and the Kibbutzim. The Oneida Perfectionists, a conservative Protestant Christian group, operated for several decades in up-state New York in the mid-nineteenth century. Beginning with the biblical observation that there would be no marriage or giving in marriage in heaven, and the biblical command to be perfect as your father in heaven is perfect, founder John Humphrey Noyes attempted to create a perfect heavenly system regarding marriage on earth. He developed a social arrangement which was termed complex marriage. All of the male members were seen as married to all of the female members.

Complex marriage was based upon a system of natural birth control used in the community which prevented unplanned birth. Each month, a man would have sexual relations with one woman. Each month a different woman would be chosen. No man or woman would have intercourse with more than one woman during any given month. Particular relationships were strongly discouraged. The administration of the system was given into the hands of the older women (perceived to be lowest in the sexual pecking order) and thus gave them a great deal of power.

The Kibbutzim which grew up in the modern state of Israel developed a system of what would be considered free love. Sexual relations with consenting adults were allowed rather freely, and children were raised communally in a free atmosphere of positive sexuality. Both Oneida and the Kibbutzim criticized the common pattern of sexual relationships based on monogamous marriage. They both offered a means of separating love and sex from economic considerations and the joys of children without the economic and time consuming burdens of constant child care. In each system, adults had a guaranteed job and home irregardless of their personal attachments. Children were raised communally and thus parents were free during the day to pursue their assigned activities and had time in the evening to spend with their children. If parents separated, children were assured of care and the continued presence of both parents, and the mother had no break in support.

The Children of God have evolved as a fairly typical communal group. It grew out of the communalism which was an essential part of the Jesus People Movement. It has a system of communal production and consumption which is similar to that of Roman Catholic and Anglican orders. Its system of sexual relationships was presaged by that at Oneida, and is closest to that of the contemporary Kibbutz movement in Israel.

J. Gordon Melton is Director of the Institute for the Study of American Religion and Specialist in Religion at the University of California, Santa Barbara. The author of such standard reference works as the *Encyclopedia of American Religions* (1987-1992) and the *Encyclopedic Handbook of Cults in America* (1992). Dr. Melton is widely recognized as a leading authority on non-mainstream religions.

Appendix A

Flirty Fishing Interview

The following is a conversation with Ammi and Joan recorded in Bangkok in November 1992. Both are prominent in leadership within The Family. They are long standing members, Ammi joined when she was 17, she is now 36. Joan is approximately 40 and has been a member for 20 years.

Millikan: After the MO Letters came out, talking at FFing, there appears to have been a delay of up to a year before some of the homes actually took it seriously as something that was being asked of them. What happened with you?

Ammi: It did come to a stage in which we were faced with a choice. IT was put a bit like this: ". . . if you want to be part of it and be in the Family then you have to let us know if you agree with, FFing, or not. You can either stay behind or come with us."

Millikan: Where were you when you started?

Ammi: I was in Hong Kong in a very small house, there were two couples and myself and the children. It was there that we started a very, inspiring, very fruitful FFing ministry. Hong Kong is a very important international business center. We were working with international people. We went to the very top hotels, The Mandarin, and the Captain's Bar. That was our home spot. It was there that I first had sex during FFing.

Millikan: How did you make up your mind that you would go all the way in FFing? How did you decide that the man you were talking with was the right one?

Ammi: It was quite unusual it was not like the ordinary. I had been close to a number of people. Some I had become quite intimate with, but it had never got to that point.

Millikan: What were you looking for?

Ammi: We had to be prayerful in the way we applied FFing. We wanted to be a witness to Jesus so we had to be sure that it would not be misunderstood when we applied it, otherwise we would not get anywhere. Actually another sister had met this man and she had become quite close to him. He was a Jewish diamond merchant. She had met him and he seemed very sweet and receptive. He invited her out to dinner and she asked if she could invite some of her friends. This way we were able to witness or do something or even help her to decide if she should go all the way. We all went out together. I went with another brother who was my date for the evening, and there was another Family couple. During the evening he asked me to dance with him. I remember it had been a bad day for me, I was having a battle with something. For, when I was dancing with him I couldn't really find much to say in the way of preaching or, socking it to him with the word. But there was a tenderness a sweetness there so we sat down. He was a sweet man. Later during the meal I said privately to the sister: "He seems like a very precious man." We left them, but it didn't really work out into a FFing situation.

The next day, he called me at our flat. He asked me to go out with him. At first I was really offended. I thought, "Heh, who do you think you are? What about the other really precious sister who you were with last night? What is this, pick and choose?" I didn't know if I liked it at all. The night before I sensed that it might be coming and I knew now that he was asking me to dinner with the possibility of it leading on to something afterwards. So I was not sure. I talked it over with one of the brothers who was there. He said, "He is such a precious man. Go ahead and go to dinner with him." He knew what that could lead to. But I wasn't sure if I liked it. But I was open. So I just said to the Lord, "You have really got to show me." Anyway, he asked me to dinner that night, and I went.

During dinner, I knew this guy needed something. When he sat at the table he seemed like an ordinary guy. But when he stood up, he was huge, he was very over weight, he was enormous. He had the sort of weight that you knew would give him a complex. I don't even remember when I made the decision to go with him afterward.

He was terribly apologetic saying, "I am sorry I am so big. This is probably going to be terrible." I was saying to him (she takes on a sweet cooing voice) "That's OK . . . you are doing great, . . . It's just in your head . . . you are wonderful . . ." It was hours, and he was so big, to be frank with you I could almost not get around him. He was huge, it was not as if I had years of experience, to be able to say to him, "Now let's do this or try this." I was just there by myself thinking: "Now what do I do?" I just knew it was so important to him to be successful. I knew that if this didn't work, he would be saying to himself, (she takes on the serious tone of someone grappling with a great emotional difficulty) "Here I am I came to SE Asia, I met this cute little blond girl and I blew it." I just knew he would leave there in some sort of condemnation. I was just praying in my mind, "This cannot happen. This can't happen. Lord you have got to make it the way he wants it to be." Well we kept at it for a couple of hours and he made it. I was exhausted. All the time I was saying, "Don't give up, come on, . . . You're doing great, . . . come on, you can do it . . . you're wonderful."

Afterwards we went into a little parlor, and I said that I had done it because I wanted to give him a gift of love from the Lord. He said, "Oh, no I could never be as loving as you people. I have never seen anything like this, you guys are so far in front of me I can't believe I have experienced something like this." I said, "Oh yes you can believe. It is not me. I am not such a loving person. It comes from Jesus. And you can have him and all you need to do is pray." He became as sincere as a little child and said, "Oh yes I would like to." So he prayed with me and that was my first experience of sex in FFing and my first soul.

Joan: We did our best to love them and let the love of Jesus come through us to them. We gave so much and they received it. Many of them cried like babies. For many it was the first time they had really been told and shown that they were loved. It put them in a position where they could not respond in any other way. It was humbling for them. They could only reciprocate and be open in some way.

Ammi: There was a spiritual thing about it. For you see, I could not still reconcile that he had "picked and chosen" between us. It was all the same love and we all said the same thing. I thought it was funny because the other sister was very beautiful, a really nice girl, a precious sister. But then he told me that all his life he had had a "fantasy," as he called it. He believed that some day he would travel to South East Asia and meet a girl with blond hair who had the name . . . (he used my system name, which I was using at that time). You know some people live in a dream world, they believe if they had that one day then everything would be OK. But it was amazing to me that he had actually dreamed about it in this way. I know it was the Lord who put the vision there for him. That was what brought him to the Lord. As for me, it was quite incredible to have him tell me that. It was amazing. He was a very precious man."

Millikan: How many men did you have sex with while FFing?

Ammi: (laughs easily) I would have to sit down and work it out. Over the five years that it went on, I would say something like 50. In Hong Kong there was quite a lot of FFing. That was definitely the place where that ministry was just right. There were so many lonely travelers.

Millikan: How many nights a week were you out?

Ammi: We rotated, because I was involved in Child Care and the others had things to do in the rest of the work. I would say two or three times a week.

Millikan: Did you always go out in pairs?

Ammi: (with some indignation) Oh yes . . . we always went out in pairs. Sometimes it was more than that. We would go with three or four.

Millikan: Would it take two or three meetings before it came to sex?

Ammi: It is a very respective place the Captain's Bar. That's why they liked to see us come. We were obviously not just meeting people and taking them up to rooms. Most nights we would meet people and talk with them and then we would leave by ourselves. As a matter of fact people very much enjoyed our company. We were good for the place.

Millikan: It is a remarkable experience for someone as young as you to go through.

Ammi: But the team I was with was a remarkable group as well. They were just as much fighters as I was. The boys as well. I really admired them. They cared just as much for these guys as we did. They weren't just sending us girls out to do the FFing for them. We would receive so much support from our little home. We would arrive and they would want to know, "What happened girls?" We were all in this together.

If we had a precious Sheep, the boys and the other girls would meet him. We would have him over for dinner and they would witness to him like a family affair. If one of us was out witnessing they would make sure that there was someone waiting when we came home, they would make snacks for us and so on.

Millikan: Joan, you were married at the time of FFing, how did your husband deal with you FFing?

Joan: Once FFing started we had to come together as a family in order to make it.

We prayed a lot more. And there were times when the only times we could make it easier on your mate was to encourage one of the sisters if they were free to share. I would say, "While I am out tonight, would you mind spending a little time with my husband?" It was really difficult, it was like real crucifixion.

Millikan: Was this where Sharing got started?

Joan: It opened it up in that way. Although Sharing made it a lot easier, it was still hard. That was when the family started to grow closer together. You had the feeling that you were helping each other to win souls. Everyone was working together for the same cause.

Millikan: What happened if your partner did not like it and could not handle the situation?

Joan: Well some did not go out at all they had trials about it. At first they were told, "Well don't worry about it. Leave it for a while and think about it later." But eventually if people did not jump in and at least try, then it became like a doubt. If people arrived at the point where they not only did not do it but said that they thought it was wrong; they ended up leaving. It became a division.

Millikan: There were girls in the Family who became pregnant as a result of FFing. What do you think about the rights of the father. Did you let the fathers know what was going on?

Joan: In most cases yes. We would tell them that this was a special gift that the Lord had given to them.

Millikan: But what about married men? What would you do in situations like that. It would be the assumption, surely, of most men in these circumstances that there was little chance of pregnancy. What would you do if the man had a wife?

Joan: It never entered into our minds to divide the men from their wives. If anything you would try to encourage them to go home and be a better husband and father and stop running around so much. Many of them were doing it all the time. They may have been doing it a bit with us. But we were trying to make their lives more meaningful. Even if there was a child I don't think it affected things.

Ammi: It was definitely up to the man's discretion. The sister would not do anything to jeopardize the man's relationship. We would never turn up and say "Heh I've got a child here . . . ."

Millikan: But there are certain legal matters and responsibilities. You could for example claim financial support from the Father in certain places.

Ammi: I don't know of anyone who did that. We were not in it for that. We knew the Lord was going to look after us.

Joan: Usually the men were very careful to fill us in on their situation. They would let us know whether we could write or where we could write to. We were always very sensitive to this we never wanted to hurt anyone. In the end all we wanted to do was bring them close to the Lord and for them to be better fathers and better businessmen that helped others.

Millikan: Did some of these men fall in love with you?

Ammi: I can think of a couple of situations in my experience where this happened. But we made it very clear to them where our loyalty lay. They knew that we would never think of coming out of the Family. Although we knew we were meeting a need in their lives, which they very much longed for and looked forward to, they usually lived in another country. The relationship was based on when they could come through the area again. It enabled them to keep a special place in their hearts for us.

Appendix B

Partial Analysis of the Racial Make Up of the Family (World Services, February 9, 1994)

In recent months we have conducted a survey of Family Homes to determine the racial make-up of the current D.O. members of The Family. This was the first time that we can recall conducting a survey of this nature. Our members come from approximately 75 countries and, as a result, our communities are very cosmopolitan. There is also a large amount of intermarrying, and this has resulted in quite a blur in racial distinctions in our second and third generations. Unfortunately, at the time of drafting this report, only around 80% of our Homes have reported back with these statistics. However, these Homes are from all geographical areas of our missionary work, so we believe these results could be reasonably extrapolated to provide a fairly accurate portrayal of the racial mix of the entire Family.

We have chosen to use the term "race" rather than the more precise term "ethnic," since trying to neatly pigeonhole each member into an ethnic category proved to be much too complicated of an undertaking. The survey was therefore conducted on several broad racial categories. The one exception to this was the ethnic/religious category Jewish. Due to recent allegations against our group of anti-Semitism, we thought that it would help to dispel this misconception if we were able to precisely note how many Jewish members we have. The categories we decided on were: Caucasian, Asian, African (including African-American, African-Brazilian, etc.), Latin,* Jewish, Mixed Race (Other than Latin),** and Other.

(* By "Latin," we mean anyone of Latin American origin who does not fall into any of the specific categories excluding "Other." If a member is an African-Brazilian for example, he would be listed under African. If he or she is of mixed South American Indian and European parentage then he or she would be listed as Latin. We realize that Latin is not a racial grouping, but in order to keep this survey simple, we settled on this.)

(** "Mixed race" is when the mother is one race and the father another.)

We also divided the survey up between adults (those over 21) and minors (those under 21). The following are the results of the survey:

Race	Adults (over 21)	Minors (under 21)
Caucasian	1,458	3,899
Asian	377	380
African	29	25
Latin	549	1,368
Jewish	50	28
Mixed Race	92	1,986
Other	1	6
TOTAL	2,556	6,900

At the present time The Family has a total population of 9,337 full-time members, composed of 3,047 adults and 6,290 minors. (It is interesting to note that the ratio of adults to minors is almost exactly 1:2.) The above table therefore represents approximately 75% of our total membership, (84% of our adults and 70% of our minors.)

Taking the results above, we can come up with what could be the make-up of the hypothetical global Family Home (borrowing from the popular conception of the Global Village) of 100 people. This Home would consist of 33 adults and 67 minors. Among the adults would be 18.8 Caucasians, 4.9 Asians, 0.4 Africans, 7.1 Latins, 0.7 Jews and 1.1 mixed race person. Among the minors would be 34.1 Caucasians, 5.8 Asians, 0.4 Africans, 11.7 Latins, 0.5 Jews and 14.5 of mixed race.

The percentage of Jewish members in The Family (1.12%) is almost four times that of the percentage of Jews in the world population. According to sources that we have on hand, there are approximately 17.8 million Jews (figures obtained from the World Almanac 1994 edition), which represents about 0.3% of the world's population.

Geographic factors should be taken into consideration when assessing our African/African-American population. Our work was never very extensive in Africa, in fact there were only a handful of Homes that existed there, and then only for a few years in the late '70s. Thus, The Family's outreach to people of African origin has only actually been active amongst the approximately 70 million people of African descent resident outside of Africa. They represent approximately 1.2% of the world's population, which although 50% greater, does not render insignificant the percentage make-up of 0.8% African/African-Americans, etc., in The Family.

Almost half of our number are other than Caucasian. Almost 1,000 of our children that we received information on (22%) are from racially mixed marriages. If this percentage is extrapolated for all our children it is estimated that over 1,350 of The Family's minors would be racially mixed.

We feel the other figures speak for themselves in that they show The Family to be a fully integrated, multicultural, multiracial society.

Notes and References

Chapter 1. "Heaven's Children":
The Children of God's Second Generation

Aries, Philippe (1962) *Centuries of Childhood: A Social History of Family Life.*New York: Vintage Books.

Bettelheim, Bruno (1969) *Children of the Dream.* New York: The Macmillan Company.

Book of Remembrance, Vols.I & II, March 1983. World Services, Zurich, Switzerland.

Davis, Deborah Berg (1984) *The Children of God: The Inside Story.* Grand Rapids, Michigan: Zondervan Books.

Davis, Rex and James T. Richardson (1976) "The Organization and Functioning of the Children of God" in *Sociological Analysis* 37:321-339.

Foster, Lawrence (1981) *Religion and Sexuality: Three American Communal Experiments of the Nineteenth Century.* New York: Oxford University Press.

Homer, Michael W. (1993) "New Religions and child custody cases: Comparisons between the American and European Experience" presented at the International conference on New Religions and the New Europe, March 25-28 London School of Economics.

Jacobs, Janet (1984) "The Economy of Love in Religious Commitment: The Deconversion of Women from Non-traditional Movements" in *Journal of the Scientific Study of Religion* 13:155-71.

Richardson, James T. and Rex Davis (1983) "Experiential Functionalism: Revising Orthodoxy in the Jesus Movement" *Journal of the American Academy of Religion* 51: 397-425.

Wallis, Roy (1979) "Sex Marriage and the Children of God" in *Salvation and Protest: Studies of Social and Religious Movements* (ed.) Roy Wallis. New York: St.

Martins Press.

_____(1982) "Charisma, Commitment and Control in a New Religious Movement," pp.73-140 in *Millennialism and Charisma*, edited by Roy Wallis. Belfast: The Queens University.

Chapter 2. Update on "The Family": Organizational Change and Development in a Controversial New Religious Group

This paper was developed in final form while the author was a Visiting Professor in the Law School and in the Department of Studies in Religion at The University of Queensland, Brisbane, Australia. Appreciation is expressed for this support, and for the sabbatical leave from the University of Nevada, Reno.

Adams, R. and R. Fox (1972). "Mainlining Jesus: The New Trip." *Society* 9(4): 50-56.

Anthony, Dick (1990). "Religious Movements and Brainwashing Litigation: Evaluating Key Testimony." In T. Robbins and D. Anthony (eds.), *In Gods We Trust*. New Brunswick, NJ: Transaction Books.

Barker, Eileen (1983), "The Ones Who Got Away: People Who Attend Unification Church Workshops and Do Not Become Members." In E. Barker (ed.), *Of Gods and Men*. Macon, GA: Mercer University Press.

Barker, Eileen (1984). *The Making of a Moonie: Choice or Brainwashing?* Oxford: Blackwell.

Beckford, James (1978a). "Accounting for Conversion." *British Journal of Sociology* 29(2): 249-62.

Beckford, James (1978b). "Through the Looking-glass and Out the Other Side: Withdrawal from Rev. Moon's Unification Church." *Les Archives de Sciences des Religions* 45: 95-116.

Beckford, James (1985). *Cult Controversies*. London: Tavistock.

Bird, Fred and W. Reimer (1983). "Participation Rates in New Religious and Parareligious Movements." *Journal for the Scientific Study of Religion* 21(1): 1-14.

Davis, Rex and J.T. Richardson (1976). "Organization and Functioning of the Children of God." *Sociological Analysis* 37(4): 321-339.

Drakeford, J.W.(1972). *Children of Doom*. Nashville, TN: Broadman Press.

Enroth, Ronald, E. Ericson, and C. B. Peters (1972). *The Jesus People*. Grand Rapids, Michigan: Eardmans.

Galanter, Marc (1980). "Psychological Induction in the Large Group: Findings from a Modern Religious Sect." *American Journal of Psychiatry* 137: 1574-79.

Galanter, Marc and C. Diamond (1981). "'Relief' of Psychiatric Symptoms in Evangelical Religious Sects." *British Journal of Hospital Medicine* 26: 495-98.

Kilbourne, B. and J. T. Richardson (1982). "Cults versus Families: A Case of Misattribution of Cause?" *Marriage and the Family Review* 4(3&4): 81-101.

Kilbourne, B. and J.T. Richardson (1984). "Psychotherapy and New Religions in a Pluralistic Society." *American Psychologist* 39(3): 237-251.

Kilbourne, B. and J.T. Richardson (1986), "Cultphobia." *Thought* 61(241): 258-266.

Lang, K. and G. Lang (1961). *Collective Dynamics*. New York: Crowell.

Lewis, James (1986). "Reconstructing the 'Cult' Experience: Post-Traumatic Attitudes as a Function of Mode of Exit and Post-Involvement Socialization."

Sociological Analysis 46: 151-59.

Lewis, James and D. Bromley (1987). "The Cult Withdrawal Syndrome: A Case of Misattribution of Cause?" *Journal for the Scientific Study of Religion* 26(4): 508-22.

Richardson, J.T. (1980). "Conversion Careers." *Society* 17(3): 47-50.

Richardson, J.T. (1982a). "Conversion, Brainwashing, and Deprogramming in New Religious Movements." *The Center Magazine* 15(2): 18-24.

Richardson, J.T. (1982b). "Financing the New Religions: A Broader View." *Journal for the Scientific Study of Religion* 21(3): 255-268.

Richardson, J.T. (1985a). "The Active Versus Passive Convert: Paradigm Conflict in Conversion/Recruitment Research." *Journal for the Scientific Study of Religion* 24(2): 163-179.

Richardson, J.T. (1985b). "The 'Deformation' of New Religious Groups: Impacts of Societal and Organizational Factors." In T. Robbins, et al. (eds.), *Cults, Culture, and the Law*. Chico, CA: Scholars Press.

Richardson, J.T. (1985c). "Psychological and Psychiatric Studies of Participation in New Religions." In L. Brown (ed.), *New Perspectives in Psychology of Religion*. Pergamon Press.

Richardson, J.T. (1991). "Cult/Brainwashing Cases and the Freedom of Religion." *Journal of Church and State* 33(1): 55-74.

Richardson, J.T. (1993). "Religiosity as Deviance: Negative Religious Bias In and Misuse of the DSM-III." *Deviant Behavior* 14: 1-21.

Richardson, J.T. (1994). The Social Psychology of 'Brainwashing' Claims." In J. Hadden and D. Bromley (eds,) *Sects and Cults in America*. Greenwich, CT: JAI Press.

Richardson, J.T. and Rex Davis (1983). "Experiential Fundamentalism: Revisions of Orthodoxy in the Jesus Movement." *Journal of the American Academy of Religion* LI(3): 397-425.

Richardson, J.T. and B. Kilbourne (1983). "Classical and Contemporary Brainwashing Models." In D. Bromley and J. Richardson (eds.), *The Brainwashing/Deprogramming Controversy*. Toronto: Edwin Mellen Press.

Richardson, J.T., Mary Stewart, and R.B. Simmonds (1979). *Organized Miracles*. New Brunswick, NJ: Transaction Books.

Richardson, J.T., Jan van der Lans, and Frans Derks (1986). "Leaving and Labelling: Voluntary and Coerced Disaffiliation from New Religious Movements." *Social Movements, Conflict, and Change* 8: 385-393.

Robbins, Thomas and Dick Anthony (1982). "Deprogramming, Brainwashing, and the Medicalization of Deviant Religious Groups." *Social Problems* 29: 283-297.

Robbins, Thomas, Dick Anthony, and J. McCarthy (1983), "Legitimating Repression." In D. Bromley and J. Richardson (eds.), *The Brainwashing/Deprogramming Controversy*. Toronto: Edwin Mellen.

Shupe, Anson, and David Bromley (1980). *The New Vigilantes: Deprogrammers, Anti-Cultists and the New Religions*. Beverly Hills, CA: Sage.

Shupe, Anson and David Bromley (1994). *The Anti-Cult Movement in Comparative Perspective*. Forthcoming, Greenwich, CT: JAI Press.

Solomon, Trudy (1981); "Integrating the 'Moonie' Experience: A Survey of Ex-members of the Unification Church." In T. Robbins and D. Anthony (eds.), *In Gods We Trust*. New Brunswick, NJ: Transaction Books.

Solomon, Trudy (1983). "Programming and Deprogramming the 'Moonies': Social Psychology Applied." In D. Bromley and J. Richardson (eds.), *The Brainwashing/*

Deprogramming Controversy. Toronto: Edwin Mellen.

Straus, Roger (1976). "Changing Oneself: Seekers and the Creative Transformation of Life Experience." In J. Lofland (ed.), *Doing Social Life.* New York: Wiley.

Straus, Roger (1979). "Religious Conversion as a Personal and Collective Accomplishment." *Sociological Analysis* 40: 158-165.

Shapiro, Eli (1977). "Destructive Cultism." *American Family Physician* 15: 80-87.

van Zandt, David (1985). Ideology and Structure of the Children of God." Unpublished Ph.D. dissertation, University of London.

Wallis, Roy (1976). "Millennialism and Community: Observations on the Children of God." *The Sociological Review*

Wright, Stuart (1984). "Post Involvement Attitudes of Voluntary Defectors from Controversial New Religious Movements." *Journal for the Scientific Study of Religion* 23: 172-

Wright, Stuart (1987). *Leaving the Cults: The Dynamics of Defection.* Washington, D.C.: Society for the Scientific Study of Religion.

Chapter 3. The Family: History, Organization, and Ideology

1. For treatment of the history of The Family see Roy Wallis: "Observations on the Children of God," *The Sociological Review,* Vol. 24, No. 4, pp. 807-829; Rex Davis and James T. Richardson: "The Organization and Functioning of the Children of God," *Sociological Analysis,* Vol. 37, Winter 1976, pp. 321-339. More extensive treatment may be found in David Van Zandt: *Living in the Children of God,* Princeton University Press, Princeton,1991.

2. Van Zandt, David E. *Living in the Children of God.* Princeton University Press: Princeton,1991.

3. Berg, David "I Gotta Split," in *Daily Bread,* vol. 4, World Services, Zurich, 1987, page 75.

4. Berg, David. "The Colony Revolution," in *Daily Bread* vol 6, World Services, Zurich, 1988, page 202.

5. Van Zandt, 1991.

6. Berg, David."Going Home -Go Mobile!" in *Daily Bread,* vol 9, World Services, Zurich, 1990, page 444.

7. Van Zandt, 1991.

8. Numerous public statements have been issued by The Family. See, for example, "Our Replies to Allegations of Child Abuse," World Services, Zurich, 1992. With each new accusation or police action, The Family releases statements to a large number of organizations and individuals.

9. Wallis argues that Berg's soteriology is Arminian but not antinomian. See Roy Wallis, "Recruiting Christian Manpower." Society, 15 (May-June 1978) 72-74. However, other observers have argued that, especially in the area of sexual morality, the group has moved toward antinomianism (Van Zandt, 1991).

10. Statements of The Family's ideology are widely available. See for example, "Our Statement of Faith," World services, Zurich, 1992.

11. Berg, David "When the Comet Comes." in *Daily Bread* vol. 2, World Services, Zurich, 1985, page 301.

12. Berg, David "They Staged the Whole Thing." in *Daily Bread* vol. 1, World

Services, Zurich, 1983, page 463.

13. Berg, David. "Why Anti-Semitism." *Daily Bread* vol. 1, World Services, Zurich, 1983, page 399.

14. Berg, David. "Revolutionary Sex," *Daily Bread* vol. 5, World Services, Zurich, 1988, page 329.

15. For a complete statement of The Family's official position on sexual practices see: "Attitudes, Conduct, Current beliefs and Teachings Regarding Sex," (official policy statement) World Services, Zurich, 1992.

Chapter 6. Sexuality and the Maturation of The Family

1. A fairly complete set of the Family's literature has been deposited in the American Religions Collection at the Davidson Library of the University of California—Santa Barbara. The collection is in the Special Collections Department and does not circulate but is available for use by any scholars and researchers who come to the library.

2. Father David is the religious name adopted by the founder of the Children of God/The Family, David Berg. It is the most common name I have heard used by members of the Family in referring to him, though he is frequently called by the more familial "Dad."

3. This paper is one of several upon which this author is currently working. A paper upon the organization changes in The Family will be forthcoming in the fall 1994.

4. The primary study of the literature has been enhanced by interviews with a number of members and former members who lived in the Family through the important years 1978-82, interviews with current leaders in the Family, and the review of a variety of material written by former members currently in a hostile relationship with the Family. These additional resources were all helpful in reaching some assessment of what was occurring during the period when the Children of God made their transition into the Family as it exists today.

5. A very helpful text in tracing the background of the Family is David E. Van Zandt, *Living in the Children of God* (Princeton, NJ: Princeton University Press, 1991). This study is based upon filed work done in the late 1970s, but includes a brief postscript written just prior to publication in 1991. That postscript, unfortunately, is not as accurate as the main body of the text.

6. These Mo Letters include *Revolutionary Women* (#250, June 20, 1973); *Revolutionary Sex* (#258, March 27, 1973); and the 1970 talk a reissued as *Revolutionary Love-Making* (#259,). Response to the letters led to a forth epistle, *Women in Love* (#292, December 20, 1973). Also important was an earlier letter, "*Mountin' Maid!*," (#240, December 27, 1970), written earlier but released for general distribution in 1973.

7. Allowing for the specific differences in religious orientation and communal mission, the Children of God/The Family and the Kibbutzim are remarkably similar in their sexual mores and child rearing practices. In each, the economic imperatives on the family unit have been removed by the collective lifestyle, and during their first generation of the Kibbutzim, members engaged in a wide variety of experimentation in family organization and sexual relations, before

settling into a mature system of monogamous relationships which might or might not result in legal marriages. Unmarried adults are allowed to engage in sex with any other consenting adult. Children are raised and educated collectively. Sexual education is integrated into their school work from an early age. The sexes share common rooms from infancy through high school and they share a common shower until they reach high school age. In the beginning the high school youth shared a common shower, but they requested separate showers (as the adults had) and it has become common practice to allow it. High school students are discouraged from sexual relationships, but graduates are free to engage in sex as they feel led. See Melford E. Spiro, *Kibbutz: Venture in Utopia* (Cambridge, MA: Harvard University Press, 1956).

8. Arthur converted, joined the family, and as of 1993 is still a member.

9. (#293, January 3, 1974).

10. See Father David's discussion of this point in *Male and Female* (#529, September 5, 1976).

11. *Revolutionary Women*, Op. cit., p. 1925. See also the 1970 letter released in 1973, *Mountin' Maid!* (#240, December 27, 1970).

12. *You Are the Love of God!* (#699, June 5, 1978)

13. *The Law of Love* (#302C, March 21, 1974).

14. Ibid., p. 2413.

15. See the various letters issued through 1976 and into 1977 especially *Four Fishing Failures* (#533, April 6, 1976); *FF Tips* (#548, May 4, 1976); *The FFers Handbook!* (559, January 1977); *FFing Behaviour!* (#563, December 1976); and *Afflictions* (#569, November 25, 1976).

16. *Our Declaration of Love* (#607, October 9, 1977); *Law vs. Love* (#647, July 23, 1977); and *Is Love Against the Law?* (#648, January 1978).

17. *Love vs. Law!*, op.cit., p. 5010. This same point was reiterated on page 5018 of *Is Love Against the Law?*:

    28. *GOD'S ONLY LAW IS LOVE! THERE IS NOW NO OTHER LAW*, no Mosaic law, no church law, no laws against adultery. —Those laws don't exist as far as *we're* concerned. They are only to regulate the *ungodly*, as he says in I. Tim.1:9, and by which the unrighteous who are violating the laws of God will be judged.

    29. *YOU HAVE TO JUDGE EVERY SINGLE CASE ON ITS OWN MERITS* and its own conditions as to whether whatever's being done is done in *love*. And as far as I know, *most* of what we do is certainly in love, if not *all*. We're trying to do it *all* in love, that's for sure. We're trying to do it *because* of love and because we *need* God's love.

18. *The Law of Love*, op.cit., p. 2414.

19. See particularly *Love vs. Law!*, op.cit., for an expression of this idea.

20. One can see the present statement of the Law of love and its consistency with the late 1970s in Why Do Ye Stone Us? (#2835, December 1992). Also published in *Good News!* (#554, July 1993). A reflection on the changes brought about during the 1980s was made in Questions and Answers on Sex, Freedom & Relationships! (#2718, July 1991). Also published in *Good News!* (#486, November 1991).

21. The major abuse into which the national and international leadership fell was the demand for money which they used in some cases to support a lifestyle plainly out of keeping with that shared by most members. However, in relation to flirty fishing, a different type of abuse results which is insightful. As the

practice of flirty fishing spread, women who wished to participate were forced to go through a lengthy process of being approved by the higher leadership. This process would often involve waiting until a leader happened to visit a local center or a trip out of the country to the leader's residence. It is of some interest that authority in this case was exercised by blocking member's participation in FFing, rather than active recruitment into it.

22. Cf. *Jesus Babies!* (#739, June 24, 1976).
23. *Sex Questions and Answers*, Parts 1-3 (#815-817, 1979).
24. (#818, July 1970, 1980).
25. (#779, November 8, 1978).
26. This practice can hardly be described as an adult-child sex act, as has been hinted at in some writings on The Family. It offered no sexual satisfaction to the adult, and had as its object the speedy drifting off to sleep of the child.
27. Van Zandt (op.cit, p. 170-71) overstates the case when he suggests, "Sexual sharing among children who are as young as eight or nine years old is not uncommon." The implication of Van Zandt's conclusion is that children were being involved with adults in intercourse. Such is not condoned either literally or by inference in the literature. The expression of childhood sexual "sharing" was clearly to be limited to exploration of their bodies, nudity, and masturbation.
28. *The Story of Davidito* (Zurich, Switz.: The Family of Love, 1982), especially the chapter entitled "My Little Fish!", has been frequently cited as further evidence of inappropriate childhood sexual contact. Leaving aside for the moment the question of one's agreement with the Family's child rearing practice, *The Story of Davidito* is quite consistent with the plainly stated policies articulated elsewhere. "My Little Fish" includes pictures of Davidito over the first three years of his life. He is shown cuddling with other children, exploring the breasts of an adult woman, and baby-like sucking the breast of the same woman. There is no hint of sexual intercourse between adults and The Family's children.
29. (#902, April 4, 1977). This letter though written in 1977 was not released until 1980.
30. As noted, at the time *Child Brides!* (#902, April 4, 1977) was written (1977) and distributed (1980), there were no teenagers in the movement to speak of. The Family had been founded only ten years previously, and except for a very few teens brought in by their parents converting, all the young [people were ten and younger. By the time teens appeared in number in the mid 1980s, this letter had become obsolete, and no marriages as described in the letter were ever made.
31. Van Zandt (op.cit., p. 53) overstates his case again in his discussion of these 1979/1980 letters. While there is a consistent theme of educating children about sex, allowing children to explore their sexuality without threat of adult reaction, and suggesting youth be able to enjoy sex with their contemporaries, there is no mention of any adult/child sex.
32. (#999, May 20, 1988).
33. Ibid., p. 7698.
34. *The Devil Hates Sex!—But God Loves It!* also raised the question of incest in some less than clear remarks. It appears that the passing references treat it much as early teen marriages as Maria is quoted as saying, "Well, we'll just have to tell the kids [i.e., s of the Family] that its not prohibited by *God*, but you'd better watch out because its *dangerous.*!
35. *The Video Ministry* (#977, March 1981).

36. *Mugshots!* (#979, 1980).
37. *Nudity Can Be Beautiful* (#1006, March 1981): 7793.
38. From viewing a number of these videos, it is obvious that the women copied each other in a set style of dancing that adhered to a rather limited dance style.
39. In the several videos this author has viewed, several women were involved in some sexual contact including kissing, fondling and mutual masturbation. It should be noted that no minors appeared in any of the love videos.
40. The dance videos were taken out of circulation in 1987, and in 1990 all copies ordered erased and/or destroyed.
41. Within months of suggesting the love videos, Father David found that they did not live up to the ideal he had in mind. Thus he wrote in Glorify God in the Dance! (#1026, August 24, 1981) that the love videos should be stopped SO AS NOT TO TAKE A CHANCE WITH OUR INEXPERIENCE IN PRODUCING SOMETHING THAT IS MORE UGLY THAN IT IS BEAUTIFUL. He also warned that in some countries that the possession of such videos were against the law. He also ordered that in the future that the film makers avoid the showing of the pubic areas and actual sex organs and that men no longer appear in any of them.
42. The great majority of the people I have interviewed (including some who participated in the dance videos) never saw the love videos.
43. Cf. *Fire & Ice!* (#1213, October 2, 1982).
44. At best, from today's perspective, the videos represent a naive idealism operating in the context of a sexually liberal culture of their Greek and Brazilian neighbors. The present Family leadership has admitted the mistake in making such videos.
45. At the beginning of 1982, Father David even had to issue a letter noting that he had not lost his commitment to FFing. See *The 7 F's of FFing!* (#1083, January 1, 1982), especially paragraph 96.
46. It should be noted that in such a liberal atmosphere that some Family members did not participate. According to interviews, the liberality of sexual behavior varied considerably from one home to the other. Also, on person I interviewed told of leaving Rio with her spouse and developing a ministry in rural Brazil to stay away from the sexual scene in the city.
47. Herpes would remain an ongoing concern and steps to keep it from spreading were introduced and periodically updated and revised. See the most recent set in *Family Special News Magazine!*(#166, May 1990).
48. *Ban the Bomb!* (#1434, April 1983).
49. See "Questions You Always Wanted to Ask!" published in the *Basic Training Handbook* (Zurich: World Services, 1987): 293-300.
50. *Teen Sex!* (#2061, September 1985). This letter was published in *Good News!* for November 1985 and republished in the *Basic Training Handbook*.
51. *Teen Marriage Rules!* (#2589, September 1989). This letter was also published in *Good News!* #416 (March 1990).
52. It must be remembered that there is a fifteen to twenty year gap in the Family between the oldest of the now (1994) young adults (now in their early twenties) and the majority of the older members (now in their early 40s).
53. *Questions & Answers on Sex, Freedom & Relationships!* (#2817, July 1991). Published in the November 1991 *Good News!*
54. (#2313, March 1987). Published in *Good News!* #305, February 1988. Follow-up to the new approach to FFing was given in a series of issues of *Family Specials*

News Magazine! (#62-67, May & June 1987)).

55. These new rules were laid down in a series of policy letters including as special AIDS Edition of *Good News!* (#287, October 1987). Subsequent statements were included in the November 1987 issue.

56. "The PER!" (2865, March 1993). Also published in *Good News!* (#553, July 1993).

Chapter 7. Keeping the Faith and Leaving the Army: TRF Supporters of the Lord's Endtime Family

Notes:

1. This research was supported by the Nuffield Foundation whilst working as research officer for INFORM (Information Network Focus on Religious Movements). Research on the Family was undertaken on visits to four different Family homes between 1991 and 1993—three in the UK and one in the USA; on visits to a TSer's home, conversations with TSers and attendance at a TS gathering in 1993 where there were some 150 people. The methodology so-far used has been one of interviews and participant observation as well as use of the group's own literature and material written on the group.

2. In 1979 TRF was distinguished from IRF (Individual Report Form) by which individuals who had left the Family could receive Family literature by sending in a Report Form monthly and at least $10. The classification, however, lasted only about 18 months.

References:

Horton, R. "African Traditional Thought and Western Science" in *Africa*, 37, 1-2.

Richardson, J. & Davis, R. "Experiential Fundamentalism: Revisions of Orthodoxy in the Jesus Movement," 1983.

Wallis, R. "Sex, Marriage and the Children of God" in *Salvation and Protest: Studies of Social and Religious Movements* (ed), New York: St. Martins Press, 1979.

Wallis, Roy. "Charisma, Commitment and Control in New Religious Movements," in *Millenialism and Charisma*, edited by Roy Wallis, Belfast: The Queens University.

Chapter 8. The Children of God and The Family in Italy

1. MO Letter No.180 "Arrivederci Roma!", September 1972, now in *The MO Letters 151-300*, Hong Kong: Gold Lion Publishers, 1976, pp.1497-1505.

2. *Ibid.*

3. MO Letter No.184 "Are the Children of God Catholics or Protestants?", September 1972, in *The Mo Letters 151-300*, op.cit., pp.1521-1530.

4. MO Letter No.192 "You've Gotta Be a Baby! Pope—Papal Audience—Pope Blesses Children of God", October 1972, in *The MO Letters 151-300*, op.cit., pp.1580-1587.

5. See Tribunale Penale di Roma (Criminal Court of Rome), November 15, 1991,

In re Berg and others, unpublished decision in the collection of CESNUR (Center for Studies on New Religions, Torino, Italy) and in the archives of the Criminal Court of Rome (RG 3841/84).

6. Gabriella Valpondi, former member of the Children of God, at the talk show *Detto fra noi,* Italian public TV, channel 2, hosted by Piero Vigorelli, April 24, 1991. David E. Van Zandt, a sociologist who did first covert and then overt participant observation of the Children of God and The Family of Love in the 1970s, claims that flirty fishing was going on in a club in Florence where Jeremy Spencer, a convert to Berg's movement from the rock band Fleetwood Mac, also occasionally played, but it is unclear whether any of the flirty fishers was Italian (see David E. Van Zandt, *Living in the Children of God,* Princeton: Princeton University Press, 1991, p.190).

7. See Tribunale Penale di Roma, doc.cit., p.5.

8. Michele C.Del Re, *Nuovi idoli, nuovi dei,* Rome: Gremese, 1988.

9. Michele C. Del Re, "Plagio criminoso e lecita persuasione nei culti emergenti", in *Studi in memoria di Pietro Nuvolone,* vol.II, Milan: Giuffré, 1991, p.79.

10. Tribunale Penale di Roma, doc.cit., pp.3-5.

11. *Le dottrine fondamentali e le linee di condotta delle comunità missionarie indipendenti comunemente note come The Family,* Italian ed., Rome: The Family, and Zurich: World Services, 1993, pp.78-79. It is beyond the scope of this paper to discuss when exactly and to what extent the unorthodox practices of the 1970s and early 1980s have been abandoned. That important changes took place around 1987 has however beem recognized also by scholars not particularly sympathetic to The Family such as D.E.Van Zandt, *Living in the Children of God,* op.cit.

Chapter 10. New Religions and Child Custody Cases: Comparisons Between the American and European Experience

Originally Presented at the International Conference on New Religions and the New Europe Sponsored by CESNUR, March 25-28, 1993, London School of Economics.

1. Even before the revolution unorthodox creeds from Europe such as the Quakers, Shakers, Mennonites, Moravians and Huguenots, appeared and thrived in America. After the Great Awakening and the first mass revival movement, there were born on American soil, the Mormons, Spiritualists, Adventists, Christian Scientists and Jehovah Witnesses. More recently, in the 1960s when Americans began to look east, new religious movements such as the Unification Church and Hare Krishnas have spread in the United States. Legal problems concerning new religious movements are often discussed in legal journals both in the United States and Europe. *See, for example,* Thomas Robbins, William C. Shepherd and James McBride, eds., *Cults, Culture and the Law: Perspectives on New Religious Movements* (Chico [California]: Scholars Press, 1985). For discussions of new religious movements in Europe *see* Francis Messner, *Le sétte e le nuove religioni in Europa. Aspetti giuridici, in Libertá Religiosa Diritto e Fenomeno delle Sétte* (special issue of *Sétte e religioni*) (Bologna: Edizioni Studio Domenicano, April-June, 1992), pp. 223-258. *See also,* Michele C. Del Re *Culti*

emergenti e diritto penale (Napoli: Jovene, 1992); and Paola Braggion, *I nuovi movimenti religiosi e la libertá religiosa* (Unpublished doctoral dissertation, University of Milan Law School, 1990).

2. For a study of the practice of Mormon polygamy, see, Lawrence Foster, *Religion and Sexuality: The Shakers, the Mormons and the Oneida Community* (Urbana and Chicago: University of Illinois Press, 1984); Richard S. Van Wagoner, *Mormon Polygamy, A History,* 2d ed. (Salt Lake City: Signature Books, 1989); Jessie L. Embry, *Mormon Polygamous Families, Life in the Principle* (Salt Lake City: University of Utah Press, 1987).

3. For a study of Mormonism's abandonment of polygamy see, D. Michael Quinn, "LDS Church Authority and Plural Marriages, 1890-1904," *Dialogue: A Journal of Mormon Thought* 18:1 (Spring 1985): 9-105.

4. Concerning Mormon Fundamentalists see, D. Michael Quinn, "Plural Marriage and Mormon Fundamentalism," in Martin E. Marty and R. Scott, eds., *Fundamentalism and Society* (Chicago and London: The University of Chicago Press, 1993), pp. 240-293. The best study of the Short Creek group of Mormon fundamentalists is contained in Martha S. Bradley, *Kidnapped From That Land, the Government Raids on the Short Creek Polygamists* (Salt Lake City: University of Utah Press, 1993).

5. For additional examples see Richard S. Wagoner, *Mormon Polygamy, A History* 2d ed. (Salt Lake City: Signature Books, 1989), pp. 200-17.

6. The United States Supreme Court determined the practice of polygamous marriages was illegal in the landmark decision of *Reynolds v. United States,* 98 U.S. 145 (1879). Although one Supreme Court Justice suggested that *Reynolds* was wrong and would eventually be reversed, *Wisconsin v. Yoder,* 406 U.S. 244, 247 (1972) (dissenting opinion of William O. Douglas), subsequent challenges to this prohibition have failed. *Potter v. Murray City,* 760 F.2d 1065 (10th Cir.), cert. denied, 106 S. Ct. 145 (1985), and a more recent opinion made such a reversal unlikely in the near future. *Employment Division v. Smith,* 494 U.S. 872 (1990).

7. Recent European decisions concerning polygamy are centered on Muslims rather than fundamentalist Mormons, who do not exist in Europe, although there were a number of American missionaries in France in the 1850s who purported to teach the doctrine. See, for example, Lucy Carroll, "Recognition of Polygamist Marriages in English Matrimonial Law: The Statutory Reversal of *Hyde v. Hyde* in 1972, *Journal of Institute of Muslim Minority Affairs* V:1 (1983-84): 81-98, which discusses the reversal of a nineteenth century decision in Great Britain involving a Mormon marriage, taking into account new realities of Muslim marriage relationships in Great Britain. See, also, Luigi Manconi, "Due casi singolari in Italia: Musulmani bravi bigami," *La Stampa* (August 30, 1991), p. 17. (article referring to two cases interpreting Italian law which allows immigrants legally domiciled and working in Italy to seek legal immigration of spouses.

8. *Washington Post,* 20 March 1993, p. B7.

9. *Washington Post,* 21 March 1993, p. A18.

10. For the origin of the Children of God and its relation with The Family, from an internal perspective, see "Our Family's Origins," Bulletin by World Series, April 1992.

11. It is ironic because this is very similar to the language used in the 1890 Manifesto of the Mormon Church which was intended to prohibit polygamy in

the United States but not in Canada or Mexico. See, "Position and Policy Statement," issued by World Services, April 1992.

12. The facts concerning this raid are set forth in Bradley, pp. 112-81; and Ken Driggs, "Who Shall Raise the Children? Vera Black and the Rights of Polygamist Utah Parents, *Utah Historical Quarterly 60:1* (Winter, 1992), pp. 27-54.

13. In re State in Interest of Black, 283 P.2d 887 (Utah, 1955). See also *Hall v. Hall,* 326 P.2d 707 (Utah, 1958).

14. The most recent example involves the Davis County Cooperative Society, also known as the Latter-Day Church of Christ, which has 1,000 active members and assets totalling $150,000,000. It is alleged that half brothers and sisters are marrying each other as well as uncles and nieces. See, *Salt Lake Tribune,* 22 March 1993, pp. B1-B2.

15. *Salt Lake Tribune,* August 6, 1991, p. 1.

16. See, e.g., *Sanderson v. Tyron,* 739 P.2d 623 (Utah, 1987) (Finding that parent practices polygamy is, alone, insufficient to support custody award); *State v. Musser,* 175 P.2d 724 (Utah, 1948) (A person cannot be prosecuted for expressing opinions of belief and personal convictions).

17. Matter of Adoption of W.A.T., 808 P.2d 1083 (Utah, 1991).

18. See Lucy Carroll, "Recognition of Polygamist Marriages in English Matrimonial Law: The Statutory Reversal of *Hyde v. Hyde* in 1972, *Journal of Institute of Muslim Minority Affairs* V:1 (1983-84): 81-98.

19. Luigi Manconi, "Due casi singolari in Italia: Musulmani bravi bigami," *La Stampa* (August 30, 1991), p. 17. (article referring to two cases interpreting Italian law which allows immigrants legally domiciled and working in Italy to seek legal immigration of spouses.

20. The Family has attempted to explain the publications of the Children of God and prior teachings of its founder "Father David," in "Our Replies to Allegations of Child Abuse," Bulletin of World Services, June 1992; "Position and Policy Statement," Bulletin of World Services, April 1992.

21. David E. Van Zandt, *Living in the Children of God* (Princeton: Princeton University Press, 1991), (a sociologist); and Deborah (Linda Berg) Davis, with Bill Davis, *The Children of God: The Inside Story* (Grand Rapids, Michigan: Zonderban Books, 1984), (a former member and daughter of the founder of the Children of God); and Jose Maria Baamonde, *Los Ninos des Dios* (Buenos Aires: Ediciones Paulinas, 1991), (a Catholic counter-cultist).

22. See, Massimo Introvigne, *Il cappello del mago: I nuovi movimenti magici dallo spiritismo al satanismo* (Milano: SugarCo, 1990).

23. "Religious Persecution—In a Democratic Society? Will *You* Be *Next?*," The Family, June, 1992.

Chapter 11. From "Children of God" to "The Family": Movement Adaptation and Survival

Durkheim, Emile. 1915/1964. *The Elementary Forms of Religious Life.* New York: Free Press.

Hunter, James Davison. 1991. *Culture Wars: The Struggle to Define America.* New

York: Basic Books.

Marx, Karl and Fredrich Engels. 1964. *On Religion*. New York: Schocken Books.

Melton, Gordon. 1992. *Encyclopedic Handbook of Cults in America*. New York: Garland.

Moses David. 1978. "The Re-Organization Nationalization Revolution." #659, January (Mo letter).

Richardson, James T. and Rex Davis. 1983. "Experiential Fundamentalism: Revisions of Orthodoxy in the Jesus Movement." *Journal of the American Academy of Religion (3): 397-425.*

Van Zandt, David E. 1991. *Living in the Children of God*. Princeton: Princeton University.

Wallis, Roy. 1982. "Charisma, Commitment and Control in a New Religious Movement," pp.73-140 in Roy Wallis (ed.), *Millenialism and Charisma*. Belfast: Queens University.

—— 1987. "Hostages to Fortune: Thoughts on the Future of Scientology and the Children of God," pp.80-90 in David G. Bromley and Phillip E. Hammond (eds.), *The Future of New Religious Movements*. Macon, GA: Mercer University Press.

Wilson, Bryan. 1970. *Religious Sects*. New York: McGraw-Hill.

Wright, Stuart A. 1983. "Defection From New Religious Movements: A Test of Some Theoretical Propositions," pp.106-121 in David G. Bromley and James T. Richardson (eds.), *The Brainwashing/Deprogramming Controversy*. New York: Edwin Mellen.

—— 1984. "Post-Involvement Attitudes of Voluntary Defectors From Controversial New Religious Movements. *Journal for the Scientific Study of Religion 23(2):172-82.*

—— 1986. "Dyadic Intimacy and Social Control in Three Cult Movements." *Sociological Analysis 47(2):137-150.*

—— 1987. *Leaving Cults: The Dynamics of Defection*. Washington, DC: Society for the Scientific Study of Religion.

Wuthnow, Robert. 1978. "Religious Movements and the Transition in World Order," pp.49-62.

—— 1980. "World Order and Religious Movements," pp.57-75 in Albert Bergeson (ed.), *Studies of the Modern World System*. New York: Academic Press.

Chapter 12: Island Pond Raid Begins New Pattern

References:

Burlington Free Press, numerous articles

The Hartford Courant, Hartford, CT

Rutland Herald

Boston Globe

Religious Freedom Alert, Washington, DC

Vermont Magazine, Mar, 1991

Correspondence and Interviews with members and former members of the Northeast Kingdom Community Church, Island Pond, VT

Interviews with reporters of the *Burlington Free Press*
Data Base research from the files of Friends of Freedom, Hunt Valley, MD

Chapter 14. Scholarly Studies on the Children of God/The Family: A Comprehensive Survey

Notes:
1. This survey is restricted to publications in the English language.
2. In the late 1960's Berg, his wife, his children and their spouses were known as "Teens for Christ." The designation "Children of God," which was soon officially adopted, was originally given to them by a reporter. They later changed their name to the "Family of Love," and more recently to simply "The Family" (see Wallis 1976, pp. 810-811). Wallis (1977, p. 12) states that the designation "The Family" was already used by the mid-1970's. The Family is described as "A Fellowship of Independent Christian Missionary Communities." In their relationship to the public, members of The Family frequently identify themselves as Christian missionaries. A more recent publication (Lynch, 1990) states that the Family is also known as "Heaven's Magic," an unfamiliar designation in books and articles on The Family.
3. See Melton (1992), where reference is made to the hearings conducted by the Senate of the State of California and by the New York State attorney general (*Final Report on the Activities of the Children of God* 1974).
4. While Zandt states clearly that his work is based on early ethnographic research, he offers no explanation why there is a lapse of 8 years between his research and his completion of his dissertation(in 1985) and why his book was published in 1991, six years after his dissertation was completed.
5. Apparently, COG members took the initiative and contacted Melton in January 1993. Several scholars are now involved in studying The Family from different academic perspectives.
6. In a personal communication, Melton explained that Van Zandt's work was consulted but purposely omitted because it presented an earlier phase of the Children of God and, consequently, offered little new to justify its inclusion in the bibliography. This paper agrees with Melton, but suggests that Van Zandt's methodology was in fact new. No other author had previously used the anthropological methodology of participant observation to study the Children of God.
7. By 1986 Wallis seems to have reestablished contact with COG. He wrote to David Berg who addressed his queries in one of MO's letters. Wallis may have been working on a manuscript about the movement, but the writer of this paper could find no evidence that it had been published or completed. (See MO Letter DO 2334, 6/87)
8. For more detailed studies on one particular Jesus Movement organization, one may profitably consult Richardson, White, and Simmonds (1979).
9. Within the movement, David Berg is known as "Moses David," "Father David," or simply "Mo." He is also sometimes referred to as "Dad" and "Grand-dad."
10. According to The Family's own 1988 figures, just over 60% of its members were under 18 (Van Zandt, 1991, p. 166, footnote 3). In the same year, according to

The Family's own statistics, there were a little over 12,000 members scattered throughout the world (ibid., footnote 4). In a recent (1993) publication, "The Family: An Introduction and an Invitation," the members of The Family claim that the movement has "around 3,000 full-time adult members and their approximately 6,000 children."

11. A two-page letter, entitled "Children of God?/Family of Love?/The Family!" briefly outlines the three stages of the movement. The letter was signed by Don George in the name of The Family. An eight-page information package, "The Family: An Introduction and an Invitation," contains a similar brief account of the movement's history.

12. Van Zandt is fully aware of these issues which he discusses at some length in an Appendix (1991, pp. 173-196).

13. In more traditional theological terminology, Van Zandt seems to suggest that COG viewed witnessing and litnessing as "sacraments."

14. For a lengthy description of how flirty fishing is justified see Richardson and Davis (1983, p. 406-420). Confer also Wikstrom (1977) who calls the female members who practice this custom "Happy Hookers for Jesus."

15. One should emphatically note that, in the case of The Family, Berg's anti-institutional and anti-social teachings and activities have not led to violence.

16. Several members of The Family were present at the annual meeting of the Society for the Scientific Study of Religion held in Raleigh, North Carolina, October 28-31, 1993. A number of scholars, including the writer of this paper, is on The Family's mailing list. Daniel Alexander, on behalf of The Family, has written a lengthy open letter to the Producers of NBC's NOW show (aired in September 8, 1993) complaining about the way Family members have been depicted in the media. And official complaints against the treatment of members of The Family in various countries have been circulated.

17. One must note that it is debatable how common were both customs.

18. The Family also distributes an information package entitled "The Family: Making the World a Better Place!" Besides an overview of their beliefs and practices, this package contains 1) a lengthy statement of their faith, 2) a summary of their lifestyle, attitudes, and home life with special reference to the care given to their children, 3) an outline of their family-based education system, 4) a rebuttal of the allegations that they practice brainwashing, and 5) a list of quotations from the "MO Letters" refuting false accusations against The Family.

References:

Barker, Eileen. 1989. *New Religious Movements: a Practical Introduction.* London: Her Majesty's Stationary Office.

Beckford, James A. 1985. *Cult Controversies: the Societal Response to New Religious Movements.* New York: Tavistock Publications.

Bromley, David G. and Shupe, Anson D. 1981. *Strange Gods: the Great American Cult Scare.* Boston: Beacon Press.

Cohen, Daniel. 1975. *The New Believers: Young Religion in America.* New York: M. Evans and Company.

Davis, Rex and James T. Richardson. 1976. "The Organization and Functioning of the Children of God." *Sociological Analysis* 37:321-339.

Davis, Deborah. 1984. *The Children of God.* Grand Rapids, MI: Zondervan Publishing House.

Drakeford, John W. 1972. *Children of God: a Sobering Look at the Commune*

Movement. Nashville: Broadman Press.

Ellwood, Robert S. 1973. *One Way: the Jesus Movement and Its Meaning.* Englewood Cliffs, NJ: Prentice-Hall.

Enroth, Ronald. 1977. *Youth, Brainwashing, and Extremist Cults.* Grand Rapids: Zondervan Publishing House.

Enroth, Ronald M, Edward E. Ericson, and Peters C. Breckinridge. 1972. *The Jesus People: Old-Time Religion in the Age of Aquarius.* Grand Rapids, MI: Eerdmans Publishing Company.

Final Report of the Activities of the Children of God to Hon. Louis J. Lefkowitz. 1974. New York: Charities Fraud Division, Attorney General's Office.

Gordon, Ruth. 1988. *Children of Darkness.* Wheaton, IL: Living Books.

Hopkins, Joseph M. 1977. "The Children of God: Disciples of Deception." *Christianity Today,* 18 February, 18-23.

_____. 1980a. "Children of God--Update." *Update: a Quarterly Journal of New Religious Movements* 4.4:42-45.

_____. 1980b. "The Children of God: Fewer and Far Out." *Christianity Today,* 20 January, 40-41.

Jorgensen, Danny L. 1989. *Participant Observation: A Methodology for Human Studies.* Newbury Park, CA: Sage.

Kvideland, Karin. 1979a. "Children of God in Bergen." Pp. 154-176 in *New Religions,* edited by Haralds Biezais. Stockholm, Sweden: Almquist and Wiksell International.

_____. 1979b. "Symbols and Their Functions in the Children of God." *Temenos* 15:41-49.

Lynch, Dalva. 1990. "Inside the 'Heavenly Elite': the Children of God Today." *Christian Research Journal* (Summer): 16-20.

Martin, Walter. 1980. *The New Cults.* Santa Ana, CA: Vision House.

McBeth, Leon. 1977. *Strange New Religions.* Nashville: Broadman Press.

Melton, J. Gordon. 1978. *Encyclopedia of American Religions.* Wilmington, NC: McGrath Publishing Company.

_____. 1986. *Encyclopedia Handbook of Cults in America.* New York: Garland Publishing Inc.

_____. 1987. *Encyclopedia of American Religions.* Detroit: Gale Research, second edition.

_____. 1989. *Encyclopedia of American Religions.* Detroit: Gale Research, third edition.

_____. 1992. *Encyclopedic Handbook of Cults.* New York: Garland Publishing, revised and updated edition.

_____. 1993. *Encyclopedia of American Religions.* Detroit: Gale Research, fourth edition.

Oosterwal, Gottfried. 1979. "The Children of God." *Update: a Quarterly Journal of New Religious Movements* 3.1-2:35-44.

Patrick, Ted. 1976. *Let Our Children Go.* New York: E. P. Dutton.

Pritchett, W. Douglas. 1985. *The Children of God/Family of Love: an Annotated Bibliography.* New York: Edwin Mellen Press.

Richardson, James T., Mary White Stewart and Richard B. Simmonds. 1979. *Organized Miracles: a Study of a Contemporary, Youth, Communal. Fundamentalist Organization.* New Brunswick, NJ: Transaction Books.

Richardson, James T. and Rex Davis. 1983. "Experiential Functionalism: Revising Orthodoxy in the Jesus Movement." *Journal of the American Academy of Religion*

51:397-425.

Sparks, Jack. 1977. *The Mind Benders*. Nashville: Thomas Nelson Publishers.

Van Zandt, David E. 1991. *Living in the Children of God*. Princeton, NJ: Princeton University Press.

Wallis, Roy. 1976. "Observations on the Children of God." *Sociological Review* 24:807-829.

_____. 1977. "Moses David's Sexy God." *New Humanist*, May-August, 12-14.

_____. 1978a. "Recruiting Christian Manpower." *Society* 15.4:72-74.

_____. 1978b. "Fishing for Men." *Humanist* 38.1:14-16.

_____. 1979. "Sex, Marriage, and the Children of God." Pp. 74-90 in *Salvation and Protest: Studies of Social and Religious Movements*, edited by Roy Wallis. New York: St. Martin's Press.

_____. 1981. "Yesterday's Children: Culture and Structural Change in a New Religious Movement." Pp. 97-133 in *The Social Impact of New Religious Movements*, edited by Bryan R. Wilson. New York: Rose of Sharon Press.

_____. 1982a. "Charisma, Commitment, and Control in a New Religious Movement." Pp. 73-140 in *Millennialism and Charisma*, edited by Roy Wallis. Belfast, Northern Ireland: Queen's University Press.

_____. 1982b. "The Social Construction of Charisma." *Social Compass* 29:25-39.

_____. 1985. "Researching the Children of God: a Reflection and Review." *Update: a Quarterly Journal of New Religious Movements* 9.2:32-37.

_____. 1986. "Sex, Violence, and Religion: Antinomianism and Charisma." Pp. 115-127 in *Sociological Theory, Religion, and Collective Action*, edited by Roy Wallis and Steve Bruce. Belfast, Northern Ireland: Queen's University.

_____. 1987. "Hostage to Fortune: Thoughts on the Future of Scientology and the Children of God." Pp. 80-90 in *The Future of New Religious Movements*, edited by David G. Bromley and Larry D. Shinn. Lewisburg, PA: Bucknell University Press.

Wangerin, Ruth Elizabeth. 1984a. "Make-Believe Revolution: a Study of the Children of God" (Abstract). *Dissertation Abstracts International*, vol. 42, No. 12 (June 1982): 5176a-5177.

_____. 1984. "Women in the Children of God: 'Revolutionary Women' or 'Mountain Maids'." Pp. 130-139 in *Women in Search of Utopias: Mavericks and Mythmakers*, edited by Ruby Rohrlich and Elaine Hoffman Baruch. New York: Schocken Books.

Ward, Hilary. 1972. *The Far-Out Saints of the Jesus Communes: a First-Hand Report and Interpretation of the Jesus People Movement*. New York: Association Press.

Weber, Max. 1968. *Max Weber on Charisma and Institution Building: Selected Papers*. Chicago: University of Chicago Press.

Wikstrom, Lester. 1977. "Happy Hookers for Jesus: Children of God's Sex Revolution." *Update: a Quarterly Journal of New Religious Movements* 1.3-4:59-63.

Wright, Stewart A. 1983. "Defection from New Religious Movements: a Test of Some Theoretical Propositions." Pp. 106-121 in *The Brainwashing/Deprogramming Controversy: Sociological, Psychological, Legal, and Historical Perspectives*, edited by David G. Bromley and James T. Richardson. New York: Edwin Mellen Press.

_____. 1984. "Post-Involvement Attitudes of Voluntary Defectors from Controversial Religious Movements." *Journal for the Scientific Study of Religion* 23:172-182.

_____. 1986. "Dyadic Intimacy and Social Control." *Sociological Analysis* 47:137-150.

_____. 1987. *Leaving Cults: the Dynamics of Defection.* Washington, D.C.: Society for the Scientific Study of Religion.

_____. 1988. "Leaving New Religious Movements: Issues, Theory, and Research." Pp. 143-165 in *Falling from the Faith: Causes and Consequences of Religious Apostasy,* edited by David G. Bromley. Newbury Park, CA: Sage Publications.

Wright, Stuart A. and Elizabeth Piper. 1986. "Families and Cults: Familial Factors Related to Youth Leaving or Remaining in Deviant Religious Groups." *Journal of Marriage and the Family* 48:15-25.

Chapter 15. The Children of God, The Family of Love, The Family

1. I have chosen to use the term "The Family." Although this is not the name by which the group is best known to the outside, it is the name they now use themselves. It is the purpose of this report to give an account of the present activities and beliefs of the group so it would be inappropriate to use any other name.

2. From the Letter "Flatlanders," G.P. 57, 13/03/71, *Vol. 1*, p. 484: referring to two-dimensional rather than three-dimensional beings. [This image ultimately derived from Edwin A. Abbott's novel, *Flatland.* Editor.]

2. *Young Adults* until 1993 were called EA's Experimental Adults—they are are young people between the ages of 18 and 21. The change in name is consistent with a move to elevate the role of young people within the movement. EA's was considereble by the young people as demeaning.

3. From the conversation in Melbourne. Jan. 1994.

4. As early as 1974, Berg was talking about the need for people within the movement to exercise some judgement about the things which came from the leadership. even his. For example, "I don't want anything done about anything unless your councils meet together and agree together, even if they are suggestions from me. If they don't think it's wise or best or well to do it, I don't want'm to do it." ("Share the Know." DO 301A,2/74,DB6,p.2.)

5. Eileen Barker, *New Religious Movements: A Practical Introduction.* Her Majesties Stationary Office. London. 1989; page 33.

6. *Why Disasters?*—Is Death a Curse or Blessing DFO959 26 November 1980, *MO Letters* Vol.8 page 7402.

7. *Why Disasters?*—Is Death a Curse or Blessing DFO959 26 November 1980, *MO Letters* Vol.8 page 7402.

8. *Why Disasters?*—Is Death a Curse or Blessing DF0959 26 November 1980, *MO Letters* Vol.8 page 7405.

9. *The 7 Ways To Know God's Will!* - At the birth of the Family!—Huntington Beach GP 829 Summer 1968, *MO Letters* Vol. 7 page 6283.

10. *Difficulty in Communications!* - Have mercy on the Departed Spirits! DO 1846. 18/9/84. *Daily Bread* Vol. 11, page 441.

11. *MO Letter* 1566:16.

12. *The Book of the Future*, page 162.

13. *The Book of the Future,* page 164.

14. *Ibid,* page 165.

15. *Holy Ghosts* January 27, 1974, GP 620, *MO Letters* Vol. 5 page 4774.

16. *Holy Ghosts* January 27, 1974, GP 620, *MO Letters* Vol. 5 page 4775.

17. *Holy Ghosts* January 27, 1974, GP 620. *MO Letters* Vol. 5 page 4775.

18. *The Children of God: The Inside Story*, by Deborah (Linda Berg) Davis, with Bill Davis; Zondervan Books, Grand Rapids, 1984.
19. *Wars and Rumours Wars!* DFO 1327. 11/82 *Lifelines* Vol. 14 page 45.
20. *The Book of the Future* page 66.
21. *The Book of the Future* page 74.
22. *The Book of the Future* page 76.
23. *Ibid.*, page 93.
24. *Ibid.*, page 93.
25. *The Read Victors of the Tibulation!*—We're More Than Conquerors! (Rom. 8:37)—The *Other* Side of the Tribulation! DFO 1624, 9/83, *Good News* Books 16 & 17 page 290.
26. *The Book of the Future.* page 97.
27. *Ibid.*, page 98.
28. *Ibid.*, page 120.
29. *Ibid.*, page 176.
30. *The Oil Shortage! What it Means to You!* DF0938, 29 September 1980, *M0 Letters* Vol.8 page 7072.
31. *Ibid.* page 18Of.
32. *The Book of the Future,* page 186f.
33. *The Book of the Future,* page 197.
34. *The Book of the Future,* page 198.
35. *The Book of the Future,* page 201f.
36. *The Book of the Future,* page 219.
37. *Here and Now For There and Then* DFO 1092, 1/11/81, para 49.
38. From a conversation with Joe, in London.
39. *Trust the Lord!*—On Husband/Wife Relationships," DO 2135, 29/11/83, *DB3,* p.211.
40. *The Talisman!* - Animism and the Sphinx! - A Family Emergency Just Before Tim Concerned's Defection! DFO 1369 23/1/79 *Lifelines* Vol. 14 page 230.
41. *Everything YOU wanted to know about SEX! Questions taken from the "Confidential Questionnaires" with answers from the letters by* **Father David and Maria.** *MO Letters* Vol.7 page 6244 42.
42. *Everything YOU want to know about SEX!,* undated *MO Letters* Vol. 7 page 6244.
43. *Happy Daze!* - Are you Still in *That Old House?* - or a *New House!* D0958 6 December 1980, MO Letters Vol. 8 page 7394.
44. *A Father Applies the Rod!* - Dad's Phone Call with Ho. 4 December 1980 DO952-8, *MO Letters* Vol. 8 page 7236.
45. *A Father Applies the Rod!* - Dad's Phone Call with Ho. 4 December 1980 D0952-8,*MO Letters* Vol. 8 page 7238.
46. *A Father Applies the Rod!* - Dad's Phone Call with Ho. 4 December 1980 D0952-8,*MO Letters* Vol. 8 page 7239.
47. *More from Esther* DO952-17, 1 January 1981, *MO Letters* Vol. 8 pages 72567.
48. *New Year's Eve Praise!* D0957 31/12/80 Vol. 8 page 7373.
49. *Afflictions* DO 569, 25/11/76. In *Daily Bread* Book 1, page 56.
50. From a draft copy of a letter called "equality" sent to me from Maria in January 1994.
51. *The Spiritual Warfare Depends on Us! The Majesty of Choice!* DO 2327, 6/87.
52. "Finish the Job!" DO 1939. 6/85. *DB3.* p. 13.
53. *What Did You Do Today to Save a Soul?,* DO 2089, 1/86, *DB3,* p. 180.

54. *The Millennium!*, ML# 1197:93, 5/81.
55. DB, No. 1, p. 8, DO 302C.
56. *King Meets King!* May '76, ML#502 pars 19.
57. Part of a conversation between myself and Andy in Australia. 17/7/93.
58. Answers to Questions no. 8, DFO 1566, in Good News Book 11. page 126.
59. From conversation in Melbourne January 1994.
60. From a conversation with Joy Hartington—National Area Shepherd in Australia—in October 1992.
61. *Ibid.*

The Family: Where Does It Fit?

1. Cf. Mo Letters 296 *Abrahim the Gypsy King!* and #300 *Abrahim: How Arabs Became Gypsies!*
2. On the healing teachings of Albert B. Simpson see *The Lord for the Body* (Harrisburg, PA: Christian Publications,1959).